THE ALGORITHM

THE
ALGORITHM

HOW AI CAN HIJACK YOUR CAREER
AND STEAL YOUR FUTURE

HILKE
SCHELLMANN

HURST & COMPANY, LONDON

First published in the United Kingdom in 2024 by
C. Hurst & Co. (Publishers) Ltd.,
New Wing, Somerset House, Strand, London WC2R 1LA

A Cataloguing-in-Publication data record for this book is available from the British Library.

ISBN: 9781805260981

www.hurstpublishers.com

Printed in Great Britain by Bell and Bain Ltd, Glasgow

For my daughter

```
01001000  01100101  01101100  01101100  01101111
01001000  01100101  01101100  01101100  01101111
01001000  01100101  01101100  01101100  01101111
01001000  01100101  01101100  01101100  01101111
01001000  01100101  01101100  01101100  01101111
01001000  01100101  01101100  01101100  01101111
01001000  01100101  01101100  01101100  01101111
01001000  01100101  01101100  01101100  01101111
01001000  01100101  01101100  01101100  01101111
01001000  01100101  01101100  01101100  01101111
01001000  01100101  01101100  01101100  01101111
01001000  01100101  01101100  01101100  01101111
01001000  01100101  01101100  01101100  01101111
01001000  01100101  01101100  01101100  01101111
01001000  01100101  01101100  01101100  01101111
01001000  01100101  01101100  01101100  01101111
01001000  01100101  01101100  01101100  01101111
01001000  01100101  01101100  01101100  01101111
01001000  01100101  01101100  01101100  01101111
01001000  01100101  01101100  01101100  01101111
01001000  01100101  01101100  01101100  01101111
01001000  01100101  01101100  01101100  01101111
01001000  01100101  01101100  01101100  01101111
01001000  01100101  01101100  01101100  01101111
01001000  01100101  01101100  01101100  01101111
01001000  01100101  01101100  01101100  01101111
01001000  01100101  01101100  01101100  01101111
01001000  01100101  01101100  01101100  01101111
01001000  01100101  01101100  01101100  01101111
01001000  01100101  01101100  01101100  01101111
01001000  01100101  01101100  01101100  01101111
01001000  01100101  01101100  01101100  01101111
01001000  01100101  01101100  01101100  01101111
01001000  01100101  01101100  01101100  01101111
01001000  01100101  01101100  01101100  01101111
```

CONTENTS

CONTENTS

PROLOGUE

can't believe what I am seeing: It is early 2018, and I am attending a business psychology conference at a chain hotel in Chicago. I have flown here on a tip by someone who calls himself an artificial intelligence (AI) evangelist. I am late to this session on using artificial intelligence in hiring, but upon sneaking in through the side door, I am struck by what is being shown up front—the future is already here!

On the screen is a video of a white man looking into the camera. Graphic dots dapple his eyes, eyebrows, nose, and mouth and a square resembling that of facial recognition software surrounds his face.

On the upper-left corner, percentages for his face are listed:

- **Smile:** 0 percent
- **Brow Raise:** 100 percent
- **Brow Furrow:** 0 percent
- **Frown:** 0 percent

On the upper-right side, it says:

- **Joy:** 0 percent
- **Disgust:** 0 percent

- **Valence** (the pleasantness or unpleasantness of an emotion): 20 percent
- **Engagement:** 100 percent

The AI, developed by a company called HireVue, analyzed the man's facial expressions and emotions, explains Nathan Mondragon, the company representative onstage. I learn later that HireVue's technology has been used by large companies, including Delta Air Lines, Unilever, and Hilton.

HireVue's AI, Mondragon says, analyzes not only facial expressions but also tone of voice and the words job applicants use during video interviews allegedly to predict a job seeker's success in a particular job.[1] That is quite a promise.

At the time, I was stunned and fascinated. It sounded like magic. A more objective, scientific way to hire people? A tool so powerful that it could almost read our minds and therefore predict whether we would succeed? What company wouldn't want this product?

YOU ARE A ZERO

Lizzie,* a young makeup artist in the United Kingdom, didn't feel the magic of HireVue. Instead, she thinks the tool cost her her livelihood. During the pandemic, she was laid off using a HireVue one-way video interview.

Lizzie had been working at a MAC Cosmetics makeup counter in a department store for just over three years when, a few months into the pandemic, the company announced that it needed to lay off half the staff. Layoff decisions would be based on employees' previous performance, a HireVue assessment, and sales metrics.

---

* Lizzie asked to have her last name withheld for fear of retribution.

Lizzie hated one-way video interviews because there was no human on the other side to talk to; instead, she had to stare at her screen and answer prerecorded questions alone in her room. But she wasn't too worried about it since the same type of HireVue interview three years earlier got her hired into the job in the first place. "I never saw the score, but I got the job, so I can only assume that it went well," she said.

Lizzie was surprised when her manager informed her that the company was letting her go. She asked why she was laid off. "I scored full marks on my performance. But then on HireVue, I scored zero," said Lizzie, recalling what her manager told her.

She lost her job and her income. "It was a very stressful time because I didn't know what the future looked like." But she just couldn't believe the low interview score. Together with two other laid-off makeup artists, she found pro bono employment lawyers and started legal action against her former employer. "We all believe that we'd lost our jobs unfairly," said Lizzie.

When Lizzie reviewed the data her former employer had on her, she found that the second HireVue interview, the basis for her layoff, was never scored. But no one caught the problem, even when she appealed the decision. Her performance had been rated well and she had been a successful salesperson, she said, but because of a mistake in the AI program, she was let go. The "revolution" and fair decision-making that AI vendors promise were definitely missing in her case.

PROMISES AND WARNINGS

As a society, we are entering a new era when we are hearing many promises of the transformative power of AI. This book is a case study of one major application: how companies and institutions are using AI to hire, monitor, promote, and fire employees at scale. Even experts, vendors, and HR managers describe this unfolding world as a new "Wild West," where unregulated algorithms rule the world of work.

By exploring how AI is used in our workplaces, we will be better prepared to question its usage when we encounter it everywhere else. And, as it turns out, there is good reason to prepare ourselves. There is trouble ahead.

One former executive even compared companies in the HR tech world to Theranos, the discredited start-up that promised to revolutionize health care with tests that only needed a few drops of blood. The two executives, Elizabeth Holmes and Ramesh "Sunny" Balwani, were later found to have lied about the capabilities of their technology and are both serving prison sentences for defrauding investors.

"There's a lot of companies that aren't quite Theranos but are similar. That's way more common than we would think," said Eric Sydell, the former executive vice president of innovation at Modern Hire, an HR tech vendor.

A former employment lawyer, Matthew Scherer, who specialized in vetting AI hiring software, has a similar opinion after taking a closer look at many of these tools: "The vast majority of the tools that are available today are not ready for prime time."

Maybe you have applied for a job lately and wondered why you never heard back. Have you been passed over for leadership training or for a promotion or a pay raise? Have you been laid off?

You might be blaming yourself, thinking you did something wrong or you didn't deserve the opportunity, but what if it was something else? These negative outcomes may not be due to anything you did or did not do. They might have happened because of a faulty algorithm.

An algorithm is merely a set of tasks that is coded into computer software. "Artificial intelligence," or its subset called machine learning, often includes algorithms that are trained with data.* The trained model then sifts through a vast body of new data (possibly much more than a human being ever could process) to reveal patterns that help predict outcomes. At least, that is what is promised.

But what's really happening inside the algorithms that are increasingly ruling our lives? It's hard to tell, and that's intentional. AI is now quietly taking over the high-stakes decision-making in hiring, promoting, and even firing.

Right under our noses, but mostly out of our sight, the world of work (and of course medicine, banking, policing, etc.) is fundamentally changing because of AI. It can be difficult for job seekers and employees to understand the ways these black box machines impact our lives and how to outperform the algorithm to get promoted or find a dream job.

AI is already everywhere in the world of work: 99 percent of Fortune 500 companies use algorithms and artificial intelligence for hiring,[2] but few people are aware of its broad application. "The dawn of robot recruiting has come and gone, and people just haven't caught up to the realization yet," said Ian Siegel, CEO and founder of the online job board ZipRecruiter. "What percentage of people who apply to a job today will have their résumé read by a human? Somewhere between 75 percent and 100 percent are going to be read by software. A fraction of that is going to be read by a human after the software is done with it."

HireVue has been at the forefront of revolutionizing another part of the hiring process by allowing job applicants to record their responses to prerecorded questions without the presence of a human interviewer. As of late 2022, this approach has been utilized in over thirty-three million interviews, according to the company.[3]

---

* Machine learning is a subset of AI that is commonly used in HR technology. *Artificial intelligence, machine learning,* and *algorithms* are often used interchangeably.

The promise of AI in the hiring process is that these tools will find the most qualified candidates at a lower price in less time without bias. Vendors sell the idea of democratization of the hiring process: every candidate gets a fair shake because the algorithm looks at every résumé and scores every candidate in the same way.

Another difference to traditional hiring is the scale and scope: A human hiring manager can only discriminate against a limited number of people. If an AI system that turns out to be biased is used on all job candidates in a large corporation, hundreds of thousands of people could potentially be affected. That's why many critics believe that the rise of algorithms making high-stakes decisions, including hiring, is one of the most important civil rights issues of our time because discrimination could be rampant in these automated systems.

I was thrown into this world by chance: In late 2017 at a conference in Washington, DC, I first heard about automatic hiring. I needed a ride to the train station, so I got into a Lyft and asked the driver how he was doing. I usually get a "Great, thanks" reply, but this driver's reaction was different. He hesitated for a second and then shared with me that he'd had a weird day because he had been interviewed by a robot. That got me interested. "Wait. A job interview with a robot?" I asked. He had applied for a baggage handler position at a local airport, and instead of a human being, a "robot" had called him that afternoon and asked him three questions. I had never heard of job interviews conducted by "robots" or algorithms.

Once I started looking into this new world, I understood why many companies are desperate for a technological solution: it is impossible for their human hiring managers to weed through the deluge of résumés and applications sent through online portals like Indeed, Monster, ZipRecruiter, and a company's own website. IBM and Google, for example, each receive around three million job applications a year;[4] Unilever, around 1.8 million;[5] and Delta Air Lines, over three hundred thousand applications from flight attendant candidates.[6] At Goldman Sachs, around 230,000 people applied for internships in 2022.[7]

When job platforms like Monster.com and Indeed.com first started, they were supposed to give everyone an easy chance to apply to any job—leveling the playing field. Instead, these platforms have led to a deluge of résumés overwhelming companies, which are now using more and more technological solutions to sift through applications.

This need and the simultaneous development of AI have led to an exponential growth of the human resources technology industry (HR tech) that offers thousands of solutions to companies. Veteran industry analyst Josh Bersin estimated in 2017 that the recruiting industry was valued at around $200 billion.[8] IBISWorld, a market research company, estimated in early 2023 that the global HR and recruitment industry is worth over $760 billion.[9]

Using AI drastically reduces the time and the human labor it takes to hire an applicant, which saves companies lots of money. IBM has fully embraced algorithmic hiring solutions and laid off 30 percent of its HR workforce by early 2019.[10]

But AI is not only being used for hiring new employees. Companies now use predictive analytics to figure out which of their employees is a "flight risk"—someone likely to leave the company within the next year—who is a high performer, who is a bully, who should be promoted, and who should be let go.

Since the start of the COVID-19 pandemic, more than half of large employers now use AI to monitor at least some of their employees.[11] Productivity metrics are tracked by eight out of the ten largest US employers.[12] And in the UK, about 60 percent of over 2,000 workers polled in

2022 believed that their company was surveilling them, according to research by the Trades Union Congress.[13]

This book is the story of the rise of artificial intelligence to rule the world of work. In the following chapters, I remove the cloaks of secrecy surrounding this industry and show how algorithms are making life-altering decisions on humans: AI is now being used throughout the entire "life cycle" of employees, from hiring to retirement.

I have talked to over two hundred people, including AI enthusiasts, vendors, lawyers, professors, HR managers, job applicants, regulators, experts, whistleblowers, organizational psychologists, and really anyone who wanted to talk to me about this profound change in the world of work, and found people who have been harmed or have witnessed the discrimination some of these tools have inflicted. In my own tests, many tools did not deliver on their basic promises.

I am not advocating that we go back to solely human hiring practices, especially not at scale: people of color, women, those with disabilities, and other marginalized groups have been underestimated and overlooked by human hiring managers for decades, resulting in discrimination and pay and employment gaps.[14]

But if we want to make sure that every member of our society has a chance to find (fulfilling) work that puts food on their table and a roof over their head, we need to ensure that employment opportunities are based on merit and qualifications and not based on where you're from, your gender, whether you have a disability, or what your hobbies are.

As algorithms take over the world of work, we need to pay attention now to make sure we are not scaling up already entrenched biases and obfuscating discriminatory hiring and employment practices under the guise of "objective AI."

Right now, these algorithmic tools are most often used for hiring hourly employees in retail, fast food, warehouses, hospitality, and call centers, but over the past few years, AI is also being used more often in white-collar professions. Algorithms are now ubiquitous for recent college graduates who are looking for entry-level jobs, especially in finance and banking. They are also being used to hire teachers, flight attendants, nurses, and even data engineers. Every job board, from Indeed and Monster to ZipRecruiter and LinkedIn, uses some form of AI.

In a recent survey, almost 90 percent of business leaders said that their AI tools have rejected qualified candidates.[15] That's not okay. Why are we automating a badly functioning system? In human hiring, almost 50 percent of new employees fail within the first year and a half.[16] If humans have not figured out how to make good hires, why do we think automating this process will magically fix it? And why do we think people analytics can find a more diverse set of employees to promote into leadership positions when humans have failed at this for years?

This book is an in-depth investigation into all kinds of AI tools that quantify humans at work. I am advocating going beyond these tools: We need to talk about how we hire, promote, monitor, and fire human beings—with or without AI. We also need to talk about how to change the incentives inside companies so managers can hire the right people and understand whether their hires are successful versus being rated on how many days it took them to hire someone, which is an often-used benchmark today. And we need to talk about how we want to treat humans in an AI-driven world.

To me, this new era is just the starting point and it's on all of us to learn how the workplace is fundamentally changing. AI is not going away; in fact, it will soon touch every corner of our lives and we need to know how these tools operate so we can effectively demand change. The book is an exposé and a warning about AI hype.

The first part of the book is a deep dive into the new world of AI-driven hiring: from discrimination based on race in résumé screeners to tone of voice and facial expression analysis and Cambridge Analytica–like methods that distill our online lives and try to find out "how we really tick."

I am telling the stories of job seekers and employees who have been subjected to these technologies and have chosen to fight back. I was also able to get my hands on some of these tools to test them myself—many tools do not work as advertised and further marginalize people, including women, people of color, and people with disabilities, exactly the opposite of what they promise to do.

In Chapter 5, I dig into the origins of some ideas such as analyzing facial expressions for clues about emotions and compare them to how previous efforts of analyzing handwriting or blood type have failed to help HR managers hire the right people.

In the second part of the book, I look more closely at how companies use AI "in the flow of work." Managers can use predictive analytics to find "hidden gems" among employees. I also reveal the different surveillance methods that many workers in the United States and around the world are already subjected to and how wellness and health programs are often undercutting employee privacy and making us extremely vulnerable.

The last chapter shows how algorithms are used to fire employees.

In the appendix, you will find tips on how to apply for jobs in the age of AI (for example, how to use ChatGPT to help you write cover letters and résumés) and what to do if you think you are being monitored at work.

A vast schism is opening up in the world of work. Company leaders want adaptable, creative workers. At the same time, the technology exists to compile all kinds of data on employees, and some of those leaders are also surveilling their employees on an unprecedented scale by quantifying their every move. Employers are starting to assess people's personalities—moving us toward what I call a predictive society in which algorithms assess and predict our behavior and ultimately might make decisions for us about where we should work.

This books reveals the profound change from human hiring practices and human oversight at work to machines quantitatively assessing and surveilling us. Contrary to public opinion, I don't believe that robots and algorithms will replace the majority of humans in the workplace in the short term, but these automatic systems will quantify and surveil our work in ways never seen before.

I invite you on this journalistic detective journey with me to meet real people who are affected by these AI tools and who have chosen to fight back to help all of us. You will also meet the people who built and use these tools as well as many other stakeholders. Through exclusive testimony from whistleblowers, countless Freedom of Information Act requests to obtain internal company documents, and my own real-world tests, I have found that these algorithms make high-stakes decisions that do more harm than good.

As you will discover, many AI companies sell their services by promising magical formulas for finding and keeping the best employees. But the results are out of sync with these promises. Again and again, we see that the effectiveness of AI tools depends on the quality of the human intelligence and understanding that goes into them as well as the proper parameters for protecting the rights and privacy of those affected. We are in the beginning stages of these algorithms dominating our lives and threatening our human future, and now is the best time to fight back—before they become so entrenched that it is too late.

CHAPTER I

Does the Algorithm Like You?

On Résumé Screeners

The need for AI in hiring is a direct result of the success of the Digital Age, which forces job seekers to face an odd conundrum: How can it be that there is a shortage of workers in the United States and other countries, yet companies are flooded with résumés and still complain there are not enough good applicants?[1]

Companies receive a lot of applications because it's easy to apply for an open position. Instead of finding job ads in magazines and newspapers and filling out individual paper application forms or mailing in a résumé, job seekers can apply on job boards like Monster, Indeed, and ZipRecruiter, which collect all job ads and make it easy to apply. Large language models like ChatGPT also make it easier for applicants; these tools can generate cover letters and résumés in seconds. And it often just takes a few clicks of the mouse to send a résumé to a potential employer.

In turn, HR departments are overwhelmed and desperate for help because their recruiters can't sift through the volume of résumés they receive. So, companies turn to algorithms and AI in hopes these technologies will surface the best candidates and help hiring managers keep track of, score, rank, and reject candidates automatically. To make their lives easier, companies use four main strategies that often involve AI to cut down the number of applicants: résumé screeners, assessments including AI games, one-way video interviews, and AI tools that conduct background checks and can scan candidates' online lives. In this chapter, we look at the first of these strategies: screening, evaluating, and ranking résumés.

If you have ever sent a résumé through one of the job boards or submitted an application on a large company's website, chances are high that AI was used to evaluate your submission. Many job seekers wonder if something is wrong with them or their résumés because they keep getting rejected or more often don't hear anything back. Why is it so hard for so many people to get hired when AI is in the mix?

There is, of course, nothing inherently wrong about using technology to make our lives easier, but it turns out that the AI tools that are meant to help companies are not always doing that. Instead, some are causing more problems and discrimination.

"SOPHIE"

Sophie* is a software developer in her late twenties. On paper, she is a dream for recruiters: she is a computer engineer, a Black woman, and a

---

* Sophie is a Black woman with a unique name trying to break into the tech industry. Because she is criticizing the hiring methods of potential employers, she has asked me not to use her real name. Sophie is a pseudonym she chose.

veteran—all desirable qualities for employers that seek to diversify their workforce, especially in tech jobs.

She graduated in May 2021 with a master's degree in data science and interaction design, basically a software developer/engineering degree, from Rutgers University in New Jersey. She has an undergraduate degree in information technology. She is a perfectionist, and so she made sure she attended and graduated from a coding boot camp on top of her graduate degree. She also taught girls how to code—all in anticipation of finding the perfect job.

When I spoke to her, we were both surprised that it took her around six months and 146 applications to find a job. She documented every application in an Excel spreadsheet.

"Every time I apply for a job, I use a tracker," Sophie said. "After I apply, I look up recruiters on LinkedIn. I shoot them a quick message. Sometimes I got a reply, sometimes I didn't." Messaging recruiters, she learned, was the best way to get interviews. Afterward, she always sent a thank-you note. "I was really trying to get myself out there."

While job hunting, she wondered why it was taking so long: "I don't understand how the tech industry makes it difficult to get in, but then they complain that they don't have enough people to hire," said Sophie. "What's the problem?"

Sophie never got an answer to this question. She recounted how throughout the process she rarely spoke to a human. Most of her applications were mediated by technology.

"It was just weird not having human interaction because it's like, 'Okay, so who is picking me? Is this robot thing picking me or is a human being picking me?'" Sophie lamented.

And she is not alone. John Jersin, the former vice president of product management at LinkedIn, has studied this problem. "I've done some analysis with teams in the past across a variety of platforms, including all of the big ones, and found that it actually takes a surprising number of applications in many cases for someone to get a job successfully. And the number of applications that it frequently takes is sometimes dozens of applications, sometimes hundreds of applications for people to get a certain job that they're looking for."

As a software engineer, Sophie has a much better understanding of the job-screening technologies than many other job seekers. When we talked, she wondered whether the low rate of follow-up she got when she applied via job boards like Glassdoor, LinkedIn, and companies' websites had something to do with the underlying data these algorithms are trained on.

Algorithms look for patterns, and she described her background and experience as nontraditional, so an AI may not have readily surfaced her résumé because it did not match with targeted patterns. She is a Black woman in tech; she grew up in a housing project in the Bronx and served in the US Navy. "I was four years active, four years reserve, and I went on two deployments," Sophie said. "I completed my bachelor's degree in information technology where there's rarely any Black people or any Black women."

Her experiences and those of many others are in stark contrast to the promise of the technology: job boards like Indeed, Monster, and LinkedIn were supposed to democratize hiring. Everyone can find the right companies, browse through thousands of open positions, and easily apply. But somewhere along the way, the system has broken.

THE RÉSUMÉ SCREENERS

After our first talk, we both dug a little deeper into AI hiring algorithms that analyze résumés. I found that some résumé screeners have been shown to be biased regarding race and gender. Thus, they may exclude many qualified applicants and many employers know and tolerate that.

Amazon is one of the few companies that has gone public with its struggles. Its résumé screener is a cautionary tale of biased algorithms.[2] A few years back, the company built an AI-based résumé screener to ingest applicants' résumés and basically compare them to patterns found in previous applicants' résumés to predict which job seekers would be successful.

The training data set included more résumés of men than of women, reflecting the gender disparity in many tech jobs. The tool picked up on male preferences and systematically downgraded applicants with the word *women's* on their résumés, as in "women's chess club" or "women's soccer team"—attributes that had nothing to do with an applicant's abilities or qualifications for a job but that weren't typically found in the majority of "successful" résumés since those were submitted mostly by men.

Amazon's engineers tried to fix the tool but couldn't. Eventually, the company had to scrap it. (Amazon said the tool was never solely used on job applicants.)

But imagine other large companies using similar tools. It could lead to discrimination against thousands or even hundreds of thousands of female job applicants if the training set is skewed toward patterns of male employees.

Amazon publicly shared its experience with AI in the hiring process, but experts told me discrimination based on training data happens more often than we think. One reason these problems aren't widely known is that vendors have no incentives to tell the public—or journalists or really anyone—that the software they built didn't work. Companies that use the products also have no interest in sharing publicly that the products they bought and used are flawed. They fear job applicants suing them for using faulty products in their hiring assessments.

Companies also fear reputational damage after seeing what happened with Amazon's disclosure and the PR backlash. That's why many companies require anyone involved in vetting and using AI products to sign nondisclosure agreements. Additionally, some of these tools are built in-house; journalists and academics rarely can access the training data or test the systems independently.

So, for now, we mostly have to rely on whistleblowers and industry insiders to learn more about this rather closed-off world.

CORRELATION BEGETS BIAS

The first source I convinced to come forward and share their experience on the record was John Scott. I encountered him when I was researching my first story on AI and hiring. A bunch of sources told me I needed to get in touch with him. Scott has been an organizational psychologist for decades. We talked briefly on the phone, and when we realized that we would be at the same conference a few weeks later, he said we should meet in person. He had some information to share.

It was early Saturday afternoon at a large chain hotel in National Harbor, Maryland, outside of Washington, DC, on the last day of the conference and I remember getting an awful-tasting chicken soup from the hotel food stand because I had skipped lunch. We sat in a ground-floor hotel lobby that looked like a small New England town, with a wall of hotel room windows overlooking this gigantic atrium.

John Scott is the chief operating officer of APTMetrics. His company helps other companies find the right assessments to check whether job applicants are the right fit. APTMetrics builds assessments and recommends tools that can be purchased from other vendors. The company also provides litigation support, and companies hire Scott to test new tools for legal compliance and potential bias.

He is a tall white man close to retirement age who is composed, well spoken, and very cordial. Everyone at the conference knew him and lots of people came over to chat with him. In between handshakes and small talk, Scott unpacked the goods.

Over the past few years, he has inspected two résumé screening tools and three other algorithmic-based hiring and selection tools that included résumé screeners. (He declined to name the companies because he'd signed nondisclosure agreements.) Most résumé screeners are supposed to analyze résumés of "successful" current employees to find the matching keywords and other patterns that predict success in a given role. The tools then analyze incoming résumés from job applicants and check for overlap. Scott loves this field and has a keen sense of what's right and wrong; he strongly feels that some of the tools he has taken a closer look at were wrong. He found biased variables and suspicious predictions in all five tools he investigated.

One tool predicted success for candidates named Thomas or Elsie.[3] It also rated positively those people who mentioned Seattle, Syria, or Canada on their résumés, or hobbies such as football, basketball, or biking. A couple of the tools used words like *church* and various nationalities to predict success in a given job.

These keyword correlations are based on statistics. Of course just being named Thomas does not mean that a person without any qualifications for a particular job would be good at that job. Scott thinks that the résumé screener probably found the names *Thomas* and *Elsie* on résumés of a few employees and that this finding was statistically significant, so the algorithm interpreted it as a predictor of success.

"Because you've got large data sets, in many cases you're going to find spurious correlations that make no sense," Scott said. "Maybe there are three or four people named Thomas who are successful, and so you get a point."

Scott says that the non-job-related variables he found the tools using had more to do with the demographic characteristics of the employees than the knowledge, skills, and abilities needed to perform the work in question.

One problem that résumé screeners have is that almost everyone puts the most important skills mentioned in a job description on their résumé, so if that's the criteria, basically everyone makes it to the next round, which defeats the point of a screener. As a result, algorithms might begin weighting other "predictors," such as first names, schools, or hobbies and other common keywords.

If I were an applicant and learned that my résumé for my dream job was rejected because my first name wasn't Thomas or Elsie, I would be livid. The rejection feels unfair because it's arbitrary and not based on any kind of evidence of inability or relation to the job requirements.

But there is more here: Employment lawyers have said that selecting job applicants based on nationality or country (*Syria* and *Canada*) could be considered "discrimination based on national origin," which is prohibited in the United States. Gender discrimination could be an issue when résumé screeners assign points for hobbies like football, which is heavily skewed toward men.

The systems also used variables that could be proxies for nationality, race, gender, political affiliations, and disabilities to predict how candidates would perform on the job, Scott said.

He is not the only one who found résumé screeners using troubling keywords.

THE PROBLEM WITH KEYWORDS

Another whistleblower who got access to these tools is Ken Willner. I met him at a conference for organizational psychologists called "The Leading Edge Consortium," which was devoted to artificial intelligence in the workplace. It was a gathering of HR folks, recruiters, a couple of academics, a few lawyers, some government workers, and psychologists—and one journalist—coming together to discuss the newest technologies in hiring.

Willner, an employment attorney, was on a panel talking with Adam Klein, a lawyer who specializes in class action lawsuits. Klein aired his doubts about how these tools work or don't work and said that he was trying to build a class action lawsuit.

Willner, on the other hand, a middle-aged white man not particularly interested in being in the spotlight, is a quiet lawyer. He was dressed down in a tweed jacket and his hair looked meticulously combed over his head. He let Klein do most of the talking. He just softly suggested that companies take their heads out of the sand and hire employment lawyers like him to do due diligence before using AI tools.

He stated that if there was a lawsuit, most judges would probably find the company—not the software vendor—liable for AI tools that even inadvertently discriminated against applicants.

Willner didn't name names but hinted at some wrongdoing he had seen. I approached him afterward and he offered to chat on the phone after the conference.

He'd retired in 2023, but when he was a partner at DC law firm Paul Hastings, Willner advised companies that were creating their own AI hiring tools in-house or buying them from vendors. When large enough companies want to buy new hiring technology from a vendor, they often have the buying power to wrestle the vendor into "opening the black box" so that the company's lawyers and consultants can make sure the tool won't cause the company legal trouble. Willner is one of the few people who has looked inside the black box.

One problem he found was in résumé screeners, which essentially predicted success based on keywords, just as John Scott explained. But an AI tool finding a pattern of keywords to make a prediction if someone will succeed in a given job is not enough. "A place where employers get into trouble," Willner said, "is if they rely solely on correlation without looking for a logical relationship between the word and qualifications for the job."

He gave an interesting example that illustrated how protected groups, including women, could be inadvertently discriminated against, which is called *disparate* or *adverse impact*: "Let's say you trained your algorithm on an employer that has mostly men in a particular job and only a few women. The algorithm could look for shoe size, and people with a larger shoe size may be associated with doing well; people with smaller shoe size may not be. That's not related logically to job performance; it just happens to be a correlation that may exist. But it also may happen to have an adverse impact on women, who have smaller shoe sizes on average."

This is obviously a theoretical example, but it describes the randomness of the correlations these machines might turn up. He counseled his clients to make sure any keywords the résumé screeners use are related to the job to ensure this part of the hiring process is fair and legal.

In one résumé screener he investigated, he found a troubling keyword that was used to score job applicants: *Afric**. (The asterisk is a wildcard character that is a placeholder for other characters in a search.) People with different iterations of the word *Afric**, including *Africa* or

African American, on their résumés got more or fewer points, depending on whether the employees whose résumés were used to train the screener were considered successful or unsuccessful. The report that Willner read stated only that the word *Afric** was used. It didn't clarify whether the word was used to up- or downgrade applicants.

He told his client that using these kinds of keywords was a bad idea: "Employers would want to be very careful before making decisions that in any way are based upon whether the word *Africa*, something that can be very clearly race-related, is contained on a résumé. . . . Either way, if an employer is making decisions based on whether the word *Africa* is in a résumé, it is looking for trouble on the discrimination front."

This means that at least some of these résumé screeners take words into consideration that have nothing to do with applicants' ability to perform a certain job but have to do with who they are or what racial group they belong to—traits that shouldn't be considered when making hiring decisions. In fact, predicting whether an applicant will be a high or low performer based on racial identity treats one group of applicants differently from others, and many would probably consider this discrimination.

Out of the dozens of software screenings Willner has done over the course of his career, he has found problematic variables in about a quarter of them. Each instance of discrimination was caught only when an outside lawyer or expert examined the screeners. It was not caught by the algorithms' developers.

Although the employers using the résumé screeners that Willner investigated removed discriminatory keywords, experts question whether this type of intervention actually solves the problem. Maybe next time the tool picks up *Hispanic* or *Latin** as a pattern? Willner worries that companies don't check these tools for potentially discriminatory keywords and don't understand how keywords should be related to the job. If the way these algorithms infer success on the basis of random and demographic keywords isn't fixed, these systems are bound to make the same kind of mistake again.

In another tech investigation, Willner found an instance of gender discrimination when the word *softball* was scored negatively and the word *baseball* positively. This could be an example of gender discrimination, he said, because softball is predominantly played by women and baseball is predominantly played by men.

"If you get a positive correlation and someone wants to rely on it," Willner said, "then you might expect that their reason would be because it promotes teamwork. Someone who has played on a baseball team has demonstrated good teamwork and learned good teamwork skills. But that's not really any different for softball. So it's really important when you find keywords to be able to give a job-related reason why that keyword is important."

Such a connection would be hard to make in this instance. Softball and baseball are very similar team sports, so why would the algorithm weight one differently from the other? Likely because successful people whose résumés were used to build the algorithm were predominantly men, and some of those men played or liked baseball. *Baseball* then became associated with success in the job even though it actually has no meaningful relation to the job, except that a few successful workers happen to like baseball.

Mark Girouard, another employment lawyer I spoke with, found similar problematic keywords in a résumé screener. "Two of the biggest predictors of performance were having played high school lacrosse or being named Jared," said Girouard, an attorney at Nilan Johnson Lewis in Minneapolis, Minnesota. Based on the training data the system was fed, the computer correlated those two variables with positive performance.

"That was probably a very simple tool where the data set it was fed was 'Here's a bunch of individuals who are strong performers and here are their résumés.' The tool just finds those correlations and says, 'These must be predictors of performance,'" Girouard said.

"So, could somebody say, 'Playing lacrosse in high school—maybe you are very good at teamwork? Teamwork is something that's job relevant here'?" I asked.

But if teamwork is an essential quality for the job, why does only lacrosse and not other sports such as softball or volleyball or basketball or even choir matter?

Girouard said I was thinking like a human trying to find meaning in the algorithm's output. "You are making a connection that the tools are not making, because you are saying that there is some kind of theoretical reason why playing football would have something to do with the success there—as being aggressive or being a go-getter. But all the tools are saying is people who have *football* on their résumé tend to do well. And therefore we should take people who have *football* on their résumé without really thinking of the why. And that's what's missing: the why."

For this résumé screener, there was no deeper meaning associated with the applicant's name or even what sport they play or are interested in.

"The people who were rated as high performers also happened to have those things in their résumés, even if there isn't a logical correlation," Girouard said.

It was just a statistical correlation that says nothing about a person's ability to do this job. And it probably happens because résumés are semi-unstructured and it is not as easy for a digital tool to ingest and rank text on résumés as one might think. Some applicants label one section, for example, "Relevant Experience," whereas others may call it

"Work History," so to be on the safe side, some tools ingest all words on a résumé, which then can lead to résumé screeners predicting success by first name or hobby.

Although statistically many recruiters spend only six or seven seconds reading a résumé, Matthew Scherer, senior policy counsel at the Center for Democracy and Technology, prefers humans over digital résumé screeners.[4] "I would take six seconds of most HR recruiters looking at a résumé over what most of these machines do, seven days a week and twice on Sunday," he said.

"In those six seconds, their eyes will go to the parts that matter on the résumé. I don't care if a résumé parser reads every single word on the résumé and looks at what extracurricular activities they engage in, that shouldn't matter for the job."

He added that hobbies and extracurricular activities should be excluded from the decision-making process because, more often than not, they are based on social and cultural factors and are probably not connected to the person's actual ability to perform the job.

The problem is that many companies simply let the tools run without supervision; not many people are looking under the hood to see what the machines are actually doing.

Hiring and other employment decisions in the United States are governed by a set of laws (Title VII of the Civil Rights Act and others) and the uniform guidelines—a list of principles created by different government agencies in 1978.[5] Surprisingly to me, these laws and guidelines do not mandate which screening tools employers can use or that a company needs to use a tool that picks the most qualified candidates or makes accurate predictions. "They could hire only Lakers fans if they wanted to," said Aaron Konopasky from the Equal Employment Opportunity Commission (EEOC) Office of Legal Counsel, even when basketball has nothing to do with the job. "There are no sort of general requirements that the employer has to make rational decisions or great business decisions or anything like that."

When hiring, employers in the US are not allowed to discriminate against applicants because of their race, color, religion, sex, national origin, age, disability, or genetic information.[6] So if an employer wants to hire only Lakers fans, for example, for an administrative assistant job at a healthcare company, even though the job has nothing to do with basketball, that would be fine if protected groups go through the screens or assessments in roughly equal proportions.

But if an assessment tool, including résumé screeners, causes a negative impact on groups of candidates based on sex or race,[7] an employer's hiring tools could be challenged in court and hiring managers might be asked: "Why do they need to know what my favorite sports team is? What possible role could that be playing in predicting whether I am going to be a good accountant or not?"

Thus, Konopasky recommends that employers choose tools that are accurate and predictive and that work. He also suggests that companies ask vendors which variables are being used during the selection process and question why potentially problematic ones like hobbies, which are probably not relevant to the job, are even used. "You have to ask, 'What has been done to make sure that this thing is making the kinds of decisions that we want it to make?' rather than focusing on some sort of irrelevant factor or duplicating past discrimination."

The EEOC has never updated the uniform guidelines. But the commission has investigated individual companies. In 2022, the EEOC filed a lawsuit against a Chinese company, under the brand name "iTutor-Group," which hired English speakers to tutor students in China. The EEOC alleged that the company used algorithmic tools to automatically reject applications from women over fifty-five years old and men over sixty years old. The EEOC stated that more than two hundred applicants in the United States were harmed.[8] The lawsuit is significant, because it was the first lawsuit by the EEOC which involved a company's use of AI, according to Reuters.[9] In 2023, iTutorGroup settled the suit and agreed to pay $365,000.

In early 2023, the EEOC investigated DHI, a company that operates a job platform for talent in tech called Dice.com, for potentially allowing discrimination based on national origin. Some job descriptions on the site stated that applicants on certain visas were preferred ("OPT," "H1B," or "Visa" near the words *only* or *must*), possibly constituting discrimination against American citizens. In an agreement with the EEOC, DHI consented to use AI to scrap these kinds of keywords from job postings on Dice.com.[10]

GENDER-BASED DISCRIMINATION

And sometimes when AI meets the unintentional behavior of job applicants, that can cause systematic discrimination as well. I learned this from John Jersin, the former vice president of product management at LinkedIn.

There are numerous ways unfair practices, including gender bias, could creep into a job platform's algorithm, possibly hurting thousands or tens of thousands of applicants who use these sites to find a job. The stakes are high.

"We are talking about people's economic opportunities, their careers, their ability to earn income and support their families, and we're talking about these people not necessarily getting the same opportunities presented to them because they're in a certain gender group," Jersin said.

THE DATA IT TAKES

The potential discrimination I have uncovered is hidden in the pile of data we all produce when we visit job platforms, sign up for their services, and apply for jobs. The most problematic type is behavioral data—the trail of data we leave when we are interacting with the platform.

"What actions you're taking on the platform can tell us a lot about what kinds of jobs you think are fit for you or which kinds of recruiters reaching out about opportunities are more relevant to you," John Jersin said.

We all think that we are unique individuals, and we are, but it turns out that our background is often intertwined with our behavior. When Jersin and his colleagues took a closer look at job platforms, they found that, overall, men and women behaved slightly differently from each other, which could have led to discrimination against women.

It's not a secret that many men (of course not all!) apply to jobs even when they only partly have the experience and skills needed to do the job, whereas many women (of course not all!) only apply to jobs for which they are at least 80 percent if not a 100 percent or 120 percent qualified.[11]

"So we see that men are slightly more aggressive in applying to jobs relative to the level of qualification that they have," Jersin said.

Nothing wrong with that, except Jersin knew that these gender differences could be amplified by artificial intelligence when the AI is tasked with matching people to jobs.

"You can end up with situations where you are treating groups of people differently and you might be recommending, for example, more senior jobs to one group of people than another, even if they're qualified at the same level," Jersin said.

Many job platforms don't just task their AI with finding the potential employees who are most qualified for a given job; instead, they instruct the AI to find the people who are qualified and likely to apply or have interacted with the target company before. "Most platforms are trying to optimize something like the number of applications per job or the likelihood that someone is to respond to a message," Jersin said.

The folks who are more engaged on the platform, for example, in messaging recruiters—which men on average do more often than women—the AI will likely recommend more often to recruiters. The AI doesn't "know" who is a woman and who is a man, but it detects these gendered behavioral patterns and may inadvertently recommend to recruiters more men than women based on the patterns.

The root problem is that AI tools are programmed to make decisions to rank "similar looking" applicants.

"We certainly shouldn't want our systems to work that way to pick up on these potentially minor behavioral differences and then drive this radical difference in terms of opportunity and outcome as a result," Jersin said. "But that's what happens in AI. It takes whatever data you give it and it takes these small differences and it really works hard to optimize whatever small difference exists by really digging into that, really leaning into that difference so it can get slightly better results than you would get in a random environment."

The outcome, according to Jersin, is that women, on average, receive probably fewer opportunities on job platforms than men. This is a problem that platforms need to be aware of and fix because users can't opt out of it. Unfortunately, most AI tools are not set up to course-correct.

In 2021, I spoke to representatives at Monster, CareerBuilder, and ZipRecruiter about this problem. None of the platforms at the time checked for this kind of discrimination, which worries John Jersin. He believes that this kind of problem might go unnoticed because standard bias mitigation strategies, including hiding names, profile photos, and gender pronouns, are not helping to prevent it.

AI TO FIGHT AI

At LinkedIn, John Jersin came up with an unusual solution to curtail this potential form of discrimination and have diversity by design: his team built AI to fight AI. They called the intervention "representative results."[12]

"What representative results does, it tries to catch that bias in the algorithm before it hits the end user," in this case the recruiter or the employer, Jersin said. The new AI ensures that before giving a list of job seekers to a recruiter, the recommendation system includes a representative distribution of qualified job applicants across genders.

Here is a simplified example: In City A, male Python software developers outnumber females 80 percent to 20 percent. If the AI includes behavioral data, including signals of candidates expressing interest in the hiring company and signals of men in the pool who behave on average more aggressively on the platform than women, on the first pages of results the distribution of qualified candidates may look more like 90 percent males to 10 percent females. Representative results pushes against this and roughly tries to keep the original ratio of 80 percent to 20 percent on the first few pages of the results it sends to a recruiter. It maintains the level of quality of job candidates but makes sure women are not discriminated against, Jersin said.

There is unfortunately no way to test how well representative results works, but there might be some indirect evidence pointing to it working. Aleksandra Korolova, a former computer science professor at the University of Southern California, and her team investigated this "gender skew" on LinkedIn and Facebook by posting job ads for pizza drivers and supermarket shoppers in 2021.[13] The researchers found the gender skew in job ads posted on Facebook—significantly more men were offered pizza driver jobs although the qualifications for pizza drivers and supermarket shoppers were the same—but they didn't find it at LinkedIn, where representative results was employed.

Not only does AI potentially skew the list of qualified job candidates recruiters are shown, but it also affects the opportunities job seekers see on online platforms. For example, the job ads you see on a job platform are selected by AI and might also be infected by bias and discrimination in that an AI tool is more likely to show senior positions to a person who applies to more senior positions regardless of whether their qualifications match the job requirements. And more men apply for more "reach positions" than women, so more men will likely get served more senior job ads, Jersin said.

But maybe, you ask yourself, this is not a big concern because technically anyone can seek out any job opportunity online? But who has the time to google around to find appropriate job ads? We go to these job platforms to find the right jobs for us. If LinkedIn, Indeed, or ZipRecruiter offers us these "personalized" opportunities, we may start believing that these are really the jobs "people like us" are qualified for and should be applying to.

AI picks up patterns of behavior, just not the right ones in the case of gendered behaviors, which have nothing to do with how qualified individual job seekers are but more how they have been culturally conditioned to behave.

THE ERROR FACTOR

And sometimes the problem with automatic tools is not based on complicated algorithms. Programming and clerical problems are significant as well, the experts say.

Another company former employment lawyer Ken Willner worked with discovered problems with its algorithms by accident. The company, a long-term client of his, built adaptive tests for hiring. Adaptive tests are preemployment tests that adjust to the level of the job candidate taking the test. If a job candidate answers a question correctly, the next question is harder. If they answer a question wrong, the next question is easier.

Willner's client wasn't trying to solve this particular problem. It came across it by chance. The team essentially discovered that the adaptive mechanism was upside down: folks who had answered a question right, who should have gotten a harder question, were scored as having gotten the question wrong and were served easier questions. Job applicants who answered questions incorrectly were scored in the system as having given the correct answers and received harder questions. This happened to lots of the job applicants, which meant that many were probably rejected based on this software flaw. The company fixed this problem going forward but couldn't do anything to fix it retroactively.

Brian Kropp, former managing director at Accenture, where he covers human resources, shared an equally troubling story of a coding mix-up.

"Candidate 20 got the results from Candidate 21, Candidate 21 got results from Candidate 22, Candidate 22 got the results from Candidate 23. One of their rows in their data field was off," Kropp said.

For about three months all the hiring decisions at this company were wrong. This is not the only time Kropp has seen this problem. "The number of simple programming mistakes that occur in these sorts of places are significant."

Harvard business professor Joe Fuller has identified other systemic problems prevalent across the industry. He started questioning a narrative that is all too familiar to many of us: Companies complain there are no qualified candidates, and yet they also complain that they are drowning in applications. And candidates are frustrated that it sometimes takes hundreds of applications to find a job. Both candidates and jobs are out there. "How could such a breakdown in the fundamental laws of supply and demand occur?" queried a study coauthored by Joe Fuller.[14]

He and his Harvard Business School and Accenture research team surveyed more than two thousand company leaders in the United Kingdom, the United States, and Germany and found that over 90 percent of the companies surveyed used some form of algorithm-based technology to filter or rank a candidate pool: to shrink the number of applicants considered for hire.

The team concluded this is one of the reasons why many workers have to submit lots of applications to secure a job. The technology that is supposed to make everything easier ends up filtering out many qualified candidates in the name of cost savings.

According to the research, these résumé screener tools reject too many candidates because they are optimized for efficiency. "A large majority (88 percent) of employers agree, telling us that *qualified high-skills candidates* are vetted out of the process because they do not match the exact criteria established by the job description" (emphasis in the original).[15]

Job seekers have long guessed the technology that promised to democratize access to jobs was doing the opposite: only letting very few applicants through. And for the first time we have proof that executives know and accept that résumé screening tools are broken and eliminate qualified candidates from being considered.

In general, Fuller said, companies' hiring pipelines are broken. The tools are designed to shrink the talent pool, so they are programmed to seek the words used in the job description and proxies such as a college degree or a precisely described skill. Folks with adjacent skills or no college degree, who still have relevant experience, may be excluded.

Another problem in the hiring process is ballooning job descriptions. Over time, most employers simply add new criteria to job descriptions and don't evaluate whether someone *really* needs all these skills and competencies to get the job done. In job postings for entry-level retail clerks, Fuller found the average number of skills today is thirty-one. Way too many, in his opinion.

With more and more skills listed in job descriptions, AI tools are then used to essentially exclude more and more job seekers who lack "nice to have" skills because they don't check *all* the boxes of what an employer wants. Instead of a basic filter that looks for the five skills that really matter on the job, the tools are more like a fine mesh rejecting lots of candidates and only letting a few through. The tool then ranks candidates, and that gives recruiters a sense of precision, but it's a false one, Fuller said. Some of the tools are very rudimentary. In some résumé screeners, even using slightly different words to describe the same skills as mentioned in the job description can lead to a rejection.

This narrowing of the selection criteria might also be the reason why hiring managers are so often unhappy with the candidates they take a closer look at. The ones who check all the boxes might be average, possessing all the skills they are asked to have, but might lack outstanding skills.

The day I connected with Joe Fuller, he had spoken to an executive in the UK who confirmed this hypothesis. The executive had asked his people to scrutinize their hiring process. They found that their system had rejected people who got near-perfect scores on almost all criteria and then scored a zero on the last criterion. The company ended up with a bunch of people who had middle-of-the-road scores across the board, and the hiring managers complained they couldn't find highly qualified people.

Fuller also found that some résumé screeners and in-house applicant tracking systems (ATSs) use criteria that are unfair. For example, a gap in full-time employment longer than six months can lead to automatic exclusion by almost half of the tools used by executives Fuller's team surveyed, even though a work gap has nothing to do with whether a candidate is qualified for a job.

"A recruiter will never see that candidate's application, even though it might fulfill all of the employer's requirements," the team wrote in their report.[16]

The reason why these applicants temporarily left the workforce doesn't matter to the tool. They could be applicants whose spouse or child was ill, who had physical or mental health needs, who had a difficult pregnancy, who relocated due to a new posting as a military spouse, who were incarcerated, or who were taking care of young children or their parents. None of these reasons matter: one strike and you're out.

A human recruiter might be more understanding of the reasons someone would have to leave the workforce for a while. During the early months of the pandemic, for example, roughly 3.5 million mothers with school-age children left active work in the US.[17] A human recruiter might remember that and put a résumé on the yes pile even though the applicant was out of work for longer than six months.

This six-month gap is a "pretty insidious filter," Fuller said. It doesn't matter if you are the most qualified candidate; algorithms are unforgiving. They do what they are programmed to do: "Minimize the time and costs recruiters spend in finding job candidates," Fuller said.

These systems must change. HR managers need to investigate the tools they use and understand whether the selection criteria are meaningful and lead to hiring people that are successful long term.

"How do I link my performance management system results with the personnel files, so I can see 'here are the five best performers in this job hired in the last five years'?" Fuller asked. HR managers need to start digging and really understand why these folks have been successful: "What are their common attributes? What does it say in the performance reviews? How are we measuring effectiveness, let's say, productivity? Who stayed?" HR managers also need to account for bias that may have crept into the system.

These are the questions and steps that will help companies build better tools and also understand on what grounds the machine learning software rejects candidates.

But when it comes to an applicant getting hundreds of rejections, it's hard to turn off the little voice asking if maybe they just aren't qualified. How do we know that it is not the applicant's fault when they don't get chosen? Joe Fuller believes that if a candidate is reasonably qualified for the position, a rejection is probably not on them.

He argues that AI systems are so good at rejecting qualified applicants that when companies start using programs that hire people who have previously been "hidden"—they were rejected from the talent pool by automated tools—the companies are surprised that these job seekers turn out to be overachievers. They are more productive, more motivated, more engaged than folks recruited through more traditional hiring channels. "I think it's pretty compelling evidence," Fuller said.

So, why is recruiting still broken? It's because many companies are focused on the wrong metrics: their first priority is to reduce costs and the time it takes to fill a position. Most often recruiters are evaluated by how fast someone is hired. "A recruiter eager to fill a position as cheaply and as quickly as possible will not spend time contemplating the potential of candidates from nontraditional backgrounds," wrote the team in their report.[18]

Joe Fuller's report calls it ironic that company leaders keep complaining about not having enough qualified candidates for jobs, when they know that their own hiring processes are broken and actively excluding the very applicants they claim to so desperately want: "Employers almost universally acknowledge that these negative filters cause them to inadvertently exclude qualified candidates some, if not most of the time."[19]

FIGHTING DISCRIMINATION
IN HIRING TOOLS

The hiring process needs to change, but traditionally, hiring and human resources have been seen as cost factors that don't directly contribute to the company's bottom line, although, arguably, hiring top talent might be the most important task many companies can do for their bottom line.

With the progress of AI, it might be possible to understand which new hires are successful, but I have not seen this done in the real world, maybe because it would take a long time to set up and years of tracking employees. Companies would also have to understand what makes someone productive or successful, which is a pretty hard thing to do.

I am hoping that companies learn from this and become more cautious, first analyzing and testing applicant tracking systems before they use them on job seekers and make material decisions about who gets hired and who gets rejected.

Some of what Joe Fuller found about the hiring industry might have affected Sophie as she was searching for a job. After we chatted, Sophie dug deeper to see if she could find out why she had been rejected so many times. She embarked on a little research project.

She uploaded a job description and her résumé to an online tool that helps applicants understand how their résumé will likely be scored by an automated résumé screener. From the results, she deduced that if her résumé was being analyzed only by AI, "I would never make it regardless of my skill set because my résumé is only 40 percent read by the machine," she explained.

A 40 percent match for a job description is pretty low. A 60 percent to 80 percent match rate score is what some online services suggest applicants should aim for. But for Sophie, this explained some of her experiences when she uploaded her résumé into companies' hiring systems that sorted the data into a spreadsheet. Often, the software would show her that some fields such as experience, education, or skills either were empty or had the wrong information copied into them from her résumé.

"I always had to fill in the rest of the stuff to match what my résumé says," Sophie said.

She applied to nearly 150 jobs and only ever advanced to the next round when she contacted recruiters directly on LinkedIn, essentially circumventing the applicant tracking systems.

Now Sophie sees part of her mission to detect and take down discrimination in tools: "Getting into tech, I'm excited, but I know we have a lot of work to do as far as getting rid of algorithmic biases. And this is only the beginning because history repeats itself. We're getting away from the whole racist discrimination with us people. But now we have a whole other battle having to do with robots."

In the future, there might be less possibility for a human workaround to avoid the machines because it is likely companies will employ more AI and automation, not less. But new AI tools are helping job seekers as well. Many applicants are using ChatGPT to write their résumés, cover letters, and answers to potential interview questions.

One social media user rejoiced that someone had gotten a job interview after using ChatGPT to write their résumé and cover letter: "I'm just laughing at the notion of the résumé screening bots liking the ChatGPT-written ones the best." Others commented how ironic it was that HR has been using AI tools that now have to deal with résumés and cover letters written by AI. AI versus AI—may the best tool win!

CHAPTER 2

Cambridge Analytica for Work

On Scanning Your Online Life

My ears were ringing. I couldn't believe what I had just heard: a company was selling Cambridge Analytica–like personality profiles for hiring.

If you don't recall this scandal, Cambridge Analytica, a political consulting firm, used social media data provided by Facebook to build personality profiles of people that it then sold to political groups to target messages and peddle influence. They were exposed in 2018. The consensus was that the firm had crossed the line.[1]

I found out about this tool predicting job applicants' personality profiles from social media feeds during a conversation with a CEO of an AI-based hiring start-up. We were chatting about the newest products and some of the dodgy algorithms that they saw emerging in the field.

I asked my favorite question: "What keeps you up at night?" They hesitated. I understood. It's hard to point out flaws in your own industry.

They reluctantly shared with me that there is a company that predicts personality traits based on users' social media feeds—with or without users' consent.

"A company is predicting personality traits based on someone's Twitter or LinkedIn feed? Kind of what Cambridge Analytica did for Facebook users?" I asked.

"They are a little creepy," the CEO said.

When I checked the company's website, even I got a bit of a jolt: its idea topped even the other "science fiction" tools I had discovered; DeepSense, now Humantic AI, advertised that with just an email address the company's algorithm can scan social feeds of job candidates and give hiring managers hidden insights into job candidates: "Get to know their real persona, not just the persona that they want you to see. Let DeepSense predict their culture fit, personality and behavior for you."

Scanning candidates' social media history is the second of the four strategies AI hiring programs use and what we explore in this chapter. But unlike résumé screeners, this strategy is less straightforward and perhaps a bit troubling despite sounding like a magic algorithm. Humantic's AI claims it can predict who a candidate really is. It can tell if I am conscientious, a team player, how open I am, if I am emotionally stable, how much supervision I need. It probably knows more about me than I do. And that information is just there hiding in plain sight—in my social feeds.

This kind of personality prediction software is part of new AI-based tools that are pushing into the world of work. We already covered the pros and cons (mostly cons so far) of résumé screeners. Predictive tools attempt to do more than sort the information people provide. They use our data—the more the better, including text we write at work and on our social media feeds—to analyze our personality and predict our behavior.

As I dug deeper into this world, I discovered that our digital bread-crumb trails can affect how attractive we are as job candidates and whether we keep the jobs we already have as companies can run contin-uous social media background checks on us. I also found that many of these tools don't require the consent of the person investigated.

And, perhaps most shocking, they may not even work very well at the two things they claim to do—analyze our social feeds and predict our personalities.

A NEED TO LOOK UNDER THE HOOD

I understand that for hiring managers insight into the "hidden" person-ality traits and soft skills of applicants would be helpful information to have, especially through an instant social media analysis. (We see this growing need for personality insights again in the next chapter on AI games that applicants play that may decide if they get rejected or move to the next round of hiring.)

Soft skills and personality traits are growing in importance in hiring since concrete job skills have shorter and shorter shelf lives.[2] Rapid tech-nological change and unusual events, including the most recent pan-demic, forced companies and their employees to quickly adjust to new ways of working.[3] Instead of employees who have just one specific exper-tise or skill set, what's helping companies in uncertain times are employ-ees who can easily adjust to a changing world and teach themselves new skills and knowledge. This need for soft skills assessments will accelerate in the near future, said Tomas Chamorro-Premuzic, chief innovation officer at ManpowerGroup and a professor of business psychology at University College London.

"If we accept the fact that jobs are going to be disrupted and replaced, and 50 percent of the jobs you will find in 2030 or 2040 don't exist today, and there is a devaluation of expertise and knowledge, then you have to bet on things like curiosity, learning ability, people skills, and motivation," Chamorro-Premuzic said.

The underlying idea is that we all have somewhat stable personality traits that drive our behavior and should therefore be considered in hiring decisions. Algorithms that analyze social media feeds also seem like a much better way to access candidates' key personality traits instead of assumptions based on their résumés or job interviews. Most people probably wouldn't admit that they struggle to work well in teams, for example.

"Personality testing is roughly a $2 billion industry," Chamorro-Premuzic told the *New York Times* in 2023, up from an estimated $500 million in 2019.[4]

Some companies, including Harley-Davidson, asked their employees to take a personality test and include their top strengths in their email signature.[5] In others, the results of personality tests were used to diagnose office problems, wrote the *New York Times*. ("Sally is really struggling because she's a blue, so every time she gets rejected on the phone, she stews about it.")[6]

Traditional personality test makers say that their products help employers easily find whether candidates have sought-after traits, but they take a lot of time to fill out, are costly to administer, and cause employers inevitably to lose candidates in the process. And there is always a risk that candidates might be dishonest on a traditional personality test because they want to come off as more employable.

Several tech companies, including IBM, Humantic AI, and Crystal, have developed tools that use artificial intelligence and algorithms to create an instant personality analysis from anyone's social media feed—possibly without the candidate even knowing they are being assessed.*

We start our investigation by looking into social media background checks and then test out personality prediction tools—both are assembled by checking employees' and applicants' social media feeds.

TIPPING THE POWER BALANCE

Of course, hiring managers were able to check my social media feeds before AI-based continuous background checks emerged, but that was a cumbersome task—who wants to spend hours reading all of my boring tweets from years ago? And how can hiring managers effectively and fairly compare multiple social media feeds of different candidates? Score them in an Excel sheet? How would a recruiter know what my personality is based on my tweets? Seems impractical and impossible.

These new tools offer employers an unparalleled look at—or, better, into—us through unauthorized surveillance and psychological assessment. They are fundamentally changing an already fragile power balance at work and in hiring.

Traditionally, hiring is based on information job candidates disclose to, and usually carefully package for, the organization they are applying to. There has never been a true balance of power between applicants and employers, of course, because companies get to make the final decision about who gets a job. But I used to be able to decide what went into my application. I was in charge of curating which past

---

* IBM has already discontinued IBM Watson Personality Insights.

experiences and skills I put on my résumé or CV. I was in charge of writing my cover letter and highlighting or leaving out any experiences or skills I did not think were relevant. In job interviews, I could decide which information I wanted to withhold or share and even reference checks were suggested by me.

But AI fundamentally changes this already uneven power balance to give employers (almost) all power: algorithms can now find and reject people, some of whom may not even know they were being considered for a job.

This is not limited to just hiring decisions. Some companies use AI to run continuous background checks on their existing employees to check whether their workers are exhibiting violent tendencies, post racy images, are bullies, post about politics, may cause a scandal, or are prone to self-harm.

It's not clear to me that these tools measure what they say they can measure: How does a machine deduce from my Twitter feed whether I am prone to self-harm? What exactly constitutes toxic language? Will it harm my job prospects if I'm not on social media at all? How do these AI tools come up with a neat and easy recommendation or ranking at the end of the analysis—boiling down a person's rich inner life into one definite number? Many of these obvious questions go unanswered by vendors.

But they do assure us their products work—almost all websites feature stats in the 90 to 95 percent accuracy range. Vendors share white papers and case studies on their websites to convince employers that these tools work. But do they?

EXTREME VETTING

Kai Moore glimpsed the new and dark world of continuous surveillance by algorithm, according to *Vox/Recode*.[7]

In 2020, the company Moore worked for switched payroll systems and required a new background check for every employee. Moore's employer worked with a company called Fama to run these background checks, which included an AI social media check.

Vendors including Fama, Good Egg, Ferretly, and Intelligo advertise that they can find negative personality traits and questionable behavior of job applicants and current employees on social media.

"Fama helps highlight behaviors that put brands and celebrities at risk and surfaces bad content that is often hidden in reams of publicly available data," the company wrote on their website. Fama also marketed its background checks to government institutions, claiming its AI can predict who will leak information: "This publicly available electronic information (PAEI) can offer clues into an individual's perceptions, plans, associations, and actions."

In early 2019, Fama shared with CNN Business that the company had more than 120 clients and screened twenty thousand people a month.[8]

Human resources managers could check social media accounts themselves, and some do, but it's time-consuming (and in a legal gray zone). It's much easier to outsource this impractical task to an algorithm that scores and ranks people's online behavior in seconds and comes up with one clear recommendation.

The CEO of Fama, Ben Mones, claimed that a Fama report affects an employment or hiring decision about 12 to 15 percent of the time.[9] He also said that the reports are 99.98 percent accurate based on feedback from candidates.[10]

These companies offer not only a onetime snapshot of a person— these background checks can be run continuously.

"Looking at a person's past isn't enough. People change, for better or worse. Have they recently committed a crime? Do they abuse drugs, bully others online, or share racist memes?" asserts Good Egg on its website. Good Egg advertises that its AI social media background report flags insults and bullying, hate speech, obscene and toxic language, threats of violence, violent and racy images, and people who are prone to self-harm.

That's at least what the companies promise. Kai Moore, who uses the pronoun *they*, didn't believe the background check they were subjected to actually flagged this kind of behavior. Fama's algorithms scanned Moore's social media feeds and labeled them a "consider" rather than an outright "clear," wrote *Vox/Recode*. Moore was able to see the report. It contained more than three hundred pages analyzing all their tweets, retweets, and likes. They were not amused by what they saw.

A tweet Moore liked was flagged "bad" for language because the person mentioned "a cool ass candle holder." Tweets they liked that mentioned alcohol were flagged as "bad," including this one: "Merry christmas to the toddler I saw running across trader joe's with a giant bottle of peppermint vodka and mom running after him 'no no no no no no' only." One tweet mentioning "hell" in discussing LGBTQ identity was labeled "bad" for "language." Remember, Moore did not write these tweets; they merely "liked" them, but this all added up to suggesting the company screen Moore more carefully.

Even in its own marketing material, one vendor is not shy about showcasing questionable calls. The background check company Ferretly posted a screenshot of one of its reports that flagged this post as "political speech": "can we quit all the talk about not letting mental illness stop you we're not letting us stop us that implies moral and personal failure on our part im [*sic*] not saying that you shouldn't challenge or fight what your mental illness throws at you but let's cut the guilt tripping language."

Many experts have criticized this kind of social media analysis as primitive and harmful. The technology lacks common sense and the ability to recognize context cues.

A babysitter background check service called Predictim made similar mistakes when trying to predict whether someone would potentially be an abusive caregiver based on their social media posts, reported the *Washington Post* in 2018.[11] "When one babysitter's scan was flagged for possible bullying behavior, the unnerved mother who requested it said she couldn't tell whether the software had spotted an old movie quote, song lyric or other phrase as opposed to actual bullying language."

Predictim's website disappeared shortly after the exposé in the *Post*. Clearly, the technology could not make sense of context, humor, and sarcasm.

"The automated processing of human speech, including social media, is extremely unreliable even with the most advanced AI. Computers just don't get context. I hate to think of people being unfairly rejected from jobs because some computer decides they have a 'bad attitude,' or some other red flag," said Jay Stanley, senior policy analyst at the American Civil Liberties Union, to *Axios*.[12]

"I think it's really dangerous to give these kinds of algorithms so much authority," Kai Moore said. "It's such a terrible algorithm. It's a key word search."[13]

This raises the question of how the algorithm was trained and how it knows what real threats of violence are or when someone is sharing violent song lyrics on their Twitter feed. And what exactly constitutes bullying online? What do people who are prone to self-harm share on social media? And if it can be identified, isn't there something better to do with that information than exclude people who are self-harming from employment?

Moore was lucky that their employer disregarded the social media background check and didn't fire them. Others might not have been so lucky.

PUTTING MYSELF TO THE TEST

Let's set aside the ethics of secretly looking at people's social media feeds for a second and focus on an even more basic question: Do these tools work? Because the developers building these applications don't share much on how their algorithms make decisions, testing them with my own data provides some means of seeing whether these tools accurately predict what kind of employee I would be.

I am getting ready to run Humantic AI's algorithm over my Twitter feed and my LinkedIn profile. Humantic AI's services are accessible on the vendor's website. To use the Chrome extension, I had to be approved by Humantic. (A monthly package cost about $250 at the time.)

The CEO of Humantic AI, Amarpreet Kalkat, shared with me that recruiters working for Microsoft, Lockheed Martin, and other companies had used Humantic AI's personality prediction tool. The software let recruiters and hiring managers decide how much to weight each input, aka personality trait. For the role they are hiring for, they can decide whether an ideal candidate's "Attitude and Outlook" should be zero or ten or any score in between. The same goes for team working skills and general behavior (whatever that may mean). The software then ranks the candidates based on the hiring managers' inputs.

I usually enjoy testing technologies (Hey, I might learn something new about myself!), but with this tool I am feeling a bit squeamish. Maybe the algorithm knows more about who I am than I know about myself or what I want others to know about me. What if my personality is awful according to the algorithm? What does that say about me? Will

I ever qualify for another job? Will the AI discover that I am secretly a resentful and negative person? Thinking about this feels a bit like when I was thirteen years old and met a friend's mom who was a therapist—I thought when she looked at me, she could immediately see into my tormented soul. (She probably could tell that I was an awkward teenager with lots of insecurities.) It was frightening and I felt vulnerable just like now.

INSTANT SOCIAL MEDIA ANALYSIS

I have recruited Tomas Chamorro-Premuzic to test these instant personality reports with me. He is a psychology professor and believes AI is a wonderful objective force in the biased world of human hiring.

While we arrange where to meet for an interview, I find out that Chamorro-Premuzic lives in a new high-rise development on the waterfront in Williamsburg—a fifteen-minute walk from my apartment. On a day between Christmas and New Year's, it's cold in Brooklyn and our offices in Manhattan feel far away. He suggests we meet in a quiet common room in his building on a Friday morning.

He is shorter than I expected, has dark hair and a scruffy beard. He speaks with a slight South American accent and is driven by curiosity. He wants to know all about me, my work, and why I am fascinated by artificial intelligence. He is too.

"I might be a little bit naive and optimistic, but I do think that data-driven tools and the deployment of it at scale would also help us understand ourselves and our potential," he says.

Chamorro-Premuzic believes that our personality is embedded in everything we do, including in our online lives. "The music that you listen to says a lot about your typical emotional state, your personality, your level of interest in different things, your curiosity level, your intelligence level, the movies that you watch."

This one hits me. I am not too confident in my musical taste—I admit I love singing out loud to Eurotrash songs while driving and I hope no one will ever find out. In 2020, I became a mom and during those hazy newborn days I watched a lot of *The Great British Baking Show*, *Nailed It!*, and, really, some very questionable reality TV shows. Please, Algorithm, don't judge my intelligence based on this!

There are of course more things on Chamorro-Premuzic's list that help us make sense of people than our taste in TV shows and music. Uber ratings, for example, could be helpful when hiring someone for a customer service job that requires friendliness. "Things like Uber or Lyft ratings say a lot about how cordial, agreeable, friendly, or pleasant you are. If they have an Uber rating of 3.9 [out of 5.0]—probably not. A rating of 3.9 means that that person has systematically upset and offended hundreds of drivers if they use Uber enough."

I have never checked my Lyft rating before (I don't use Uber), but now I do—and I feel relieved. Drivers have given me a rating of 5.0 out of 5.0 during my 250 total rides over the past seven years.[14] (Although a five-star rating in Lyft is the default if the driver does not take action and rate me.)[15] Is there a pattern here that says something about me?

"If you examine people for long enough, just one individual, you will understand that, first of all, people are very consistent and that's sometimes not clear to us. But when others look at us, they see us in very consistent ways," Chamorro-Premuzic says.

That is the promise of this technology, and intuitively it makes sense that our personality would be part of everything we do online—because we did it.

AI is very good at finding patterns, including finding patterns of people's personalities in large data sets, something humans really can't do without the help of computers. This is one of the reasons artificial intelligence is such a powerful force. It brings something new to the table that humans have not been successfully able to do at scale.

"Nowadays, you don't need to ask people a lot of questions to understand what their preferences are and whether they are more extroverted or introverted, more neurotic or stable, or whether they have higher or lower IQ, grit or agility," Chamorro-Premuzic says. "You can just look at their typical patterns of behaviors."

Pattern recognition technology not only is used in hiring but also is the driving force of the internet. Companies like Facebook and Google collect my likes, my clicks, my posts—everything I showcase and leave behind on their platforms.[16] From this so-called online data exhaust (mixed with data from the offline world) the software infers my preferences, needs, motivations, and personality traits so marketers can target me more precisely.[17]

Cambridge Analytica used similar pattern recognition technology. The company, infamously, used predictive algorithms to build mass personality profiles based on Facebook data to move public opinion. In the United Kingdom, Cambridge Analytica was hired by the Leave.EU campaign to try to algorithmically convince Brits to vote to exit the European Union.[18] In the United States, Cambridge Analytica was hired by Ted Cruz's presidential campaign and then to help elect Donald Trump as president.[19] The idea was to build psychometric personality profiles of every voter and then target individuals to persuade them to vote a certain way.[20] In the intelligence community these tactics are known as "psychological warfare."[21]

When I started digging a little deeper into Cambridge Analytica's methods, I was surprised to find just how similar they are to the algorithm behind my personality profile generated by Humantic AI. Cambridge Analytica essentially built psychological profiles based on the Big Five/OCEAN personality assessment.[22] The theoretical groundwork for this type of social media analysis was laid by organizational psychologists Michal Kosinski and David Stillwell, who published influential papers about the prediction of personality traits based on Facebook likes while working at the University of Cambridge's Psychometrics Centre.[23] They found, for example, that people who "liked" *Battlestar Galactica* were likely to be introverts. Facebook users who "liked" Lady Gaga were likely to be extroverts.[24] In another paper, the researchers stated that they were able to derive highly sensitive personal attributes—including sexual orientation, ethnicity, religious and political views, personality traits, intelligence, happiness, substance abuse, age, and gender—from Facebook likes.[25] They claimed that once their algorithm analyzed hundreds of a user's Facebook likes, it could predict that person's personality more accurately than the person's own spouse could.

Kosinski, now a professor at Stanford Business School, sits on the science advisory board of Humantic AI.

WHO ARE WE, AGAIN?

So, Algorithm, who is Tomas Chamorro-Premuzic? What are his "hidden" personality traits? With his consent, I run Humantic's AI over his Twitter feed: The algorithm predicts he is "Analytical," "Cautious," and "Deliberate": "Being a team player comes naturally to Chamorro-Premuzic. Chamorro-Premuzic delivers best results when working with low supervision. Don't try to be too friendly. They might not be very people oriented. Avoid direct confrontation [. . .] be formal."

As an organizational psychologist, Chamorro-Premuzic has done dozens of these tests and knows his personality pretty well. "Do you see yourself in this?" I ask.

"I think about half of it I probably identify with and the other half not," he says. "I would say definitely the need for autonomy. I work with low supervision better than with high supervision. *Team player*—yes. *Be formal*—definitely not." (Even I can attest that he prefers to be informal and I have just met him.)

"I am cautious. Yeah," he says jokingly. (He is not!) "My PR and communications department will laugh at this one, but I will tell them, especially as they are very scared every time I tweet something."

We next run Humantic's algorithm over Chamorro-Premuzic's LinkedIn feed. In this case, the AI predicts that he is "Influential," "Energizing," and "Impulsive." A few minutes earlier, on Twitter, the same algorithm predicted that he is *analytical, cautious,* and *deliberate.*

Humantic AI Twitter	Humantic AI LinkedIn
Influential	Analytical
Energizing	Cautious
Impulsive	Deliberate

"I would say I am more impulsive than cautious and deliberate. And the two are the opposite extreme," Chamorro-Premuzic says. The technology thinks there are basically two different Tomas Chamorro-Premuzics out there.

That is not the result that researchers would expect. Psychologists have studied personality traits for decades and found that they are relatively stable over time.[26] If this algorithm picks up Chamorro-Premuzic's true personality traits from his LinkedIn profile, it should generate a very similar personality profile out of his Twitter feed—especially since I ran the reports less than five minutes apart. (If personality was fluid and ever changing, we shouldn't use it in employment assessments.)

But that doesn't happen. I feel kind of bad, since Chamorro-Premuzic is so excited about the technology. "There is an element of 'throw everything against the wall and see what sticks' here," he admits.

He and I then run the algorithmic tool from another company called Crystal over his LinkedIn profile to see if this algorithm could predict his personality. This time the three keywords are "Direct," "Assertive," and "Competitive."

Crystal AI LinkedIn	Humantic AI LinkedIn	Humantic AI Twitter
Direct	Influential	Analytical
Assertive	Energizing	Cautious
Competitive	Impulsive	Deliberate

"*Direct, assertive,* and *competitive* I think is better than *cautious, deliberate,*" he says. "'Tomas gets frustrated if someone is late to a meeting.' I get frustrated very easily. Full stop. So being late to a meeting is just one of the many things that frustrates me. 'Speak very directly or bluntly.' Yes. 'Enjoys argument and debate.' Yes. 'Work independently to meet a deadline.' Yes. I would say this one is better!" He's excited.

"'Stays focused on one point.' Not necessarily. I mean, I like to jump from one to the next point. 'Assert yourself with confidence.' Definitely not. I spent the last ten years writing books on how we shouldn't mistake confidence for competence."

Another mixed bag of results.

"How accurate was it for you, would you say?" Chamorro-Premuzic asks me.

We study my "report cards." My numbers in many categories are very different. My DiSC (Dominance, Influence, Steadiness, Conscientiousness) influence score is 3 on LinkedIn and 7.8 on Twitter. For "Steadiness," the system predicts 2.8 on my LinkedIn and 7.0 on my Twitter.

"I feel like I'm a completely different person in these two predictions."

Chamorro-Premuzic agrees: "They're all very different, except emotional stability."

Same algorithm, very different results depending on which social feed the algorithm runs over.

Seeing these results, Chamorro-Premuzic thinks there is still a need for human intervention: "AI is mostly a prediction machine. And human judgment is the ability to know what to do with a prediction." He recommends spot-checking algorithms. Especially when the predictions don't line up. "Well, maybe I should look for other data and see if it's consistent. Maybe I should explore why there is a difference. Maybe I should look at your job history and see, you know, what's the signal and what's noise? And that's why you need competence and you need expertise."

Unfortunately, we humans don't always rise to this challenge and ask the right questions to critically examine technology that is put in front of us.

TRUST THE MACHINE

While researching the use of artificial intelligence in employment, I spoke to a lot of hiring managers. Most pointed to one main problem they were hoping AI would solve: they are overwhelmed by the number of job applications they receive. AI promises a quick fix. One hiring manager, who started using an AI-based résumé screener because his recruiters were drowning in résumés and he needed a technical fix, told me that his people are not checking whether the algorithm works, since artificial intelligence never makes mistakes.

Researchers at Georgia Tech built a lab experiment that illustrates this lack of skepticism of technology all too well: in the experiment, the researchers created an emergency fire alarm with fake smoke, and most participants followed a robot, which they knew had trouble navigating the space, into a brick wall even though they themselves knew where the closest emergency exit was located. "Even when the robot pointed to a dark room with no discernible exit, the majority of people did not choose to safely exit the way they entered," wrote the researchers.[27]

Humans often blindly follow whatever technical devices tell us because many of us believe technology is superior and more objective. That's how technology goes unchecked and dodgy algorithms might cause real harm without anyone noticing.

Tomas Chamorro-Premuzic has another explanation for the discrepancies in my Twitter and LinkedIn predictive personality results: I might use one medium more than the other. That might be true, although both the Crystal and Humantic AI tools claim that even a writing sample of about five hundred words is enough to pull a personality profile out of any text. I counted the words in my LinkedIn profile—there are more than five hundred words.

Which brings me to my next point: If the algorithm doesn't have enough data, or not enough "good" data, to predict my personality, shouldn't it at least warn the user that is the case and *not* generate a profile? Or maybe it could at least display a disclaimer that the prediction will have a very low accuracy rating and therefore shouldn't be used to make high-stakes decisions, including hiring.

The problem is that once we see the ranking of candidates and their numbers on the dashboard, we believe they are real even though they might just be a prediction with a low accuracy rating, meaning the prediction could be totally off, but the way the technology is presented makes us believe it works.

It's a problem we see in a lot of algorithms—accuracy versus the need for results. Hundreds of AI-based start-ups and companies have entered the human resource market over the past few years and are under tremendous pressure to make money. It might not make much business sense to have an algorithm alert the user that it doesn't have enough data and shouldn't be trusted.

So, instead, companies often build different accuracy levels into their algorithms. The problem is that each accuracy level still showcases the same neat and clear results. So a facial recognition algorithm used by a police department might claim that someone is a match, but when one looks at the fine print it may state that the accuracy is 60 or 70 percent—not very high, especially for the high stakes of the criminal justice system.

A police officer shouldn't arrest someone based on a low confidence score, but Robert Julian-Borchak Williams, a Detroit resident, was arrested early in 2020 because of a wrongful facial recognition match by an algorithm.[28]

In retrospect, I shouldn't have been so nervous before I took these AI tests. In my and Tomas Chamorro-Premuzic's cases, none of the algorithms agreed on who we were.

WORD GAMES

I talked to the two companies about the predictive personality results and was surprised to learn about their methods.

Humantic AI's CEO Amarpreet Kalkat told me that his company's algorithm uses natural language processing libraries to analyze the text that is fed into the system. For the average user, that makes it hard to understand how the tool generates results—which words in the text or which words in tweets it specifically predicts upon.

Crystal's creators described to me in-depth how they validate their tests internally. Crystal asks some users to take traditional DiSC personality tests answering lots of questions. If the user rates their results as accurate, this data is used as ground truth for the AI-based model. The AI then takes in all the text that is associated with this user: "That information is things like the phrases they use on LinkedIn profiles, different words, job titles, employers, pretty much any information that is associated with that user," said Drew D'Agostino, CEO of Crystal.

To predict my personality, Crystal's AI compared the words I used on LinkedIn to the words other Crystal users with a traditional personality test on record have used on LinkedIn. Whoever I have the most words in common with, the system then bases my personality prediction on that user's traditional personality test results.

It seems odd that job titles and other descriptive words, including location names, are fed into the model since I probably used similar words to describe my job history as did other reporters who live in New York City. Does that mean I might have the same personality as others who use similar words and live and have worked near me? Or those who work in the same profession? Crystal acknowledged that there are no independent studies verifying that its method works.

John Scott, who evaluates assessment tools, thought that in theory instant personality tests could be efficient and cost effective. "The problem exists when the data that underlies some of this is filled with errors or the design of the algorithms is filled with errors," he said about

Humantic AI's and Crystal's software. "It's this going after the latest technologies that has resulted in a commercialization of these assessment tools that exist at the expense of sound, professional practice and good science."

I didn't want to rely on my own small experiment alone to make a judgment call about these two tools. So, together with a computer science, a psychology, and a sociology professor and other colleagues at NYU, we worked with four graduate students from NYU's Center for Data Science to run a larger experiment comparing Humantic AI and Crystal. Our team recruited more than ninety students at NYU and used their LinkedIn pages, résumés, and Twitter profiles to audit these two companies' algorithms, basically repeating in a nutshell what Chamorro-Premuzic and I did in a more scientific way and with a larger sample size.[29]

In an early testing phase, we made an unsettling discovery. We uploaded the same exact résumé to Crystal as a raw text file and as a PDF and got slightly different personality predictions off of identical documents.

When we ran Humantic's AI separately over participants' Twitter and LinkedIn profiles, the software returned different personality predictions for many of the people in our study—just like it did for Tomas Chamorro-Premuzic and me, contradicting many research studies that show that personality traits are mostly stable over time.[30]

When we compared Crystal directly to Humantic AI, the two tools assigned different DiSC scores to the study participants.

I reached out to Humantic AI and Crystal and invited the companies to comment on this study. Crystal this time did not answer my queries. Humantic AI's CEO Amarpreet Kalkat noted that the sample size of the study was on the smaller side, with 94 students, and that since

2021 "Humantic AI algorithms have undergone three major revisions" and that the company is now primarily focusing on giving personality insights to sales teams. (To me, giving sales teams advice on how to approach people is a less high-stakes usage of AI then using these kinds of algorithms for hiring.)

Unfortunately, these and other untested and unverified algorithms are still out there, making the process of finding a job even more opaque and delivering questionable benefits to busy hiring managers.

But there are still other AI tools that promise to accurately find personality traits of job applicants, which we explore next.

CHAPTER 3

The Games We Play

On Creative AI Tests

Since I started researching how artificial intelligence is used at work, I've heard about AI-based video games. Instead of boring assessments, applicants play video games so companies can learn whether they are the right person for the role.

If résumé screeners are not reliable and secretly scouring people's social media doesn't work, maybe playing games is a better approach. I mean, who doesn't want to play video games to get a job?

The idea is alluring and these games are in widespread use for jobs that attract recent college graduates to large companies, especially in finance.

And that's how Martin Burch encountered the technology when he was looking for a new job. I call him Patient Zero, because he is the first person I know who requested his data from the companies he applied to and initiated legal action.

Burch is in his mid-thirties and has worked with data for Dow Jones and *The Wall Street Journal* for years, moving from New York to London to Barcelona. In 2021, he applied for a data analyst position at Bloomberg in London, a role that was similar to the work he was already doing.

"There are not very many companies at Bloomberg's level when you are looking for a job in data processing," Burch said. "This job looked like it would be a good way for me to slightly pivot my skills and do something that I really enjoy and work with the best people."

On Sunday, May 2, 2021, Burch wrote a cover letter highlighting why he would be qualified for the job and submitted an application. He immediately got a response from Bloomberg that asked him to complete a digital assessment by a Canadian company called Plum. "Please note your application will be withdrawn should you not complete the assessment," read the email. He wanted the job, so he followed the link and started playing a gamified assessment right away.

THE ADVANTAGE OF GAMES

If you have applied to a job at McDonald's, Boston Consulting Group, Bloomberg, Deloitte, Kraft Heinz, IBM, Colgate-Palmolive, Hyundai, Whirlpool, McKinsey, Postmates, or many other companies, you might have been asked to play a suite of video games.

As we have seen, since the dawn of job platforms like Indeed and Monster, many employers say they are drowning in applications, especially for entry-level programs, which are popular with recent college graduates. Very few of the applicants have extensive work experience, so hiring for potential and personality (versus skills and experience) seems to make a lot of sense.

"The fundamental premise is that we all sort of have certain predispositions and they'll lead us to be more versus less successful," said Frida Polli, the former CEO of AI games vendor Pymetrics: "There's been a lot of research showing that different cognitive, social, and emotional or personality attributes do make people particularly well suited for role A and less well suited for role B. That research predates Pymetrics and all we've done is essentially make the measurement of those things less reliant on self-report questionnaires and more reliant on measuring your behavior." (In 2022, Pymetrics was acquired by Harver, a vendor that offers a suite of assessments, from soft skills analysis to interviews and background-checking services. The Pymetrics game suite has been incorporated into the broader Harver platform. Frida Polli became the chief data science officer at Harver, but resigned in April 2023.)[1]

It doesn't matter which positions someone is applying for, the games can work for many different jobs, the vendors say. It's all about how much the individual applicant's traits overlap with the traits that current employees exhibit.

Digital games are also increasingly used to find the right employees for internal promotions or leadership positions, said Caitlin MacGregor, CEO of Plum, the company that built the game Martin Burch was asked to play.

The vendors of algorithmic games for hiring that I spoke to said their tools reduce human bias and focus on applicants' innate talents, human potential, and soft skills.

Intuitively, this feels right: because of our personalities, some jobs feel like they are better suited for us. But there is also a counterargument: I have certainly met many doctors and teachers who all had different personalities and they each have found ways to be successful in similar jobs. Introverts and extroverts and people with other personality traits can succeed doing the same job. I understand that people don't want to hire jerks, but aren't skills more important? I am pushing the argument here, but I hope my accountant was not hired because they have the same personality as their colleagues, but first and foremost because they have the skills to be a good bookkeeper.

But in hiring, personality is a growing focus.[2] Skills matter, but only to a point and less and less so. Rapid technological change and unusual events, including COVID, forced lots of companies and their employees to quickly adjust to new ways of working and to pick up new skills.[3]

"Five years ago, everybody wanted to hire Ruby on Rails [programming language] developers. That was the hottest thing and you couldn't get enough of them. Now nobody wants to hire Ruby on Rails developers. The shelf-life of those hard skills is just getting smaller and smaller," MacGregor said. "We need to be focusing on potential first and then be looking at eligibility as one of the decision-making criteria."

Caitlin MacGregor herself cofounded Plum in part because a former boss had taken a chance on her when she started her first job. MacGregor had no relevant experience, but her former boss believed in her potential and that she could start a new business arm of the charity. Her job was to create a social enterprise for the charity, building a sweatshop-free, locally made, custom apparel company. Through this challenge she found her entrepreneurial side.

"If my boss hadn't seen my potential, there was nothing on paper that said that I knew anything about manufacturing and supply chain management in the apparel business. I had to learn everything from scratch," she said. And she succeeded.

POTENTIAL FIRST, SKILLS SECOND

As noted earlier, instead of specific expertise, many business leaders say that what's helping companies in uncertain times—be it a pandemic or a volatile start-up environment—are employees who can easily adjust to a changing world and teach themselves new skills and knowledge.[4] But how do hiring managers deduct from a résumé or in a job interview that an applicant is a team player or adapts easily to new challenges? That's almost impossible.

And that's where AI games come in.

"Ultimately, I just had this light bulb go off," Frida Polli said of her time at Pymetrics, "thinking, 'Okay, we know how to measure soft skills. We know how to measure the things that recruiters and candidates are looking to understand about themselves in a much more scientific, objective way. We don't have to tea-leaf-read off a résumé.'"

Safe Hammad, the chief technology officer and cofounder of game-based assessment provider Arctic Shores, believes there is a further benefit of AI games. Behavioral tests embedded in AI games reduce candidates' ability to fake their answers compared to traditional personality tests and job interviews: "When I ask a question about how would you react if you're in this position, you're not thinking, 'Oh, how would I react?' You're thinking, 'Oh, what does the person asking me want me to say that's going to give me the best chance of getting that job?' So without asking questions, it's a lot harder to fake and it's a lot less subjective."

AI games are also more enjoyable for job applicants, said Matthew Neale, vice president of assessment products at Criteria. Most people hate lengthy skills assessments or answering lots of personality test questions, but most applicants enjoy playing video games. While an applicant is playing, their in-game behaviors reveal aspects of their personality.

For example, a sociability score wouldn't be predicted by putting a candidate in a virtual room and measuring how many folks they approach. It's more abstract. "Actually, you really wouldn't realize it," Hammad of Arctic Shores said of his company's assessment tool. "There are a few tasks where we ask you to choose left, choose right, and press you a little bit and we come out with a measure of sociability," he said. "For me, it's magic. I understand the science a little bit underneath. I certainly understand the mathematics, but it's like magic."

Martin Burch, the data engineer turned job applicant, was asked by game maker Plum to play a sorting game. The assessment showed him three different shapes in two rows and asked him to choose which shape should be the third one on the third row, testing his pattern recognition abilities.

The software wanted him to solve more and more sorting tasks. After a while, he wondered what these games had to do with the job. "What does this question about the patterns on these blocks have to do with my abilities to scrape data from websites? Shouldn't we be testing my abilities in the job?" he asked himself.

Burch is not the only one with that question. Sophie, the navy veteran turned software developer from Chapter 1, had similar questions when a company she applied at asked her to play a game called Cognify. "For me," she said, "being a military veteran being able to take tests and quizzes or being under pressure is nothing for me, but I don't know why the Cognify test gave me anxiety. I think it's because I knew that it had nothing to do with software engineering. That's what really got me."

Sophie has a graduate degree in information sciences, with specialties in data science and interaction design. She didn't understand how solving a timed puzzle or playing video games that feel like Tetris could lead to a meaningful calculation of her potential to succeed in software development.

"I'm just like, what? I don't understand. This is not relevant," she thought as she played the games. "Companies want to do diversity and inclusion, but you're not doing diversity and inclusion when it comes to thinking; not everyone thinks the same. So how are you inputting that diversity and inclusion when you're only selecting the people that can figure out a puzzle within sixty seconds?"

LOSING A GAME VERSUS LOSING A JOB

Sophie and Martin Burch felt that the assessments weren't really optional. Burch needed to complete his to be considered for the job at Bloomberg, so he finished it. He took the Plum test on a Sunday. The next day, which was a bank holiday in the UK, he received an email from Bloomberg. It contained bad news: he had been rejected.

The turnaround time was surprising for Burch as was the rejection itself. He was working at a direct competitor, his experience lined up with the job description, and he had a track record of success. But still, he was no longer being considered.

He emailed a recruiter at Bloomberg and asked what happened. An answer came from Sophie Wallis, the former manager of campus recruiting at Bloomberg: "Looking at your application on our system I can see that your application was rejected due to not meeting our benchmark in the Plum assessment that you completed. Unfortunately on that basis we are not able to take your application any further."

Burch had been rejected by an algorithm. This didn't sit right with him. He knew he was qualified for the job, and he wasn't going to give up so easily.

"There are lots of reasons why you might not be the right fit for a job," he acknowledged. But he didn't understand how adding blocks in a row or answering questions in a personality quiz has anything to do with predicting whether he can scrape websites in a structured way, which was one of the main skills needed for the job he applied for.

Experts call this *lack of face validity*, when someone does not understand how a test or assessment is related to the job. (Plum said that it ensures that it matches talents that are job relevant.) Whether an assessment has face validity is a concern for organizational psychologists like Charles Handler, who for over twenty years has helped companies find the right tools for their recruiting processes: "If you have an applicant saying, 'Why are they asking me this?' you got a problem."

That's exactly what Martin Burch asked himself. He had worked for years at a leading news organization. Through that work, he learned that he had some rights to his own data. "At that point, I got out the good old GDPR tools."

General Data Protection Regulation (GDPR) is actually a pretty recent landmark data protection and privacy law. It gives residents and citizens in the European Union and in the United Kingdom the right to learn from companies how their personal data has been used. With that knowledge in mind, Burch reached out to Plum and requested his data. That is what makes him Patient Zero, the first person I'm aware of who used the law to dig deeper and find out more about why he was rejected for a job.

I also reached out to Plum and spoke with the CEO, Caitlin MacGregor. She told me that her company's products are evidence based: "Psychologists have done the research, and past experience and past education, [that information] is not a strong predictor of future performance. It can tell you if somebody can hit the job running. It can tell you, 'Can somebody do this job?' But it will not tell you if they will do it well. It won't tell you if they will be a low performer or an average performer or a top performer. You can't get that data from past experience and past education if you want to know if somebody is going to perform well and stay in the role. You need the data that we assess for."

The messaging around AI games sounds like a dream come true, where anyone can be matched to the perfect job based on their innate abilities and traits: "It is understanding what are those behaviors, that when you do them, it's like your bucket gets filled, it drives you," MacGregor said. "This [software tool] is quantifying what drives each individual person and the competencies and behaviors right down to 'this might drive you and this drains you.'"

People who are good at executing don't need to be micromanaged. They will drive themselves to fulfill a task because they love the satisfaction. Plum's "games" measure problem solving, personality, and social intelligence. Caitlin MacGregor said that this is a more holistic understanding of a person—albeit reduced to the ten talents the company screens for.

Plum's process starts with a job analysis—what does an employee need to be successful in this job? An eight-minute survey of multiple-choice questions asks stakeholders at the employer company to figure out which five of the ten traits that Plum tests for are the most important for the role. (Caitlin MacGregor avoided answering questions about what happens if a trait or skill important to a job is not part of the ten Plum traits.)

Then, the Plum applicant assessment consists of three parts. The first is a pattern-matching test—you are given three shape patterns in two rows and only two shapes in the third row and you have to add another one shape that fits the sequence; a personality test; and a situational judgment test, where applicants read short stories of potential problems in the workplace and are asked how they would react.

MacGregor gave me an example of a fictional candidate named Maya: Maya scored a 95 percent match for product manager, but only a 65 percent match for director of operations. She may have experience in both roles, but the assessment showed that, as a product manager, she is more like the other top 5 percent of the workforce at the company, so that's where she would be a better fit and excel.

This is a prediction, a forecast, a prognosis, so it's interesting for me to hear that CEOs like Caitlin MacGregor say so authoritatively that job applicants, like the fictional Maya, would be better in one job than in another.

It's striking that some hiring managers are okay with considering only a candidate's personality when making a decision of whether the individual should advance to the next round or be rejected. Experts say that there are many reasons why someone might fail or succeed at a new job: the managers, the team, the company culture, a personal situation, their skills, their past work experiences, their personality. It's fascinating that most assessments take only the traits and skills of the candidates into consideration.

I wonder if we will ever be able to consider applicants, and the teams they are about to join, more holistically. Unless this work is done, it may be magical thinking that some AI tools have found the right formula.

In the meantime, Martin Burch received his scores from Plum:

Problem-Solving: 75.06

Social Intelligence: 35.401

Industriousness: 20.598

Orderliness: 76.299

Stability: 32.487

Self-Regard: 29.822

Intellectual Disposition: 34.812

Experiential Disposition: 10.135

Enthusiasm: 42.673

Assertiveness: 4.333

Compassion: 73.42
Mannerliness: 88.818

Burch didn't get much of an explanation and he wondered what the numbers meant. Were these percentages? Was 88 a high score or a low score? Which scores were relevant in Bloomberg's assessment? (I asked Plum and the numbers are out of 100; the higher, the better.)

For regular job candidates who do not inquire about their data, the results are more vague. Test takers learn about their three most important traits.

I took the Plum assessment, as well, and my three most important traits were *communication, teamwork,* and *persuasion.* Burch and I compared notes on the tests we took and are pretty sure we took the same one; Plum has only one suite of games. But I am not sure how *communication, teamwork,* and *persuasion,* the traits I scored highest on in the same Plum test Martin Burch took, are connected to the twelve categories of results he got from Plum. How is persuasion related to enthusiasm, intellectual disposition, and industriousness, for example? It seems like Plum's assessment is trying to measure certain traits, then somehow translates them into other traits. The company told me that essentially there is an associated algorithm for each Plum Talent/Competency. For example, *communication* consists of these competencies: explaining key concepts with clarity, listening and attending to others, and responding to an audience and showing empathy. The competency *explaining key concepts with clarity* is composed of the following traits: *enthusiasm, assertiveness, orderliness,* and *social intelligence.*

This inquiry raised more questions. For one: How do these AI games work under the hood? I was given a glimpse when I reported on Pymetrics. The company sent me a link to try out its suite of games myself.

PLAYING WITH PYMETRICS

Once again, I am a bit nervous getting started. Maybe my personality traits aren't as "good" as I hope? Maybe the game will find out I am secretly mean and vindictive?

I take a deep breath and start playing. One of the first games in the Pymetrics suite is kind of vintage, with an early video game aesthetic. Think pre-Pac-Man.

I see a white background with either a blue, orange, or yellow balloon. I am tasked with inflating one balloon at a time. Every time I click "pump," the balloon expands just a little and I receive five virtual cents. My goal is to earn as much money as possible. But if the balloon pops before I press "collect" and receive my money, all my digital earnings for that round disappear.

As I play, the system is collecting different data points about my behavior—taking in all the signals, from my mouse movements to intervals between clicks.

As a player, I learn as I go: I quickly figure out that the orange and yellow balloons pop faster, so I make sure to collect my money earlier, after just a couple of pumps. But I can pump the blue balloons more than twenty times, earning over two dollars, which is more than I can make with the other balloons.

While playing the balloon game, I figure out a strategy and earn more money using this insight. Maybe the software is scoring me as a risk-taker and that's hopefully a good thing?!

After pumping up thirty-nine balloons, I have earned $14.40. A message appears on the screen: "You stick to a consistent approach in high risk situations. Trait measured: Risk."

The video games are not super engaging, but I understand that they are not designed solely for my entertainment.

While I'm playing, the machine learning–based system measures eight cognitive, social, and emotional traits, including generosity, fairness, emotion, and attention. I feel doubly vulnerable: a job application is a high-stakes setting and playing a game that will "reveal" my innermost personality traits is kind of scary.

In a real-world job application setting, the system would compare my traits to those of successful employees already working in the job for which I'm applying. If my traits line up with theirs to a similar degree, I'd advance to the next round of hiring. If my traits don't line up, I most likely would be rejected for this particular job.

During the game playing, my mind has random meta conversations with myself. I keep asking myself what this game might be testing as I am pumping balloons. What does it mean to share virtual money with strangers or hit the arrow keys to match the direction the arrows on the screen point? Other games are more straightforward: series of numbers flash on the screen one right after another and I have to note down the sequence.

For some of the tests, like the one where I have to press my spacebar as fast as I can, I am just confused. They don't feel like they are related to any kind of job I can think of.

THE SEARCH FOR HIGH PERFORMERS

When a new client signs up with Pymetrics, the company must select at least fifty employees who have been successful in the role it wants to fill. These employees play Pymetrics' games to generate training data. Next, Pymetrics' system compares the data from those employees with game data from more than ten thousand people randomly selected from over two million to find what makes this batch of successful employees special compared to the rest of the population.

"It's basically understanding how people that are successful in a role are different from what we call a baseline group," Frida Polli said. The system builds a model that identifies and ranks the skills most specific to the client's successful employees and also makes sure the model is fair.

Pymetrics prides itself on finding traits in job applicants that it says are hardest to train for, including flexibility, learning ability, and decisiveness. The company says it utilizes the same "state-of-the-art" data science recommendation engines used by Netflix, Amazon, and Spotify.

But as every user knows, Netflix's and Amazon's AI-based tools don't always get it right. That's not a problem with an AI tool that recommends products to me—it's Amazon's loss if its AI gets my preferences wrong and I don't buy anything. The stakes are much higher when AI games are used for hiring and giving promotions: if an AI tool gets my personality wrong and rejects me even though I am a well-qualified candidate, I wouldn't be so happy.

Experts see a couple of issues when it comes to using successful employees as a benchmark: Who decides who is successful? If successful employees are selected on the basis of annual performance reviews, that might be a problem because it's been shown that managers rate women and employees of color more negatively because of their own biases.[5] Are employees perceived as high performers because their manager likes to grab a beer with them or are these folks objectively high performers? And what does it mean to be a high performer, anyway—how is that objectively quantified?

Another issue is sample size and diversity within the sample. If the size of the sample is too small and includes many white men, who are selected as high performers, there is always a risk that the tool will pick up their traits and preferences and not the traits and preferences of other qualified applicants who might be of a different race and/or gender.

Matthew Neale from Pymetrics' competitor Criteria shared an example that explains why looking only at high performers and comparing them to the general population, as Pymetrics does, might be risky in hiring. Neale's company was tasked with finding assessments that could be used to hire high-performing healthcare workers for the client's organization.

Neale wanted to understand how high-performing healthcare workers may be different from the general population—is there something that makes them special? In an approach that at first mimicked Pymetrics', Criteria had "successful" employees take a test and then compared the findings to the general population. "When we looked at just the high performers," Neale said, "we found the high performers are more warm and agreeable, more friendly in their approach when they are interacting with others than what is typical in the general population."

He continued, "If you only looked at that data of the high performers, you might say, we need to go and hire people who are warm, friendly, and agreeable."

But that would have led the company down the wrong path.

"When you bring in the poor performers," he said, it turns out, "well, they're just as warm and friendly and agreeable as the high performers." High- *and* low-performing healthcare workers are warmer, friendlier, and more agreeable than the general population.

If companies only check high performers against the general population in searching for what makes their high performers special, they might find something that distinguishes the high performers from the general population, but that might not be a predictor of success.

If this company had hired healthcare workers based on how friendly and warm they were, they would have hired people based on a criterion that had nothing to do with being successful in the job. It would have been like basing high-performing basketball players' success on their height, which is taller than the average person. But low-performing basketball players are also taller than the average person.

Neale was able to narrow down what distinguished high-performing healthcare workers at this organization from low performers to how organized, diligent, and conscientious they were toward their work.

When I talked to other experts, they shared additional concerns about Pymetrics' and other AI game vendors' products.

Pymetrics says its games are derived from cognitive and neuroscience tests. Because of that, one expert suggested that Pymetrics' games could uncover signs of mental health issues, something that is not allowed to be assessed or questioned in the United States before a company makes an offer to an applicant.[6]

John Scott, the COO (chief operating officer) of APTMetrics, who found all the wrong keywords in résumé screeners in Chapter 1, is often brought in to check whether new technologies are fair and legal. He questioned whether some of these AI games really measure personality traits or just measure how well someone plays the games. "Is blowing up balloons really a measure of risk-taking?"

So, maybe I am a crazy risk-taker in a video game, but does that make me a risk-taker in my job when something more is at stake than a score in a game? The longer I think about it, this could be me: I love taking risks in video games because there isn't any harm, but in real life I tend to be more guarded.

"And, second, is risk-taking a characteristic necessary for this job?" Scott asked. It may just so happen that many successful accountants at a company that played Pymetrics' games are risk-takers compared to the general population, but taking risks may not be required for the job at all.

Tomas Chamorro-Premuzic, the organizational psychologist and chief innovation officer at ManpowerGroup, generally sees predictive analytics as a breakthrough technology, but even he is skeptical about Pymetrics' games. He and his two coauthors in his book *The Future of Recruitment* have strong opinions about companies like Pymetrics, which borrow heavily from experimental psychology, neuroscience, and other fields, including the balloon-pumping game in their software suites.

"These tasks are not designed to predict work-relevant behaviors or even to measure individual differences but to study cognitive processes or group dynamics. This means that scientific evidence for their relationship to job performance is limited or nonexistent," the authors wrote.[7] "While they are developed by psychologists to measure human behaviors, they might not be suitable to predict the real world outcomes relevant in recruitment unless carefully matched to specific job tasks and locally validated."

In other words, Chamorro-Premuzic and his coauthors state that it is unknown whether these tests can predict job performance. (Pymetrics said that the company used best practices for showing job relevance of the traits that it measures.)

Pymetrics shared a document that outlines the history and a scientific explanation of its games. I read the description of the balloon-popping game called BART and felt like a fool. While playing, I had figured out that the blue balloons took much longer to pop (which Pymetrics thought players would not be able to do), so I was able to amass more money playing the game, which I'd been tasked to do. My behavior came off as being a risk-taker, I assume, which I naively thought was a good thing—who doesn't want an employee who takes risks and pushes the company forward?

But the document Pymetrics shared via email, which normally requires the recipient to sign a nondisclosure agreement which I wasn't asked to sign, says that taking risks in the balloon game is associated with a tendency toward gambling and workplace maverickism. "Conversely, low-risk scores on the BART have been associated with more conservative behavior and higher positions of power."

Figuring out that the blue balloons took longer to pop than the yellow and orange ones—which doesn't say anything about my risk-taking tendencies—could have bit me in the behind if I were a real job applicant. My results in the game would have probably indicated that I was not cut out for a leadership position.

Claudia Prostov, a college graduate in her twenties, isn't so sure about Pymetrics' games either. She received her BA from the University of Mississippi in 2020 and applied to jobs through Indeed, Glassdoor, LinkedIn, and her school's career website. Late that year, Prostov applied for an operations associate role at McDonald's and was invited to play Pymetrics games.

She was curious about the assessment, so to prepare herself, she read about the games online. But she felt self-conscious when playing them: "I feel like I did things a little bit too fast," she said. "I was almost overthinking what the game meant as I was playing it."

I agree with Prostov. I felt self-conscious the whole time I was playing the games, constantly wondering why the software was asking me to do this or that.

Pymetrics identified Claudia Prostov's strongest traits as *focus*, *generosity*, and *fairness*. But that's not how she thinks of herself. She feels misrepresented—she believes *decision-making* and *effort* are her strongest traits. McDonald's informed her that she didn't advance to the next stage in the company's hiring process.

THE COGNIFY CHALLENGE

Cognify's suite of games is less about finding an applicant's personality and more about predicting their abilities.

"We know from years and years of research, like decades in research, that people who are good at processing information, learning new information, and solving problems tend to do better in the job," said Matthew Neale, the vice president of assessments at Criteria, which sells Cognify's suite of games. "This is a really well-understood individual difference between people."

Neale and his team decided to build puzzles and games to measure problem-solving and processing skills. "We know that it's related to job performance. And so this de-risks the whole situation because I understand what I'm measuring in someone," he said.

The first game I play is a version of Tetris, except that the puzzle pieces don't come at me at a certain speed. I get a grid and have to move the pieces in there—it's a timed exercise and it's supposed to measure my problem-solving skills and my visual and spatial abilities. It's fun and not super hard, but I keep forgetting that I am being timed. It feels like I am pretty slow.

The next game is harder. I get a target number at the bottom of the screen and math equations in a bubble. I have to click the right equation before the bubble evaporates.

I always thought I was really good at basic math equations because I helped elementary school kids with their homework when I was in high school and I also worked as a waitress in college in Germany. Groups of friends going out in Germany tend to split the bill, leaving the server to do the math. But now in the game, there are tons of bubbles coming up and I have to hit them super fast. This game is hard! I am getting annoyed at myself when I miss a bubble and I'm not sure how good I am at the game. Maybe I am not fast because I haven't played video games in a while?

I am also not sure if I ever had a job in which I had to solve math problems on the fly. What does that tell an employer about my abilities?

I then have to read a couple of work documents and mark all the mistakes in it—it's a basic English exercise. Although English isn't my first language, the game is surprisingly easy, but I definitely need more time to get to the end of each document.

Cognify's team chose to highly engineer the games and run them with close human supervision so employers know why a certain candidate is chosen. Cognify uses around twenty variables of data and the team knows which variables predict what.

Other tools will directly utilize every click, every drag, every time interval, every mouse move—generating potentially hundreds or even thousands of data points. But that makes it more complicated to understand which signals the system records and what these data points are measuring. "It's an order of magnitude easier when you have fewer features, variables, and predictors in the equation," Neale said.

If game developers have hundreds or thousands or hundreds of thousands of predictors, it's not clear how each predictor is related to a job.

"You lose the ability to say, 'Well, this is why this person got this score and this person got that score. This is what that person did when they were playing the game to get a better score,'" Neale said. It will be much harder for developers to describe why this is a good test for a particular role and why a company should trust the algorithm's results if they can't be adequately explained.

By closely combing through the data points, his team also found features that are predictive but possibly unfair.

"There are some situations where we will reject the recommendations made by the machine learning algorithms," Neale said. When the team built a puzzle-based game, the computer learned that the inspection time, the time before a job applicant starts a game, is a really important factor. "What the algorithm identified was that people who need less inspection time, who make the first move faster, are on average better problem solvers than people who take a long time to make that first move." It looks like a neutral predictor.

And that would be true if everyone had the same chance to sit down in a quiet place and quickly learn about the game without interruption. But, of course, our lives are more complicated. Some of us might need another minute to read or understand instructions. Others might not have a quiet room available at home.

"If you are completing the assessment in an environment where there are more disruptions, where you are less likely to be alone, where you are more likely to have people walking in on you, then you can be more easily interrupted in that initial inspection time. And that would harm your performance in the game," Neale said.

It wouldn't be fair for an AI system to predict that applicants who have a shorter inspection time are better problem solvers based on just that one predictor, which can easily vary because of outside factors and may not reflect someone's true abilities.

"Who is more likely to have an interruption while they are doing this kind of job application game? Who might be more likely to have someone walking in on them? Who might be more likely to have a kid come up to them and say, 'I need something'?" Neale asked. Mothers, of course. It would not be fair to penalize mothers, who are more likely to be interrupted. It's also not fair to penalize any applicant based on a possible distraction—we all get phone calls or emails at inopportune times.

"That is an aspect of fairness and equity that the humans and the experts bring to this kind of situation that the AI doesn't know about," Neale said. "That is why we decided to tinker up there and intervene."

The team decided not to include this signal in the algorithm.

But this kind of conscious turning off and turning on of variables can only happen if researchers closely investigate how the AI tool analyzes job applicants' data.

For Matthew Neale, this is the difference between game designers, who often come from a data science background, and folks who have a psychology background. Data scientists, more often than not, just want more and more data, including data from résumés, social media profiles, and AI games to predict the outcome they are after. Matthew Neale is a psychologist and has a different approach: "Our domain is more 'what information should we be looking at?' How do we design these application experiences to get the right data? And then indeed we can bring in the data scientists to analyze that information. But if you are not paying any attention to or exercising control over the data that you're feeding into the algorithm, then you are in a situation where there's high risk," he said.

That's why he and Criteria are using only data related to the job. The team made a conscious decision not to use just any data that is readily available, like social media feeds, if it lacks connection to the position.

"You're ending up with data that is poor quality and is less reliable. It puts you at risk of making employment decisions that, at the end of the day, are not legal," Neale said. "The levels of prediction that you're getting from here, the levels of signal that the providers are talking about, are often really low."

It also raises the issue of consent, because most people haven't agreed to let their Twitter feed be used in hiring decisions.

Sophie, the navy veteran and coder who sent out 146 applications for software developer positions until she found a job, also encountered AI-based games. She even practiced for them on YouTube, where a whole brigade of how-to video makers is trying to help people succeed in job assessments.

Sophie applied to IBM and had to do a Cognify assessment that she felt was not relevant to the job she was applying for. I played the recording of my interview with Sophie for Matthew Neale, who knows a lot of about the Cognify game suite. "For me, being a military veteran, being able to take tests and quizzes or being under pressure is nothing for me," Sophie said. "But I don't know why the cognitive tests gave me anxiety, but I think it's because I knew that it had nothing to do with software engineering—that's what really got me." She had actually practiced online but felt she was slower than others and took it to heart when she was rejected. "Any job that gives me a Cognify test—I'm automatically just going to say no," Sophie said.

"It's obviously always disappointing when someone doesn't have a positive experience playing one of our assessments, particularly one that we've put so much effort into building to be an engaging experience for candidates," Matthew Neale acknowledged.

"The intention behind Cognify is to look at people's ability to learn, to process information, to solve problems. I suppose that these kinds of skills are relevant in software design," he said. "That's the connection that I would draw between the assessment and the role."

In addition, Neale said that IBM did its due diligence. The corporation tested Cognify on its software developers and found that high-performing software developers scored higher on the assessment than others. IBM also made sure the assessment was not discriminating against different groups of applicants.

For Sophie, Cognify wasn't just another assessment that was "dumb," in her words. This one messed with her head. "At that moment in time, I wanted to give up and I was like, 'All right, maybe this industry isn't for me or maybe I'm just dumb.' And then I was just really beating myself up," she said. She was so down, she didn't apply for jobs for a few weeks.

Sophie came out of the funk only when a former student found a job. Sophie had been teaching this student, so she told herself that she couldn't be an imposter. She started applying again and eventually landed a role as a software developer.

WHAT GAMES CANNOT DO

Martin Burch, who took the Plum assessment as part of his application to Bloomberg, had a similar demoralizing experience. He had been scraping websites for years for his job, so he wondered why he had to fill in a sequence of shapes if he would still be scraping websites for the job at Bloomberg. And if he wasn't very good at shape sequencing, why did the games matter when he was already successfully doing essential functions of the job?

"These types of measures are trying to measure cognitive ability," work psychology professor Fred Oswald at Rice University told me. The tests could be related to job performance, but should it just override previous job experience? "If the job that a person is applying for is similar to what they've done in the past, how does this measure reasoning at above and beyond what's evidenced in the résumé?" It is doubtful that a reasoning test is a better prediction than previous experience.

AI games executives emphasized the importance of the science underpinning their hiring tools. Plum's CEO also took a jab at her competitors. "This is real science," Caitlin MacGregor said about her company's tool. "We beat out the gamification-type assessment companies because of the accuracy of our science."

She said that her customers' experiences also provide evidence that Plum works in practice. She knows that other AI tools are built on shoddy science: "We get very worried about the snake oil or the bad science in our industry."

MacGregor shared Plum's technical manual with me, which includes more than ninety pages of how their algorithm was tested and how her team made sure it worked. (The other companies declined to share their technical reports with me, which are supposed to lay out how these tests were validated and which, in my opinion, should be featured on every company's website.)

Matthew Scherer, a former employment lawyer specializing in artificial intelligence and hiring, read the technical report. As part of his job as a lawyer, he studied many technical and validation reports from AI vendors to assess the accuracy of their claims and help employer companies decide which specific tools they wanted to use.

He was not too impressed with Plum's report: "The entire report reads like a ninety-page effort to distract readers from the fact that, one, Plum does not measure candidates' ability to perform the functions of any specific job, and two, the things it does measure are not all that predictive of good job performance."

Scherer checked Plum's statistics in the report. How well do its tests predict job performance versus a random number generator? According to Scherer's math, "Plum's Talent Match scores tell you anywhere from 1.7 percent to 18.5 percent more about a candidate's ability to perform the job than you would get by giving random Talent Match scores to each candidate."

That means, in a best-case scenario, Plum's assessments account for 18.5 percent of someone's job performance. In the best-case scenario, 81.5 percent of an applicant's job performance rating cannot be explained by the Plum Talent Match score. In the worst case, Plum's assessments predict 1.7 percent of someone's job performance, and 98.3 percent of a candidate's job performance cannot be explained by Plum's assessments. I guess it's better than nothing. (Plum said that they have a .36 predictive validity index, which, the company stated, is a more accurate representation of the assessment.)

To Fred Oswald of Rice University, these numbers are not disappointing at all: "These numbers are pretty average." He cautions that no one has a test that can cover 100 percent of a candidate's job performance. But the question for him is if the tests are actually relevant and related to job performance.

Matthew Scherer believes the AI games are too abstract to be relevant for every job: "The information in the report does not suggest that this is an especially effective method of assessing candidates' ability to perform most of the jobs for which it was tested. That's not surprising, because it only measures very abstract/generic characteristics—far removed from the duties of any particular job."

That's the crux of a lot of games. They don't measure how well someone will perform the core duties of a job; instead, they attempt to assess whether someone has the right personality for a job.

For applicants, it's often nebulous what these AI games entail, so in response, there is a whole industry out there trying to help job seekers. Folks can watch and play the balloon game online in preparation for their assessment games and watch countless videos of people explaining other AI games used for hiring or finding internal candidates.

Unfortunately, many of these tools are calibrated to successful workers' results on the games, so no tutorial can anticipate what the AI is looking for. Some games are timed, so candidates should ensure they are not distracted and have slept well.

Even experts, including employment lawyers, who are sometimes brought into the process to evaluate AI tools, don't always know what these tools are evaluating. Companies may get in trouble if the tool (unintentionally) discriminates and causes adverse impact on any group.

Nathaniel Glasser is an employment lawyer with Epstein Becker & Green, based in Washington, DC. He and his colleague Adam Forman have been hired to check out AI tools for employers that are doing their due diligence before buying an AI tool. "What we have seen is often, not always, but often, in newer organizations, some of the start-up vendors are less sophisticated and they don't have the total understanding of the legal framework that's going to cover the use of the tool," Glasser said.

He recalled a specific situation a few years back when he and his colleague were brought in to evaluate a vendor of AI games that assessed risk-taking and trust, among other traits. Part of the due diligence was a pilot test before the company felt comfortable using the tool to make hiring decisions. The outcome wasn't what the company had hoped for: "After multiple rounds in beta prior to going live, the tool demonstrated adverse impact against the female applicants, and no matter the tweaks to the inputs and the traits and the algorithm itself, they couldn't get confident that it wouldn't continue to create this adverse impact," Glasser recounted.

Women didn't pass the tool at similar rates compared to men, and the difference had nothing to do with the job.

If the statistical differences between the scores of men and women or of different races in an assessment is related to the skills or requirements of the job, this type of "inadvertent discrimination" may be legal. For example, for firefighting jobs, applicants might have to carry two hundred pounds or more of equipment, which a supervisor might argue is essential to the job. A test like that may exclude more women than men. But if this difference is in a job-related business necessity, like carrying heavy equipment for firefighters, a company may legally be able to use that kind of test (although people could challenge and have challenged these kinds of assessments in court). But Glasser and Forman didn't think that reasoning applied to their client.

"We don't know for sure that, even if the difference is attributable to some personality difference between men and women, that is necessary for this particular job. And so we are going to look for a less discriminatory alternative that might be using a completely different method of selection," Glasser said. The legal risks were too high.

Their client decided not to work with this AI games vendor and found another assessment to use. The vendor, Glasser recalled, was a start-up at the time and since then has grown and done quite well. He hopes it learned from these tests.

A team of industrial-organizational psychologists at Rice University, Texas, which included Fred Oswald, and the Human Resources Research Organization (HumRRO) published a paper in December 2021 showing that the AI games they built to test for the most predictive personality trait in hiring, conscientiousness, didn't reliably predict it, despite the team's decades-long experience building and evaluating assessment tools.[8]

Charles Handler, the organizational psychologist and host of the industry podcast *Science 4-Hire,* said that at least five of his clients tried Pymetrics and then abandoned the tool because they didn't get the results they had hoped for.

David Futrell, former senior director of organizational performance at Walmart and a guest on Charles Handler's HR podcast, had a similar experience with AI games when he was still working at the retailer. "There's no doubt that what we run is the biggest selection and assessment machine that's ever existed on the planet. We test, every day, between ten and fifteen thousand people," Futrell said. "That adds up to somewhere north of four million every year. And it's just entry-level hires for the store."

His team has access to an incredible amount of data and has conducted many studies to test out new technologies. "When this machine learning idea first came out, I was very excited by it because it seemed to me like it would solve all of the problems that we had with prediction. And so we really got into it and did a lot of work trying to build predictors using these machine-based algorithms."

A few years back, Walmart acquired an online retailer that was using an AI games vendor. Futrell and his team took the software for a spin. "You would do these tasks that didn't look work-related at all. But they were purported to measure some underlying aspects of personality, like your willingness to take risks," he said. He personally found the games very engaging, but the results weren't promising. "We found that it just didn't work well."

In fact, the AI games were slightly negatively correlated with job performance, if anything. In other words, the games didn't seem to work at all.

SACRIFICING QUALIFIED CANDIDATES

Martin Burch wondered what he did so wrong in the Plum assessment that he was automatically rejected: "What thresholds have I failed to meet here? Is it about my ability to rotate shapes in my head and complete the IQ intelligence assessment portion of the test? Or is it something to do with these personality or emotion questions?"

In the email Burch received from Plum, he didn't get any concrete answers. The company told him that it was not the one making hiring decisions: "Plum does not perform automated decision-making. . . . The employer may choose to consider the candidate's Plum information along with several other data points (résumé, cover letter, other assessments, interviews, etc.) as part of their decision-making within the recruitment and selection process."

That seems like a good idea. If a company takes into account gamified personality tests, a candidate's résumé, cover letter, interview, and other assessments to make a decision, that seems like a reasonable approach.

Except the Bloomberg recruiter Sophie Wallis had explicitly stated that because Martin Burch didn't pass the Plum assessment, he was no longer considered for this job. She did not mention that someone had also assessed Burch's résumé and cover letter at the same time before sending the rejection. To Martin Burch, this strongly suggested that he was rejected based on the Plum score alone. (And Plum does allow employers to use cut scores, which automatically reject applicants that scored below a certain threshold.)

I have talked to other hiring companies that use Pymetrics and other AI-gamified assessments and all of them shared that they use the AI games as a screen: at that stage in the process, the game results are the sole reason why candidates are cut and others are moved to the next round of hiring, not the more elaborate process Plum laid out in the email. It takes a lot of time to assess candidates on different dimensions, so companies often don't do it.

Using AI games as a screening mechanism didn't sit right with Martin Burch. Instead of just accepting Bloomberg's rejection, he wanted to know more about the company's decision-making process, especially after he checked the European Union's GDPR (General Data Protection Regulation) laws, which state that individuals "shall have the right not to be subject to a decision based solely on automated processing."[9] He believed that his rights had been violated, as indicated by Sophie Wallis's email stating that he was cut from Bloomberg's applicant pool based on Plum's automated assessment.

The law clarifies that automated decision-making can be used if data subjects give informed consent. Burch didn't recall giving explicit consent to Bloomberg.

He decided to hire an employment lawyer in London. He also reached out to Bloomberg asking for its privacy notice and his data under the GDPR. There was some back-and-forth, but Burch felt that Bloomberg didn't answer all his questions, so he and his lawyer filed a complaint with the UK data governing body, the Information Commissioner's Office (ICO). The ICO sided with Burch, telling Bloomberg: "From reviewing the information provided, it is our decision that there is more work for you to do. As such, we now expect you to take steps to address any outstanding issues with the individual."

On March 15, 2021, after ICO's intervention in the dispute, Burch and his lawyer received a reply from Bloomberg that described how it uses assessments in the hiring process and stating unequivocally: "This initial selection decision is automatic, as defined under Article 22(1) of the U.K. GDPR." There it was.

It's something that probably reads like a normal sentence of bureaucratic jargon to most people, but this is an incredible revelation. I have covered artificial intelligence used in hiring for over five years and I don't know how many times vendors and employer companies have told me that their AI tools do not make automatic hiring decisions. I was told that there is a human in the loop to review the decisions and that no one is being rejected outright by "robots." This argument always felt off, especially because vendors argue that their tools save time and money in the hiring process, and automating rejections seems like exactly why companies want to use AI.

But in Burch's case, Bloomberg admitted it: this algorithm decided who got rejected for a data analyst job and who advanced to the next round.

"It's good to see that in writing," Burch said.

He is glad that future job seekers who apply to Bloomberg will now learn that their game-based assessment will be used to automatically reject them or move them into the next round of hiring. In addition, Burch hopes that hiring managers at Bloomberg will realize that this particular assessment is a mistake to use. He is trying to prove to them that the Plum assessment is weeding out good candidates, including himself.

If Bloomberg insists on continuing to work with Plum, Martin Burch can't do anything about it. But he is glad he showed Bloomberg that automatic decision-making may not save that much time: he figures that his inquiry must have cost Bloomberg's staff a lot of work. He is hoping other applicants will follow his lead and demand similar information. "The cost savings or the time savings or whatever savings they're getting out of this automated process, then it's kind of negated by the fact that they would have to review every one of those appeals," Burch said.

He was also happy about Bloomberg following his lawyer's lead on another matter. Bloomberg offered Martin Burch 8,000 pounds (about $9,700): "Their agreement to pay the sum in full is a clear admittance of wrongdoing," wrote Georgia Roberts, Martin Burch's lawyer at Kingsley Napley in London.

(Bloomberg didn't answer multiple requests to comment.)

AI games inferring personality traits may not work well and have low predictive value. A review of the literature, for example, concluded that personality is correlated with about 5 percent of job performance.[10] This means that about 95 percent of our work performance has nothing to do with our personality, so personality might not be a great way to assess if someone is the right person for a job.

But there is another common assessment strategy we have yet to explore.

CHAPTER 4

You Said What?

On Facial Expression and Tone-of-Voice Analysis

I am sitting at my desk at home, getting ready for a "job interview." This one is a bit different from a regular one via Zoom—there will be no humans on the other side. I am getting dressed up and putting on makeup for no one, or maybe more accurately, for the green camera light on my laptop.

In this job interview, which will be scored by AI, I will receive questions on my computer and have a few minutes to answer them and record myself. These types of one-way video interviews are widespread in hiring. Millions of people have done them, and they're used by some of the largest companies in the world.[1]

The first thing I struggle with is finding a good time to start the interview. I could do it whenever, but when should I? Am I more alert in the morning? After coffee? Before lunch? Should I start now or maybe give it another five minutes? Who knows? The whole thing feels weird. At two o'clock on Monday? I decide to just go for it.

I follow the link I have received from Retorio, the vendor that built this tool. The first window opens: "For us you are more than a CV and we would like to know more about you." Sounds good!

Then I am being asked to center my image on the screen and avoid any lights in the back. Check.

First question: "In social situations at work, what role do you find yourself in?" The software then tells me to "be yourself—it's not a test." I get a few minutes to prepare and then I have a minute to answer the question.

I think for a second, take a deep breath, and try to sound as upbeat and full of energy as I can, which is weird, since no one is here, but I want the AI to predict that I am a positive person.

"So, in social situations at work, I think I'm always interested in chatting with folks and connecting with them. And, you know, just creating a really good climate at work . . ."

It's more than a little weird talking to myself. Granted, I am less nervous than in a traditional job interview, where I would meet with recruiters and hiring managers in person or at least via video conference. I feel like I am speaking into a void and have no idea how I am coming off.

I'm offered the option to watch the video of myself answering the question. And that is the most painful part. It's cringeworthy to see myself trying to sound smart and energetic and relatable and hireable. In retrospect, I wish I would have answered some questions in a different way. Should I have avoided talking about how I love the social aspect of work? Maybe they think I am too social and don't work hard enough?

It's weird how nervous I am. I have wanted to do this since I first encountered AI-based technology at a conference in 2018. During a presentation on AI used in hiring, the HireVue representative claimed that an analysis of facial expressions, tone of voice, and the words candidates use during interviews reveals whether a candidate is suitable for a given job. It sounded like magic. Finally, an AI tool could make sure we only hired competent people, because we could tap into their innermost thoughts and behaviors.

I have hired people before and I know how hard it is. How do you know from a job interview if someone can do the work you need them to do? Of course they will say they can do everything, but I have hired enough folks to understand that professed confidence in one's abilities doesn't equal competence.

The next question in my video interview appears on-screen: "Have you ever trained for something—an event or race? If so, can you tell me about it?"

I think about it for a few seconds and off I go with the next cringeworthy answer: "Yeah, I've trained for something. I've actually trained for . . . I wanted to learn . . . One summer I decided I wanted to learn how to run five miles. And so I just started to be very clear about it. The first time I went out for a run and maybe was able to run for thirty seconds, walk for thirty seconds, run for thirty seconds, walk for thirty seconds . . ."

So far, I am not sure what to make of the experience. Maybe I am just old-school and prefer in-person job interviews because they can turn into really meaningful conversations in which the organization's people learn about me and I learn more about them as well. Doing a one-way video interview is a different beast. I am alone in my tiny little office in my apartment; no one is on the other end and I am basically recording a presentation of myself.

Next question: "Tell me about a time when you had to 'ruffle a few feathers' to get a project or task done."

"So there was a time when I wrote a new curriculum for a documentary program. And there were a lot of people at the university that had a lot of opinions . . ."

Retorio's AI is analyzing the words I say, my facial expressions, and my intonation.[2] The tool will then come up with a score showing how qualified I am for the job I am applying for.

It's weird to know a computer is secretly scoring me as I talk. Does it know more about me than I do? Is it getting a glimpse of my soul? My innermost thoughts?

Retorio gave me access to the platform, allowing me to see my score as if I were the hiring manager. I scored 93 percent! Yeah! It's weird how excited I am about this score—I don't know yet if it's meaningful, but it's hard to ignore the numbers.

I'm surprised I am so qualified. Under the Summary tab, the software states that I am *curious*, *deliberate*, *candid*, *compatible*, and *relaxed*.

My high score makes me feel better about this bizarre experience. But almost all of the interviewees I spoke with about their one-way video interviews told me they didn't like it.

One of these people is Alex Huang. In 2018, he was a young credit analyst at a local bank in Chicago. He applied to about thirty entry-level banking and finance jobs that year while he was graduating from the University of Illinois with a major in economics and a minor in statistics.[3] Digital hiring was in its infancy back then, but out of the thirty applications he sent out, about ten companies asked him to do video interviews. Today, almost all large financial companies and banks in the United States require entry-level candidates to first pass through a digital hiring tool before they are able to speak with a human hiring manager.

Huang had his dreams set on working at a bigger financial institution in downtown Chicago, but the company required a one-way video interview. He hated it. "It didn't provide me the opportunity to show who I really am. I'm more of a people person," he said in an interview with the *Wall Street Journal.*[4]

Huang's girlfriend and his group of friends at the time were all complaining about the video interviews they had to do. Huang hated the process, hated speaking in a room by himself, and he thinks it showed.

"Essentially, I never really went past the first round," he said. He also didn't get any meaningful feedback. The rejections made him feel angry and frustrated.

He even decided to withdraw an application because the company asked him to do a video interview: "In the end, I wasn't comfortable with doing them at all," he said. "I got tired of just quickly being rejected from the companies I want to work for. I decided I should approach it a different way." He requested an alternative, such as a phone conversation with a human hiring manager.

The strategy didn't get Huang the desired results. He realized that most companies run automated communication systems, and out of his three requests for an alternative to the one-way video interview, he was granted an in-person interview once. The other two times, he didn't hear anything back.

He decided not to care. Huang thinks that if a company lacks the decency to invest in its hiring strategy and conduct in-person job interviews, he does not want to work there.

Until he spoke to the *Wall Street Journal,* he wasn't even aware that some of the companies he was interviewing with might never watch the video, instead using HireVue's AI-based video interview tool to score and rank candidates. He assumed all of the interviews would be watched by a human hiring manager. He was not pleased when I told him that some of his video interviews probably had been analyzed by a machine.

"That kind of scares me—what else are they doing? What else are you hiding without telling me?" he asked.

What seems like science fiction—analyzing job applicants' facial expressions, tone of voice, and the words they use with artificial intelligence—is already reality and is used for hiring in the United States and abroad. Facial expression and tone-of-voice analysis is also being used at work to monitor employees' conference and sales calls and customer interactions in call centers.

Whereas the three AI applications we have covered so far—résumé screeners, social media scanners, and gamified assessments—have multiple drawbacks, the case for this analytical tool is supposed to be more scientific and fair, that is, if a person can get beyond their aversion to being interviewed by a computer. As it turns out, this is not a small problem.

Other experts say that this technology is digital snake oil and not rooted in science. Yet it decides the future of millions because AI-based video interviews can automatically reject applicants and are ubiquitous in finance, retail, and hospitality. Let's explore this new frontier using me as the guinea pig. I tested some of these tools and was not always impressed by the results.

LEARNING TO DO SOMETHING WEIRD

Video interviews, especially for recent college graduates for entry-level jobs at large companies, have become so widespread that many university career centers now specifically train students for them. "Students are encountering these systems earlier and earlier on," said Gracy Sarkissian, the executive director of the Wasserman Center for Career Development at NYU. (Her office also offers students an AI tool that shows them how much their résumé overlaps with a job description and what they should change to get through the machine screening.)

But one-way videos are especially hard for students to deal with.

"It's this big unknown to students," Sarkissian said. "Our job is to demystify it a little bit. To say, 'I don't know what that interview's going to look like, but here are some things you might expect. Here are some things you might want to prepare.' And let the student know what they're getting into."

Duke University's economics department gives students concrete video interviewing tips that include suggestions like: "Practice talking into a camera. It feels very strange at first to talk to a screen rather than a person. Act natural, talk slowly!"[5]

However, even with thorough preparation, one-way video interviews feel unnatural for many students: "When we are interviewing with AI, it feels like a stranger. It feels like a stranger without a face. It's a blank screen. And oftentimes you're staring at yourself and so it can be a lonely process for some of our students," Sarkissian said.

Since so many of the students Sarkissian works with at NYU must take video interviews, she recently tried one herself. "It didn't feel so natural. And I think it aligns with a lot of what I'm hearing from our students about their anxieties around it," she said. "Students desire a genuine connection with employers, and it's hard to get that connection."

Many international students and students with speech impairments are especially afraid that some of these automated systems may penalize them, because speech-to-text transcription software could be less accurate for them. In an in-person interview, many may want to disclose their speech impairment, but that's not possible in video interviews.

"They don't know how they're being assessed in these virtual interviews and that does create another layer of anxiety," Sarkissian said.

"Some students are warned that these technologies discriminate and privilege certain characteristics over others, and so they refuse video interviews altogether."

In a tight labor market where there are roughly two jobs for every job seeker in the United States, she believes that employers should reconsider some of their hiring strategies, especially if they wish to attract top talent.[6]

"Gen Z students are a values-driven generation. They want to make sure that they can connect with the culture of the organization, that the mission and values of the organization are in line with their own and that's something that's difficult to assess when you were interviewing in a virtual way," Sarkissian said.

DEMOCRATIZING HIRING

Despite the negative feelings many job applicants have toward the technology, the business of video interviews is thriving. One of the largest vendors, HireVue, announced that it conducted its thirty-three-millionth one-way job interview in November 2022, up from twenty million in October 2021.[7]

As of mid-2023, its customers include more than sixty Fortune 100 companies, and its AI video technology has been used by brands like Unilever, Delta Air Lines, and Hilton. (HireVue says that it does not confirm or disclose the identity of any customer.)

Many of HireVue's clients are not looking to fill a couple of open positions but rather are interviewing thousands of people at once. On the extreme end, one customer interviewed fifty thousand applicants for jobs in fifteen hundred locations over one weekend.

HireVue's reach expanded tremendously during the pandemic when remote hiring had to become the norm, said Kevin Parker, CEO of HireVue since 2016, who recently transitioned to an executive advisory role.

He said that HireVue's mission is to democratize hiring—give everyone an equal chance to apply for a job.

"Our founder was a college student here in Salt Lake who could not get an interview or could not get a job because the companies he wanted to work for weren't coming to Salt Lake City to interview anybody. And so he set about a process by using video to open the talent pool to more and more people."

This was in 2004. Parker says that although the underlying technology has changed, the companies that use HireVue's tools follow the same ethos from way back when HireVue was founded; instead of a small applicant pool, companies want to give more people a chance: "They've recognized over time that the old sort of ways of finding talent—whether it's looking at a résumé or only going to certain schools or hiring from certain companies—really limited the number of people they can talk to and they've really changed that and they're using technology to reach more people and interview and hire the best talent in a variety of new ways."

Human hiring managers have consistently exhibited bias in favor of certain groups, such as those who attended prestigious schools like Harvard or worked for certain companies like Google; women and people of color have been underestimated for decades.

Parker believes the way his company does hiring is more fair than the way most humans conduct job interviews. HireVue uses structured interviews, which means that everyone is asked the same questions, which reduces bias in comparing applicants. Structured interviews leave very little room for chatting, where bias can easily creep in.

We humans love to connect with other humans, and in job interviews, many of us like to make a human connection. We often ask the person across from us where they went to school, if we know the same people, have similar hobbies. It's wonderful realizing that you have a personal connection with another human being, but it turns out that when humans make hiring decisions, interviews in which people ask different questions and chitchat bring out more human bias. A hiring manager may unconsciously prefer one candidate because they went to the same college and not because that person is more qualified than others.

HireVue's customers have two options: they can review videos by humans and sort candidates by score, or they can have the videos analyzed by an algorithm and ranked by score. "We're unique in the sense that we're taking that video and now using artificial intelligence to help companies find the very best talent for the job that they have," Parker said. "We're seeing tremendous success with that."

Thorough scientific assessment, as with many bleeding-edge technologies, lags behind companies bringing their product to market. AI black boxes, such as HireVue's, make it especially difficult to test and analyze these tool because we don't have access to the input data, we don't know how the data is analyzed, and we do not have the results. We mainly have to rely on the vendors' and the client companies' words that the technology works and makes fair decisions even though some vendors themselves don't fully understand how their tools make decisions.

So my colleague Jason Bellini and I decided to learn as much as we could about the technologies and test them ourselves.

HIREVUE

In HireVue's test interview we meet Gabriella. In a prerecorded video, she says that she is hiring for a customer support representative role at "Eastmond Paper": "Some of the things we are passionate about and focused on are acting like an owner, being an industry leader, and customer obsession. Tell us some of the things you are passionate about and why you will be a great fit for the role," she says.

The next question asks Jason to solve a problem. A video starts playing, a young man is sitting at his desk with a headset: "Thanks for calling customer support. My name is Jay. How can I assist you today?"

A split screen starts with a woman saying angrily: "Yeah. There seems to be an error with my account. I have got my bills set up to auto-bill and my latest statement says that I am three payments behind and I am at risk of having my service terminated. This is my third attempt to resolve this issue and no one at your company seems to care. If you can't help me resolve this right now, I am going to take my business elsewhere."

The agent tells the customer in a somewhat dismissive voice that her credit card may have expired, which only gets the customer more upset. She demands to speak to the agent's manager. A new window opens: "If you were in the position of this customer service support representative, tell us how you would respond to this customer's frustration."

Jason starts his answer: "I am here to try to make things better . . ."

After Jason completes the interview, we talk with Nathan Mondragon, HireVue's chief psychologist. Jason jumps right in and wants to know about his performance: "I just did the interview for a job as a customer service representative. How did I do?"

"The first thing we look at is the AI score that's attached to it," Mondragon says. Jason is lucky that he learns what his result is. Regular applicants will never know. "You can see that up here, you scored a 37 percent."

"That's pretty good, right?" Jason asks.

"No," Mondragon says, smiling at Jason, a little incredulous. "That's out of one hundred."

Jason makes a face.

"So you'd be a low match, essentially," Mondragon says, giving Jason a small apologetic, but encouraging smile. He says he thinks that he himself would be a low match for the job, as well.

Maybe Jason doesn't have the right personality for the customer service job? Or maybe his answers didn't contain enough details?

"If a job applicant scores 37 percent, is an employer even going to look at their video? Wouldn't they just reject the candidate?" Jason asks.

"No, no, absolutely not. Actually, what we would recommend is that the candidates can be ranked by that, but they still go and look at the different videos," Mondragon says. "It's up to the company to decide if they want to watch."

"But they might decide, 'Hey, this guy Jason Bellini has 37 percent, not even worth our time,'" Jason says.

"If you score so low, they might say, we may not watch all the videos, but they may watch a question," Mondragon explains.[8]

Technically, companies can do that, but why would they? I have a feeling I am being misled by vendors and employer companies telling me that the AI scores they pay thousands of dollars for are essentially being ignored and humans still watch the videos. Why pay for and set up a system if it is not helping to ease your hiring burden?

In conversation, vendors and companies have never admitted to this because most applicants probably wouldn't be happy to learn that an AI outright rejected them. And maybe companies fear a public backlash if folks find out that they use this kind of bleeding-edge technology.

But in industry-only settings at conferences, where no one suspects that reporters like me will show up, some vendors have been honest about how companies should best use their products.

At an online HR tech conference during the pandemic, Mark Adams, the former vice president at Curious Thing AI, a company that sold AI-based phone interview software, was doing a demo of the AI tool and showed the tool's dashboard. "The recording of [the automated interview] is here, and I can play it back if I choose to, but generally that's not the best use of time, because the whole point of it is to reduce your screening time and just focus on candidates you want. So you can listen to it, but we don't recommend that you do that."

There, Adams spelled it out to hiring managers: Do not spend time on the interview recording.

HireVue also told me that in the end, it is not the one making the final call on who is getting rejected: "We're not making the decision about whether you get hired," Kevin Parker, former CEO, said. "We don't want to be in that position. That's still a very personal decision on the part of the hiring company."

But in an email I obtained through a state public records request, Hire-Vue's chief psychologist showed a different intention. This email is from an exchange between HireVue and Atlanta Public Schools, which began using HireVue's technology to interview new teachers and staff around 2017.

On Thursday, September 21, 2017, at 7:38 p.m., Nathan Mondragon wrote in an email: "They are excited to start using the assessment with a 33 percent cut score. This [sic] anyone scoring at 33 or lower will be a Not Pass."

When I first read the email, I had no idea what a cut score was, but when I found out more, it made sense. A cut score is a score that is used to filter people out in the hiring process. In some cases, if job applicants don't score above the cutoff, they are rejected.

When I talked to the former vice president of human resources at Atlanta Public Schools (APS) in 2020, Skye Duckett, she said that the school system only used HireVue's AI tool as a pilot study at the time and were hiding the AI scores from the principals, who make the hiring decisions, to test in the background whether HireVue's AI is better than their previous scoring system.

Duckett said that she was seeing encouraging results from the pilot and would have better data in about six months. She left Atlanta Public Schools for another job before we could follow up; I reached out to her successor multiple times, but never heard back, so I filed another Freedom of Information request and learned from correspondence between the school district and outside lawyers that in June 2021 Atlanta Public Schools received a Department of Justice (DOJ) inquiry regarding their use of HireVue. (HireVue says it is not aware of a recent inquiry and declined to comment.)

VIDEO INTERVIEWS IN THE WILD

I wanted to understand how organizations use HireVue "in the wild" to make high-stakes decisions about who gets hired. How do they understand how the technology works? What kind of checks and balances do they employ?

HireVue put me in touch with one of its clients. Shelton Banks is the CEO of a nonprofit called re:WORK in Chicago. His organization specializes in helping minorities move up in the workforce and into better-paying jobs—often sales jobs in technology companies.

Every few months, Banks needs to select people into his sales training program. Over the course of eight weekends, he teaches students how to cold call, how to excel in job interviews, and how to craft their stories. They also learn how to transfer the sales and customer service skills they've learned from their previous jobs to tech sales roles at companies such as Salesforce, DocuSign, and, recently, HireVue itself.

Banks's team needs to find people they think will succeed in re:WORK's program and will also secure a job after graduating from the program, so they need candidates to interview well.

Banks is Black and originally from the South Side of Chicago. He understands where his students are coming from. He himself dropped out of high school and didn't get a college degree and at times struggled to find employment until someone gave him a chance. His students are trying hard, but many don't have family or friends who could help polish their résumé.

"Nobody teaches you how to interview. Your grandparents are like 'show up on time and give it your best,'" he said. "Going on the interview, it's trial and error."

His students, who are 95 percent Black and brown, struggle to find well-paying jobs and are mostly from underserved or underprivileged backgrounds—terms that Banks hates. "We've been training candidates from what we like to call 'untapped and overlooked' communities."

His weekend program, which people are paid to attend, has been successful in raising people's incomes. "Roughly eight to nine hundred bucks a month is what some people are making, either working retail or driving Uber, or just kind of odd jobs, and when they leave the program, they typically make around $63,000 a year."

When he joined the program in 2017, Banks wasn't eager to try AI in his search for people to join the job-readiness program, but he soon understood that traditional job interviews weren't working. At first, he worked with volunteers to select the right applicants. Banks and his team put together a hiring rubric and asked volunteers to score people's answers on a scale from 1 to 5.

But the volunteers scored the interviews inconsistently and they often started rooting for the candidates rather than judging their answers, Banks said.

Once, Banks asked a candidate a typical question that volunteers would ask: "Tell me about a time you failed at something."

The job seeker told the team: "I've never failed at anything."

Banks started laughing. "That was horrible," he said to the candidate. "What do you mean? You are unemployed right now. You have challenges, sir, come on," he recalled saying. "But interestingly enough, a volunteer would say, 'Okay, man, that's awesome. You are confident.'"

Volunteers scored people based on their own feelings and opinions, Banks said. Some high scores didn't necessarily match the experience Banks and his team consequently had with the students in the program.

"We would invite these high-scoring people to the program and then throughout the eight weeks, we would just run into roadblocks like, 'Man, you are rough around the edges. I got you for eight weeks. . . . Who gave you this gold star?'" he said. Not only were these candidates struggling in the program, but also when Banks put them into real-world interviews, many didn't get a job.

He wanted to give HireVue's AI tool a shot and encountered some interesting surprises. He was introduced to HireVue by one of the board of directors of re:WORK, who is a partner at a venture capitalist firm that invested in HireVue. Banks was granted free access to HireVue's AI interviewing tool but wasn't overly excited when he first tried it.

"We were skeptics like most people were. 'Man, this isn't gonna work. This is going to be biased. This is gonna be a danger here,'" he recalled thinking. "And we've realized that there's danger everywhere, there's going to be bias everywhere."

The AI tool scores people on different traits that job candidates probably need in a tech sales job, including communication skills, initiative, and problem-solving abilities.

In the first round of using HireVue, candidates scored from 99 percent all the way down to 5 percent. For his first test of the AI's accuracy, Banks took only the people HireVue had labeled as the best. "Cohort of ten folks. I want to say seven of them got jobs," Banks recalled. But that process was not easy, he said. "It was difficult for me to get the seven people jobs that HireVue said were the best."

He then decided to do the opposite. He used HireVue's tool again on the next set of candidates and took the ten people the AI scored lowest. "Worst cohort of my life," he laughed. "None of them got jobs."

Banks started to believe that there might be something to the AI tool. He took a closer look at the results and noticed that HireVue gives a higher score to people who sound convincing: "They talked and used all the right words and the tone and pitch and pace was on point and understandable. But they had no context. They didn't answer the question, they just sounded great." It's something both machines and human recruiters may fall for. The *convincing* people got the jobs, according to Banks.

In other words, HireVue seemed to be overindexing a candidate's delivery over their content, but so were many human hiring managers, since it's almost impossible to predict from a job interview whether someone who says they are an aggressive salesperson really is an aggressive salesperson on the job.

The AI tool is able to pick up who sounds convincing. Banks was sold. re:WORK has been using HireVue's AI video software ever since. "Just that little piece, it changed the way we recruit and changed the way we train." He understands HireVue's AI tool is not bulletproof, but the tool's analyses are better than the human volunteer ratings. They give him a baseline of where his students are in terms of interviewing skills, which he then tries to improve during the re:WORK training.

After a bunch of testing, Banks decided he wanted a mix: each cohort now consists of roughly 60 percent of folks HireVue scored as high performers, 30 percent middle-tier applicants, and 10 percent coming from the bottom. "You get this diversity of thought and diversity of experience in the cohort," he said. He noticed that many of those who scored low on HireVue are not afraid to ask basic questions, which is important for his students' success. Folks who scored high are often too afraid to ask.

Banks decided to not only use HireVue to recruit people into the program but also, because he is teaching people how to interview well, add HireVue into the program itself. Now, partway through his students do another HireVue interview. "If you scored a 16, I will teach you something. And then I throw you back in HireVue and now you score 80." Roughly 70 percent of his students improve their score in the second HireVue interview. He essentially wants to know how far his students have come and if they can beat the machines and potentially score a job.

Sometimes Banks overrides his own calibrated "hiring" system, especially when folks are really interested in joining the program. "I see you're in the bottom bucket and it's like, man, I want to help you. This is going to be rough. But sometimes, they prove HireVue wrong."

He believes combining his human judgment with AI helps him make the best selections. "You shouldn't always listen to the tool. But the tool will help you make an informed decision," he said.

Today, he and his team use a two-week self-guided online learning management guide to gauge if people should join the program. Shelton Banks thoughtfully implemented the technology, tested it, and came up with a process that works for his training courses. What's troubling to me is that along the way, the technology was never questioned except when he and his team thought about potential bias—but agreed that bias is everywhere.

In its assessments, HireVue claims that its technology can measure cognitive abilities, including *mental agility*, *reasoning*, and *numerical ability*, out of the data it collects. The results show a "soft skills" analysis of each applicant. Candidates are scored on their communication skills and also get a score for "drive and persuasion." That category is described as someone who is goal oriented and tries to exceed in performance. Candidates are categorized as *novice, developing, intermediate, advanced,* or *expert.* Applicants are also scored for their negotiation and persuasion capabilities and their personal stability—how calm they remain under pressure.

What's interesting with any job interview—if it's scored by humans or by AI—is that a candidate only talks about their experiences. We are not seeing the candidate in action at their job. "There is just a limitation of how do you know if someone's going to do well at a job. The best way to know would be to let them do the job for a while and see how they do. And obviously you can't do that," said Lindsey Zuloaga, the chief data scientist at HireVue. "So assessing people is, in nature, kind of a proxy to getting to the actual job and the performance in the job."

Neither job interviews with humans nor AI can predict with 100 percent certainty whether someone who says they are a team player in a job interview is really a team player on the job. Just like Shelton Banks found out, some people might interview well but may not succeed in a certain role.

Even with these limitations, HireVue says that the AI scoring is an accurate reflection of a candidate's traits. How does it work under the hood?

SCORING PERFORMANCES

"It's a combination of what you say and how you say it and the emotions you portray in your facial movements," Nathan Mondragon told Jason Bellini, my former colleague and correspondent at the *Wall Street Journal* in 2018. "It's a combination of all three layers on top of themselves."

Kevin Parker, HireVue's former CEO, said that this is how hiring managers have traditionally assessed people during job interviews: taking in what applicants say, how they say it, and their facial expressions.

The algorithm is trained with video interviews from individuals already in the job who have answered the same questions and have been rated as low, middle, or high performers by the company hiring. The AI figures out which words, facial expressions, and tones of voice these incumbents have in common.

The videos of the incoming job applicants are then run against the algorithm, which tells human hiring managers whether the applicant is likely to be a low performer or a high performer by giving them a percentage ranking, just like Jason got.

In a private tutorial with HireVue, I learned a couple more interesting nuggets on how the company pulls out personality traits from these video interviews.

"There's certain language and text and language combinations and categories and libraries that indicate and link to certain personality traits," Nathan Mondragon said. "If teamwork is important and working with others is important, somebody is using word categories of *I* and *me* versus *we*, *team*, and *people*, pronoun usage is going to have an impact on that team's orientation of working with others." Here is my translation: if you use *we* and *team* a lot, it shows you are a team player at work.

It seems very elementary, one of the attendees of the tutorial concluded. For me, context is everything. Was the applicant asked to talk about leading a team or about a project that they started alone from scratch? Wouldn't that matter, since they would likely use more *I* than *we*?

In the web tutorial, Mondragon then said: "The example I gave, pronoun usage, is an example of when we looked at the text analysis using natural language processing. That is one, two, maybe five data points out of what could be fifty thousand data points. . . . No feature has a lot of impact anyway. There are thousands of features rolled together to generate the results."

I am glad to hear that no job applicant would be rejected for using too much *I* or *we* alone, but is it really true that the folks who say *we* more often are team workers? It feels like an oversimplification and it isn't saying anything about our capabilities as a team player.

THE CHALLENGE OF OVERCOMING BIAS

Bias is a real threat with AI tools. The basic question is not only whether these tools work but also whether they treat everyone fairly. "Just making sure bias isn't baked in in any way is really important," said Lindsey Zuloaga, the chief data scientist at HireVue.

Many companies prefer AI tools to human hiring, and they adopt the vendors' marketing messages and say that the tools are bias-free or less biased.

"It's a commitment to our candidates that we are ensuring consistency and fairness," said Jennifer Carpenter, the former vice president of talent acquisition at Delta Air Lines, in a promotional video about HireVue's AI-based technology. "Some of the assessments, including HireVue's assessment using AI, allow us to ensure that we are removing bias whenever we can."

Here is how many vendors do bias testing: the most frequently used method of checking fairness in hiring assessments is what's colloquially known as the four-fifths rule, which has become an informal hiring standard in the United States. The Equal Employment Opportunity Commission (EEOC), one of the regulators of work in the United States, released guidelines in 1978 stating that hiring procedures should select roughly the same proportion of men and women and people of different racial groups. Speaking to me for a piece I wrote for the MIT Technology Review, Pauline Kim, a law professor at the Washington University of St. Louis, explained the four-fifths rule. "If men were passing 100 percent of the time to the next step in the hiring process, women need to pass at least 80 percent of the time." So, for example, if 1,000 men applied and 800 made it through the assessment, that is an 80 percent passing rate for men. Now let's say that 100 women also applied. For the assessment to be considered "fair" under the four-fifths rule by the EEOC, then at least 64 women needed to make it through the assessment, because that is a passing rate for women of 64 percent (four-fifths of 80 percent). Of course, passing 80 percent of women through the assessment would be precisely fair, being the same passing rate as for men, but the four-fifths rule allows for some wiggle room.

If a company's hiring tools violate the four-fifths rule, the EEOC might take a closer look at its practices. "For an employer, it's not a bad check," Kim said. "If employers make sure these tools are not grossly discriminatory, in all likelihood they will not draw the attention of federal regulators."

One drawback is that the four-fifths rule traditionally has not been tested for intersectionality, especially people who may be discriminated against because they are part of a racial minority *and* they are women. The rule compares men with women and one racial group with another to see if they pass at similar rates, but it doesn't compare, for example, white men with Asian American or Latin American women. "You could have something that satisfied the four-fifths rule [for] men versus women, Blacks versus whites, but it might disguise a bias against Black women," Kim said.

A few years back, many developers thought that algorithms would be "naturally" bias-free if age, race, gender, and so forth weren't used. "People have been naive, though, to think that 'we are not feeding that into our model, so it can't be biased.' That's obviously not true," Kim said.

Non-job-related demographics can creep in when other features, so-called proxies, are used. For example, some employers have figured out that the farther an employee lives away from their worksite, the higher the chances of them quitting. So it might make sense to reject applicants from certain zip codes. But in the United States, and possibly in other places as well, zip codes are not benign proxies.

"Given the history of segregation in the United States, zip codes are actually highly correlated with race," said Ifeoma Ajunwa, Emory University School of Law professor and an expert in AI and hiring. "So if, for example, a hiring algorithm decided to use zip codes, technically that's not unlawful. It's not using race. But in practice, it's a proxy and it could have a disparate impact on racial minorities."

I also spoke to a talent acquisition manager at one of the largest companies in the United States. Their team screens hundreds of people every day. They had another example of a benign-seeming proxy that turned out to be racially biased.

I can't name this person because the company denied my official interview request. But this person believed it was important to share this kind of information, and so I agreed for them to speak on background. I am allowed to quote them, but I am not allowed to reveal their name or the company they work for.

In the team's research, they found that applicants who knew at least one person who worked in the store were more likely to stay at least six months. They have friends; they have a connection; they are more embedded than folks with no connections, so their work tenure is longer, which is a desired goal of the company because hiring and training new employees costs money.

So the hiring team started asking job applicants how many people they knew who worked in the store where they are applying. The company could have used this proxy as one criterion in an automated hiring tool because it's predictive, but the talent acquisition leader wanted to first dig deeper and understand why it's predictive. When they checked the answers by racial groups, they got surprising results.

"What you found was that for Asian Americans, they were very likely to know someone who worked at the store. For African Americans, it was a huge difference. They usually did not know anyone who worked in the store," they said.

The company decided not to use this criterion because, although it is predictive, it introduces racial bias. "If you implement that item, it's like you don't know if it's really that item or that it's just a surrogate for race/ethnicity," they said.

You can only find this sort of hidden bias if you know what kind of bias you are looking for and you closely examine your hiring methods and questions and the results of your algorithms. "It's really hard to know if there is bias baked in somewhere that you just don't know about and you're not measuring, right? So I think it's a continual work in progress," said Lindsey Zuloaga, HireVue's chief data scientist.

THE DANGER OF PERPETUATING BIAS

In its tools HireVue used facial expression analysis, a controversial technology. Is reading and analyzing facial expressions in job interviews fair? And does it work to predict job success?

"If you think of facial movements," said Nathan Mondragon, HireVue's chief psychologist, "there are emotions that are portrayed in different movements of the face, smiling and frowning, eyebrow movements. . . . The muscle movement of the face, smiling. Here you can see you're starting to have a smile with the lip curl," he said, pointing at Jason Bellini's video. "Those are actual database points, and they roll together to give certain emotions and traits and personality and thinking styles."

What Mondragon is saying is that HireVue can pull meaning out of the movements of the muscles in our face.

"So, some would be contempt, fear, anger, joy, surprise, happiness. Some of those emotions and traits—it doesn't mean they're important, it means they're important when it's linked statistically to performance on the job," Mondragon said. "For example, being engaging and friendly could be an important trait for a retail job or a professional sales job, but for a software developer, it might have an opposite effect."

These emotions are important if high performers in the job showcase the same facial expressions and emotions during their job interviews. That's the link.

And Nathan Mondragon says the expressions come onto our faces almost unconsciously. He tries a live example with Jason: "If I said, 'Jason, it's Friday afternoon. We just met. I'm going to give you a million dollars, but you only have the weekend to spend it all. What would be the first two things you would buy?'"

"Oh, you are asking me right now?" Jason asked. "If you give me a million dollars to spend over the weekend and I can only buy two things . . . hmm . . ."

"And there it is," Mondragon yelled excitedly, startling Jason. "Your eye went like this and down and you went, 'umm.' So two seconds of a video capture, two seconds of data, but every microsecond of the video frame is frozen and your eye movement went down and your head tilted and you went into an alternative thinking style. A lot of times 'eye going down' means a deeper thinking style, and going up can be a creativity thinking style."

Mondragon said this example of "thinking styles" is only relevant if the algorithm has found a pattern of similar behaviors in the training data. But what do candidates' thinking styles in job interviews have to do with their performance on the job?

As we have seen, in this new world of hiring, it seems like it's often too burdensome for employers to go through all the résumés they receive and it feels much easier to have an AI analyze and rank potential employees. But comparing job applicants to current employees is not without pitfalls.

I talked to law professor Ifeoma Ajunwa about this. She has studied algorithmic decision-making in hiring for years and has testified many times in front of Congress. "What if the facial expressions of the highest-performing employees are meaningful in predicting success on the job? Shouldn't we use this kind of information in hiring?" I asked.

Ajunwa answered with another question: "What is the demographic of the highest performers?" She asks because there could be historical and structural biases at play in how the group of highest performers is determined. "The highest performers on Wall Street are mostly men. Does that mean women can't be high performers if given the chance?"

We know women can be high performers. But the problem is that if a company has mostly men in their high-performer list and in their data sets, the algorithm might pick up men's facial expressions, their tones, and the words they use and equate that with high performance, even though it may have nothing to do with any skills or traits one needs for the job. It could just be facial expressions or words that more men use than women.

That could down-weight some women's expressions, just like what happened with the Amazon résumé parser that down-weighted the term *women* on people's résumés because it was trained on data from mostly male applicants.

The other question is, How did the high performers become high performers in the first place?

"That's the problem with using high performance, because you really have to ask, 'Did a company in the past give an equal opportunity to everyone to be a high performer?' And unless you can answer that question 'yes,' then your sample of high performers is already biased," Ajunwa said.

Also, if we want to diversify our workforce going forward, does it make sense to use a pool of employees hired in the past to train the AI on essentially past hiring decisions? Wouldn't we want to attract different employees?

"When you're looking at my full facial expressions and you're trying to match exact facial expressions, that's not necessarily going to create diversity in thought because you're trying to match people who are quite similar," Ajunwa said.

Science has shown that diverse groups of people produce better business results, she said. Relying on high and low performers to build a data set and not the concrete ideas and skills that are tied to the job could also bring in random features that have nothing to do with the job.

What if facial expressions have nothing to do with the job? The selection could be totally random and just rely on the features of the dominant group that was used to train the algorithm. For example, some people cry when they are angry, but the computer would infer from their tearful facial expression that they are sad.

Maybe the high performers in a company all like snowboarding, but does that have anything to do with the job? Did all the high performers go to Harvard and so Harvard best prepares candidates for the job? Or did a hiring manager in the past prefer people who graduated from Harvard?

It could be that facial expressions and the intonation in our voices in job interviews are just as random as hair color. If we look at high performers in video interviews and most people have brown hair, an unsupervised algorithm could pick up on that and choose only people with brown hair. Of course, a human would know that hair color has nothing to do with the job, but a computer wouldn't—it just looks for a statistical connection and doesn't care if the connection is random or meaningful.

Ifeoma Ajunwa believes that more transparency will be the key to understanding whether algorithms trained on high performers really work. If there is transparency, other people, including academics like her, can check the results.

"The employer may not know," she said. "And then there's no way to explain the decision to the applicant. And this strikes me as wrong, because if you think about it, when we apply for credit and we're denied, we have a right to review, we get a letter that tells us exactly why we were denied credit. But when it comes to something as important as our livelihood, as having the opportunity to feed ourselves and clothe ourselves, we don't have a right to review just because a machine or an algorithm made that decision. So this seems problematic."

Ajunwa acknowledges that most of the time applicants in traditional hiring processes are also not told why they were denied the job, but she hopes that hiring managers would know the reason why they chose one candidate over another.

Maybe this full transparency is something we should strive for in the hiring process anyway? This way, we could keep hiring algorithms and human hiring managers accountable and also discuss how we can make hiring and using algorithms at work more equitable and fair for everyone.

READING FACES

Can a computer really read our emotions on our face? What does the software do and how accurate is it? Do we all experience the same emotions and are they represented the same way on all of our faces? I have my doubts.

Many people, I bet, like me, have had their facial expressions misread over the years or have misread others'. I had one student a few years back whose neutral facial expression always looked sad. We would often ask her if she was okay or feeling sad—and she would say that she was feeling absolutely fine. We just misread her facial expression.

And to be honest, I have a personal beef with facial expressions being misread. It has happened to me a bunch because I have what some call a resting bitch face. Over the years, students have asked me if I am angry with them when I am just talking and looking normal (or so I thought!). Apparently, my neutral face is sometimes misperceived as angry. An algorithm would likely classify my facial expression as angry—just because my brows are slightly furrowed even when I am relaxed—although I might not feel anger at that moment.

So using facial expression analysis in job interviews could turn out negatively for me if high performers in the job were not using "angry" facial expressions during their job interviews. I might get rejected for my "resting bitch face." (As a side note, I now wear long bangs covering my brows, and so I haven't encountered the resting-bitch-face problem in a while.)

Another good example of misreading facial expressions is people who are smiling, but are not happy. I have often forced myself to smile in awkward situations, including in job interviews. In such instances, a computer algorithm would likely classify me as happy, although I am feeling the opposite.

To understand the science of emotions and facial expressions, I consulted an expert, Lisa Feldman Barrett, a university distinguished professor of psychology at Northeastern University in Boston, Massachusetts. She is a fast-talking middle-aged professor with shoulder-length brown hair who has studied emotions for decades.

When we spoke, she had just finished a major research endeavor tackling the exact question I wanted to ask her. Do we all express our emotions the same on our faces? (And is a facial movement algorithm able to pick this up and essentially detect our emotions?)

Here is how she described her research: "Our major question was whether there are universal facial expressions of emotion, and whether people move their faces in universal ways when they're angry or when they're afraid or when they're happy. And do they recognize certain facial configurations as expressions of emotion in a universal way?" Barrett and her coauthors from different disciplines with opposing viewpoints met weekly for more than two years and read over a thousand papers.

For many years, psychology mainly relied on Paul Ekman's studies and theories from the 1960s and 1970s that stated emotions are (almost) universal. The idea is that everyone feels at least six base emotions. These emotions are indicated by roughly the same facial expressions that almost every human can recognize, and therefore computers could detect too. (Nathan Mondragon specifically referenced Ekman's research in his explanation of the facial movement detection analysis HireVue uses.)

Lisa Barrett and other scientists used other research methods and found something else: "Now there are studies with many cultures in Africa, other studies with other cultures in Papua New Guinea, and when you start to peel away the parts of the method, all the evidence for universality really falls apart," Barrett said.

Instead of finding that everyone has similar expressions for emotions, "what you see is reliable variation," Barrett said. There are differences in how people express emotions on their faces. For example, Barrett investigated whether scowling is reliably seen in episodes of anger. And do we ever see scowling expressing emotions other than anger?

"Sure, people scowl more than you would expect by chance when they're angry, but they don't scowl with the degree of reliability that would be required to say that this is *the* expression of anger. It's one expression out of many expressions that people make," Barrett said. "So people can cry in anger; they can smile in anger; they can widen their eyes in anger. In fact, the wide-eyed gasping face that is supposed to be the universal expression of fear is more like a threat or anger face, for example, in Melanesia. . . . People move their faces in many ways and people scowl when they are not angry, when they're concentrating, when they are really focused, when they have gas."

Maybe I am one of the folks who is subconsciously scowling when I am concentrating.

Barrett said her research shows that the consensus in psychology is now that facial expressions and underlying emotions have variability, but the AI-based facial movement technologies called affective AI are stuck in the old theory of universal emotions that, she said, is outdated. "If you think about AI as being sort of a consumer of this research, they're using the very stereotypical model. That's what they've built their whole science around and it's hugely problematic."

"Computer vision is a fantastic technology for detecting facial movements," continued Barrett, like capturing how much I am furrowing my brow, but it's not helpful to guess the possible emotions behind those movements. "It tells you nothing about the meaning of those movements. It tells you nothing about the emotional meaning. It only tells you the movements. And so when a company says, 'We can read happiness and sadness and anger,' what they mean is that they can capture smiles and frowns and scowls and they don't really know what the emotional meaning is. They confuse the measurement with the interpretation of the measurement."

So, if the facial movements that a computer captures don't carry universal meaning, why would we use them in job interviews? There is no science about facial expressions you need in a given job, except maybe folks who work with customers all day may want to smile a lot to be perceived as helpful. But what facial expressions do computer engineers need? Professors? Lab assistants? Insurance brokers? Warehouse workers? And to be clear, HireVue doesn't measure facial expressions on the job that may or may not be job relevant, but it measures facial expressions in job interviews. It begs the question what facial expressions and underlying emotions or "thinking styles" in job interviews have to do with how well people perform in a given job.

"There's a difference between a movement and the meaning of the movement. It could be that some people are looking down because they're thinking and other people are looking down because they're looking at their notes. I mean, the point here is that the movements don't have inherent meaning," she said. "The face is not a window into the mind."

Lisa Barrett also said that "thinking styles" are not supported by sound science. "We just don't know what the meaning is of someone looking up or down," she said.

GIVING UP ON FACIAL ANALYSIS

As Lisa Barrett and other experts publicly shared that they didn't believe facial movement technology could accurately infer our emotions, HireVue suddenly changed its tune about using facial expression analysis in their products.

In 2018, Kevin Parker told me that HireVue was seeing "tremendous success" with its AI product.

In 2019, the Electronic Privacy Information Center (EPIC) filed a complaint with the Federal Trade Commission alleging that HireVue "engaged in unfair and/or deceptive trade practices." EPIC had a long list of concerns, among them that the methods HireVue employed to calculate a job applicant's score were not known by the job applicant and often not even known by HireVue itself.

In January 2021, after the EPIC complaint, my investigative report in the *Wall Street Journal*, another exposé of HireVue in the *Washington Post*, and other skeptical coverage—all questioning the soundness of facial expression analysis in hiring—HireVue announced that it was phasing out facial expression analysis. "It was adding some value for customers, but it wasn't worth the concern," HireVue's former CEO Kevin Parker said to *Wired*.

At the time, we jumped on a call with Parker and chief data scientist Lindsey Zuloaga. My colleague and I asked them specifically why they decided to drop the facial expression analysis that they had defended for so long. The reason, they said, was that natural language processing technology has gotten so much better and there was no longer any need to analyze facial expressions.

"We started out with this idea that it was going to be helpful to understand, and it turned out that it just overlapped with what the spoken word was communicating," Parker said.

Then why use facial expression analysis in the first place for all these years and subject people to the invasive practice if it overlapped with the words that job applicants said? Maybe because HireVue hadn't checked?

But of course the underlying problem is not gone. After HireVue started phasing out the facial expression analysis in 2021, it still defended using tone-of-voice analysis in video interviews, something Lisa Barrett says has the same underlying problems as facial expression analysis: there is no science underpinning this kind of analysis.

Then in April 2022, I read a new blog post Lindsey Zuloaga had written for HireVue. Near the end, it was quietly mentioned that a year after removing the facial expression analysis, the company was now also phasing out the tone-of-voice analysis. I checked in with her and asked why they were dropping it. She used the same argument the company had made a year earlier: there was no significant benefit from tone-of-voice analysis. HireVue will now just be using the words candidates say.

It raises the questions: Why didn't the company remove the voice analysis in 2021 when it removed the facial expression analysis? At that time or even much earlier, wouldn't it have been clear that it was not adding anything? And if it was never adding much, why did the company use it to screen job applicants for all those years? Did HireVue even know whether it worked or didn't work? Wouldn't this misuse of technology lead to lots of people erroneously getting screened out?

Today, to build a model to determine traits and competencies from job interviews, HireVue uses trained subject matter experts to manually review the video interview files and use a rubric to check whether someone demonstrates team orientation, drive for results, or other traits and competencies. These scores and the words that the applicants say become the training data for the algorithm that job applicants are compared to and ranked against.

I was glad to hear that HireVue finally dropped facial expression and voice intonation analysis. But using unscientific methods in AI tools is like a game of Whack-A-Mole. One company drops a controversial method, another rudimentary method shows up or some of these AI methods return in different products. New AI tools have cropped up that use facial expression and tone-of-voice analysis to judge job applicants or use the technology generally in video calls. It often feels like vendors just don't learn—or don't want to learn.

Brian Kropp, former managing director in talent and organizational performance practice at Accenture, has a surprising view of the many AI tech tools coming into this crowded arena. It is new technology looking for a problem to solve, he said, rather than the other way around. For example, facial expression analysis came out a few years back. Some AI vendors wanted to sell the technology and decided it might be useful to market it for companies to use in hiring. But they are missing an important point: "What problem were we actually solving?" Kropp asked.

In his view, these are solutions in search of a problem and many may not work for hiring. "The technology advances are just completely outpacing most HR executives' ability to take that technology and figure out what to do with it," Kropp said.

Even if one company decides to get rid of a controversial feature, another will try it, even though scientists have already debunked the methods. History repeats itself in real time.

PHONE INTERVIEWS

At an HR tech conference, I saw a company presentation that caught my attention. Mark Adams, the former vice president of Curious Thing AI, claimed that the company's AI could automatically find a person's personality and their competency in speaking English by conducting automated AI-based phone interviews.

The service is aimed at hiring call center employees abroad because a lot of Western companies try to outsource their customer service departments but must ensure that agents have a good command of English. The company's headquarters is in Australia and Adams said that its volume of business has tripled since the beginning of the COVID pandemic, when companies needed to switch from face-to-face to remote interviews. Many chose the fully automated solution Curious Thing offers. In 2020, the company analyzed about two million minutes of interviews. If the average interview takes about fifteen minutes, the company's AI has analyzed about

130,000 interviews. Curious Thing says it lowered hiring costs for its clients by 65 percent.

In the presentation, Adams demonstrates the tool by calling in as an applicant. A female voice starts speaking: "Welcome to the digital interview hosted by Curious Thing AI. My name is Christine. Thank you very much for joining me today. It will be a short interview of six to ten questions. Please remember, I don't think there are right or wrong answers here. You can treat this as a sharing session. Enough of me talking. I can't wait to know more about you. Let's start. Are you a US citizen or permanent resident?"

(The first question already raises my eyebrows. There might be a reason why you haven't had to answer that question in a job interview—the question is legally problematic because employers can't discriminate on the basis of national origin. But I digress.)

During the demo, Adams keeps answering standard interview questions, including these:

- "Why did you apply for this customer service representative role?"
- "Where do you see yourself in five years' time?"
- "How would you handle an inquiry from a difficult customer? Please give me an example."
- "Please tell me about a time when you found a customer difficult to understand."

He then explains how the tool analyzes applicants: "The AI is actually listening to the spoken word and then it's being streamed into text in real time. And the analysis is just done on the text of the conversation. So it's just what the candidate says, not how they say it, which is analyzed by our AI," Adams says.

A recruiter can then rank the candidates according to which criteria are most important to them: "So English, resilience, customer focus, teamwork, and so forth to really instantly get a subset of the candidates who are the best fit for this particular role based on my experience."

To test the technology, I bought a monthly subscription for $199. Mark Adams was right: it was pretty easy to set up an account and get started. From a list of attributes, I chose *resilience*, *humility*, and *adaptivity*. Other traits I could have chosen were *business acumen*, *motivation*, *customer focus*, *teamwork*, *problem-solving*, and a few others.

The first person I invited to take the interview was myself.

I dialed the number and got Christine, the digital interviewer. She asked me to answer the question about a tough work situation. I went ahead and told her I once had a boss who was a micromanager and how tough that was to deal with. After answering all the questions, I was able to see my results. I scored 0.77 on adaptability, 0.77 on resilience, and 0.78 on humility. Interesting that they were essentially the same scores.

I also scored 8.5 out of 9 on English competency and my skill level was ranked expert. I have to say I felt proud of the number—I am an immigrant in the United States and English is my second language.

I then invited myself to the same digital interview again using a different email address. I wanted to know how these systems behaved in unusual circumstances, which could show more clearly how the AI worked.

I have attended numerous HR conferences and have talked with a lot of vendors. They repeatedly told me that if someone had issues speaking, if there was a problem with the detection of another person's voice, or if there was silence, the software would recognize the problem.

So I thought I would read a text in German, my native language. After every question Christine asked, I read in German the Wikipedia entry for psychometrics, which deals broadly with measurements in psychology.

Here is what I read: *Die Psychometrie ist das Gebiet der Psychologie, das sich allgemein mit Theorie und Methode des psychologischen Messens befasst . . .* And so on and so forth. No words in English crossed my lips.

I thought after answering all the questions in German I would get an error message from the system saying it couldn't compute any scores.

I was surprised when I got a message with the results. In fact, the AI gave me a score of 6 out of 9 for English competency, and overall my skill level in English was deemed "competent."

Just to be safe, I did the test again, reading the same text in German. Again, I scored a 6 out of 9 and my skill level in English was deemed "competent."

The results surprised me, so I did a similar experiment with another AI tool, myInterview.

THE JOY OF WATCHING YOURSELF

MyInterview is a video interviewing tool similar to HireVue's. The company is based in Israel.

The company's cofounder and CEO, Benjamin Gillman, told me that around four thousand small to medium companies use the tool. Over 3.4 million candidates have interviewed with myInterview.com.

Similar to HireVue, at myInterview.com, job applicants receive questions on their phone or their computer and record themselves answering with no human on the other side. The tool then analyzes the intonation of an applicant's voice and the words they say, based on a speech-to-text transcript the tool generates.

The hiring manager is sent a match score—essentially, how good a fit the candidate is for the role. Hiring managers also see a five-factor personality score that predicts how conscientious, innovative, etcetera, the candidate is.

Gillman said the system needs only thirty seconds of a candidate speaking to give insights into how well suited they are for a given job and what their personality is.

It was odd to me that Gillman kept insisting that the tool wasn't telling HR hiring managers whom to hire because the AI literally gives hiring managers a score on how well candidates match the role and ranks applicants according to their results.

After speaking with the CEO, the company gave me a login and I proceeded with my experiments.

I decide to hire an office manager/researcher. The tool asks me specific questions about the role I am hiring for.

How important is it for your candidate to

- maintain specific attention to detail? Not important at all / Somewhat important / Moderately important / Very important
- be in control of their own tasks and deadlines to a certain extent? Not important at all / Somewhat important / Moderately important / Very important

It's hard to choose. "Maintain specific attention to detail? I would say that's somewhat important," I say, thinking out loud. "Hmm, no, *moderately important* maybe?" I click on *Moderately important*.

What does "being in control of your own tasks to a certain extent" mean? I wonder. Should they be in control or not or to a certain extent? I bet that would differ from boss to boss. And is it *somewhat important* or *moderately important* or *very important*? Hmm. It's hard to say, but this matters because candidates will be scored and matched based on these selections. After I choose all the attributes the job applicants need to have, I get to select questions.

The system works similarly to Curious Thing's: a hiring manager can easily pick different questions like, "Please introduce yourself," and, "What makes you the best person for this role?"

I then invite myself to do the interview for the office manager/researcher position I set up. "Hi, my name is, umm, Hilke Schellmann and I am applying for the role of office administrator slash, ahh, researcher position. Umm, I am, I think I am very good at running a very straightforward, clear office. I want to make everyone happy . . ." I will spare you the details of my boring answers arguing why I am perfect for the role.

After I finish recording, I watch myself again—a really cringeworthy experience, but I close my eyes and hit enter and send it in.

The hiring manager, me, then gets my results. The system says I am an 83 percent match for the role! (The match score indicates that I have an 83 percent overlap with the ideal candidate I set up at the beginning when I had to choose how important a skill or trait was.)

"HS [me!] can be described as creative, secure, and organized," it tells me. Thanks, Algorithm! I also get a personality analysis thrown in for free.

I then redo the interview and instead of answering questions for the office manager/researcher role, I respond as if I am interviewing for the job I have. I say things like, "I think I am the best person for the role because I have two graduate degrees. I have one degree in journalism from Columbia University . . ." and, "I bring all the experience I need. I have probably twelve years of experience on the job and I am ready to go. I am very agile, resilient, very interested in taking on new challenges."

With those answers I still score an impressive (or so I think!) 82

percent match with the role, which is extraordinary, since I didn't really answer the questions that I was asked.

I then answer all questions by looping the sentence "I love teamwork" over and over again. I score a remarkable 71 percent match with the role!

Next, I repeat the Curious Thing experiment. I answer all the questions in German, reading the same Wikipedia entry on psychometrics:

Die Psychometrie ist das Gebiet der Psychologie, das sich allgemein mit Theorie und Methode des psychologischen Messens befasst . . .

To my surprise, I don't get an error message. Instead, the AI scores me a 73 percent match for the role, even though I didn't speak a word of English and the things I said in German had nothing to do with the job.

MyInterview showed me the transcript the software generated. Here is the gibberish it concocted out of my German:

So humidity is desk a beat-up.
Sociology, does it iron?
Mined material nematode adapt.
    Secure location, mesons the first half gamma their Fortunes in for IMD and fact long on for pass along to Eurasia and Z this particular location mesons.
So BD r r by 2.

I wondered whether it translating my German into gibberish was just an outlier, or if this is a pattern with the algorithm. So I asked one of the graduate students I was working with at the time if she could record herself in Chinese reading the same Wikipedia text. She did and she scored an impressive 80 percent match with this job role. Again, the software tried to "make sense" of her Chinese in English and her transcript is gibberish "English" just like mine:

> So seeing you coming to show thought study, real hard in young children from dance around that table under the truly Francis cigar don't incompetent waitressing little t-shirt youthful, passions the honey on isolating it, such that I should say.

The experiment left me with many questions. If the system confuses German or Chinese with English and analyzes a transcript that is gibberish and pulls results out of that, does the AI predict anything real?

I got on a Zoom call with myInterview again and spoke with the former chief marketing officer Eliav Rodman and the former work psychologist Clayton Donnelly. I explained that, even though I spoke in German in my interviews and received a gibberish transcript in English, I still received a 73 percent match score with the role.

I was surprised when they both thanked me and said this was useful feedback.

"I love these discussions with people who are testing the system, because what you're doing here is an edge case for us," Rodman said. "Most users just use the system the way it's intended to be used and don't torture it, but we learn the most from people who are torturing it."

But what did the system do exactly?

"What it was doing is, it thought that you were an English-speaking client with English-speaking questions and it was trying to make a transcript from that," Donnelly said.

He acknowledged that the transcript was gibberish. The system produces a transcript and usually uses it to score job seekers in addition to their tone of voice. But Clayton Donnelly surprised me with what he said next: apparently, myInterview's AI engine is a thinking machine with its own intelligence: "It knows that you weren't speaking English, for sure," he said. "The content you can see—it's random nonsense."

I was honestly surprised that a "thinking machine" could distinguish transcripts of "proper English" and transcripts with random words in English, but Donnelly believes the system not only understood whether a transcript didn't make sense but also deprioritized it when tallying my results: "It scored you primarily on your audio, on your tone and pitch, not on what you said."

That is astonishing to me. How can analysis of the intonation of my voice work to create the 73 percent match score? What kind of information does the computer detect in my intonation and pitch that is related to the requirements of the job, including maintaining specific attention to detail? Donnelly didn't explain that part to me—maybe he just didn't know how the AI worked.

With a tone of disbelief, I then asked Donnelly: "The intonation of my voice was a 73 percent match with the role?"

"Yeah, well done," he said, laughing.

I shared my findings with Fred Oswald, the psychology professor at Rice University in Houston and the director of the Organization & Workforce Laboratory. He has decades of experience analyzing assessments for hiring. The last few years, he has started to take a closer look at AI tools in the workplace.

I told him how I answered all questions in German, expecting an error message or a zero score result, but received a 73 percent match to the role and a personality prediction; and how my graduate student answered all questions in Chinese, received another gibberish transcript, and was an 80 percent match to the role.

"I'm glad you're posing these challenges to the algorithms because they deserve some attention," Oswald said. He wasn't impressed by the results myInterview.com put out. "A high fit to the job based on random input doesn't seem appropriate. Results should be reliable and it should be clear why an AI made a decision, which is pretty muddled in this case."

Oswald also questioned whether voice intonation analysis is really ready for prime time. "Intonation, I don't see much research evidence. What are the situations where intonation would provide any job-relevant information? I think the argument currently has to be that we really can't use intonation as data for hiring—that just doesn't seem fair or reliable or valid. You don't need me saying that as a professor, I think it's just obvious."

He doesn't want to discourage innovation, but he believes that AI vendors need to be more thoughtful about what and how they are testing their products. Research also has to catch up quickly to test these new tools to see whether they're fair and reliable and if they work—meaning that, if the makers of the test say it's measuring personality, we need to test whether it's really measuring personality and not something else or nothing at all.

A LONG WAY TO GO

A team of German journalists tested Retorio's video interview software and showed that when they used a green screen to insert a different background behind the same fictional interviewee, such as a bookshelf, the personality scores changed.[9]

But the same kind of technology is already being used in the workplace: in call centers, for example, AI is widely used to analyze customer voices to detect anger, aggression, or stress and tracks interruptions and speech length. In insurance claims calls, some vendors say that their software can "detect unique vocal characteristics that may indicate a high probability of fraud or concealment of information." These vendors also say that their tools can be used to analyze recorded audio, including Zoom calls.

In general, AI-based video interviews have a long way to go before they can be used to not only save companies time and money but also pick the most qualified job applicants.

I did one last test with myInterview in 2021. I typed my answers into an AI voice generator and had a computer "read" my statements into myInterview with no one on the screen. My AI voice scored a 79 percent match for the role—a few percentage points higher than my score when I used my authentic voice! The tool never detected that there was no human in front of the camera and that my voice was generated by an AI tool.

In fact, this kind of candidate faking has become such a problem in the US that the FBI is investigating. In June 2022, the FBI issued a warning to companies about deepfake videos in hiring: "Deepfakes include a video, an image, or recording convincingly altered and manipulated to misrepresent someone as doing or saying something that was not actually done or said."[10]

Remote hiring and remote work have also generally led to more candidate fraud in hiring, said Lindsey Zuloaga, the chief data scientist at HireVue. "There are people trying to get a job, they legitimately want the job, and they hire someone to take an assessment or an interview for them." And on the first day, someone else shows up on Zoom. This kind of candidate fraud is a problem, but many companies are also worried about people trying to get hired for remote roles, and then using remote access to a company's system to try to steal data from the company.

"I wonder if eventually we'll just have to implement more kinds of identity verification," Zuloaga said.

Job applicants are also trying to outperform the algorithms in other ways. I have seen folks on social media using ChatGPT and other large language models to generate answers in real time during one-way video interviews. If applicants have an accent, for example, some may opt to use AI-based voice generators to speak their answers.

Hiring vendors have a lot more work to do. Meanwhile, job applicants are still being asked to use these tools.

If you wondered what happened to Alex Huang, who back in 2018 refused to do one-way video interviews in his job search, I have good news. After being invited to about thirty job interviews, Huang did find a job—through a traditional in-person interview.

When we visited Alex Huang at work, he introduced us to his boss at the time, credit manager Tony Velasquez, who has been in banking for over thirty years. Huang had started about two months earlier, and my colleague Jason and I jokingly wanted to know from his boss how he was doing. (Full disclosure: Alex Huang was next to us when we asked the question.) Velasquez turned pretty serious. "In my thirty years of doing this, he's probably one of the top three, four, or five kids who come through here," he said. "Alex has come very far very quickly. He has done very well."

CHAPTER 5

The Essential You

On the Ideas Behind the New AI Tools

I n late 2018, on a reporting trip in Seattle investigating facial recognition technologies, I spoke to developers at RealNetworks, the makers of the RealPlayer, one of the first multimedia players. After our official filming part was done, folks from the company showed my colleague Jason and me their newest project, a facial expression analysis program. The developers told us it could detect our gender, age, and emotions. When I showed my face to the camera, the program predicted that I was female and about eight years younger than I was—yay to looking younger than my actual age! But it felt weirdly personal when the tool showed me in real time how it was inferring that I felt sad or happy as my facial expressions changed.

RealNetworks is not alone in building technologies that try to get a deeper look at our emotions. As we have seen, other developers have built similar tools that infer people's emotions from their facial expressions and the intonation of their voice. These technologies are being used in stores, in health care, in hiring, and at work.

In this book, we have explored a number of strategies companies have used to identify the best candidates to hire: résumé readers, social media spying, game playing, facial movement and tone-of-voice analysis, transcribed phone interviews, and so on. All are seeking a way to find the secret formula that best explains what the candidate is like and best predicts their future performance. Here I would like to step back from looking at tools and explore where the ideas behind them are coming from.

I get that people, especially in hiring and at work, want to look "under the hood" of applicants and employees and find out who they "really" are. (Heck, I want to know myself—who I really am!) It seems intuitively right that my personality, essentially who I am, is embedded in everything I do—but is that idea correct?

The underlying assumption is a form of "essentialism": that humans have a stable character and personality traits that can be categorized and compared, and, more importantly, that we reveal our internal character traits and emotions through physical appearance and the traces we leave behind—be they facial expressions or tweets. The idea is that my "essence" is embedded in all these things I do, something Plato, Socrates, and other philosophers have long debated.

This assumption has been around for thousands of years, and in the late eighteenth and the nineteenth century it became a "scientific" endeavor. Physiognomists and phrenologists tried to scientifically infer inner characteristics and behaviors from people's outside features and expressions—just like what many AI tools are trying to do today.

At the time, scientists claimed that bumps on one's head showed personality characteristics (phrenology). Cesare Lombroso, a criminologist who examined the skulls of convicted criminals and thieves in nineteenth-century Italy, and others believed that criminals were born as such and had specific distinguishing facial features (physiognomy).

Physiognomy and phrenology have been widely discredited as pseudoscience, but a look at history makes it clear why they were such appealing ideas that keep reemerging. The newest iteration is built into AI tools that claim to reveal our personalities through analysis of our facial movements or voice intonation or Facebook posts.

BAD SKULLS, BAD PEOPLE

One of the origins of "modern" physiognomy, the idea that our innermost characteristics are revealed on the outside of our bodies, can be traced to the eighteenth-century Swiss theologian Johann Kaspar Lavater: he "analyzed character based on the shape and positions of the eyes, brows, mouth, and nose to determine whether a person was, among other characteristics, 'deceitful,' 'full of malice,' 'incurably stupid,' or a 'madman,'" wrote Blaise Agüera y Arcas, Margaret Mitchell, and Alexander Todorov in their 2017 essay "Physiognomy's New Clothes."[1]

One of the most widely known phrenologists and physiognomists was the previously mentioned Cesare Lombroso. He believed that people were born as criminals and concluded, therefore, that traits of criminality could be found in their bodily appearance, including on their skulls. In one case, Lombroso found "a depression on the occiput of the skull reminiscent of the skulls of 'savages and apes.'"[2] The central idea of phrenology was that our brain is a muscle and some regions are more active than others; therefore, we have different contours of the skull that map to the differences in the brain's development. Through reading and measuring the differences in skulls, phrenologists could objectively find personality traits, they said.

The same general idea of defining a person's inner states based on their outside appearance is at work today. With AI, developers and researchers want to objectively measure and show how humans tick and predict how they will behave. AI can't read our thoughts yet, but algorithms can measure the movements on our face, our intonation, and our words. But does that mean they reveal some essentialist truth?

"Many of the capabilities and traits AI-powered video interviewing technologies claim to understand or evaluate map neatly onto the mental faculties that physiognomy and phrenology sought to identify and leverage," wrote Luke Stark, professor of information and media studies at Western University in London, Ontario, who researches the social implications of AI.[3]

"For example, AI video interviewing company Inclusive.hr (formerly 8 and Above) claims to understand how 'adventurous,' 'cultured,' 'resourceful,' and 'intellect[ual]' a job candidate is based on a thirty-second recording of their facial expressions and voice. Likewise, phrenological analysis claimed to understand how 'conscientiousness,' 'benevolence,' and 'self-esteem' were evident in a person's character based on the 'crown of the head' and the 'top of the head,'" Stark and their coauthor Jevan Hutson wrote.[4]

In the nineteenth century, another method to get to the "essence" of a person emerged: photography was the new and exciting medium that promised to make visible what people couldn't see before. In the 1880s, Francis Galton, an English explorer, anthropologist, and eugenicist, experimented with composite photos, trying to find the "ideal typical form" of different races, scientists, criminals, and others by exposing photos overlaid on one another.

In retrospect, it seems extraordinary to us today that by superimposing photos of convicted criminals, a scientist believed he could find the "face of criminality," but we might not be so far off from these nineteenth-century methods today. AI is the new technology that promises to make things "visible," or to find patterns, that were previously unknown.

A few years back, researchers at Harrisburg University in Pennsylvania circulated a press release about a study titled "A Deep Neural Network Model to Predict Criminality Using Image Processing."[5] The researchers had used photos to build an algorithmic tool that could infer whether the person depicted was a criminal or not, the researchers claimed. "With 80 percent accuracy and with no racial bias, the software can predict if someone is a criminal based solely on a picture of their face. The software is intended to help law enforcement prevent crime." The researchers believed they had found the ultimate crime prevention tool.

After a public uproar, the paper was never published.[6] This shows what researchers are trying to use AI for today, eerily recalling the work of physiognomists of the nineteenth century—but often uncontested.

DETECTING SEXUAL IDENTITY

In another example, Michal Kosinski, an associate professor at Stanford Business School, and coauthor Yilun Wang built an AI that can identify gay people from a photo alone, they said. They called it "gaydar," based on the idea that many humans also form impressions of people's sexual orientation on the basis of their appearance.[7] (Even though we do this, it doesn't mean the impressions are true, of course.)

In the paper, the authors show composite photos of "archetypal straight faces" and "archetypal gay faces," trying to make visible the "essence" of someone's sexual orientation.

Can a software tool really detect sexual orientation in people's faces? It cannot, because our sexual orientation and our facial features have no causal relationship: facial features do not make someone gay and being gay doesn't give someone distinct facial features.

There may be some cultural connotations for how "gay" or "straight" people choose to present themselves, and maybe a computer could pick up those signals, but what's the point? This and similar tools could actually endanger people in countries where being gay or lesbian is outlawed.

Guessing people's sexual orientation is based in our own biased practices that we should work hard to get rid of—not try to replicate with AI.

But some researchers are trying to elevate non-evidence-based myths drawn from racist, classist, or homophobic tropes into "objective science," again trying to find essentialist truths in our appearance that connote our sexual orientation.

HUSKIES AND WOLVES

Physiognomy and phrenology were never able to prove that criminals were born as such or that bumps on our heads show who we are, but this kind of thinking, which includes sorting and ranking people, has been used to justify racism and white supremacy—labeling enslaved people in the United States, immigrants, and Black Africans as inferior. It was also used by the Nazis to paint Jews as inferior and used as a rationale for killing them.[8]

Although physiognomy as a science fell out of fashion in the late nineteenth century, it always had a broad appeal outside of academia because it was consistent with a lot of folk wisdom. For example, in nineteenth-century England, it became popular to judge people's character based on their appearance. In fact, many of us still do this today when we say that someone has an angry face or looks open or whatever other personality quality we connect with their appearance. At that time of rural to urban migration, judging by appearance helped newly minted city people make sense of the unfamiliar others around them. And they applied the idea to facial features, clothing, gestures, and decoration.

Today, we are asked to never judge a book by its cover, which implies that, yes, we do judge books by their covers and humans by their looks or how they present themselves. It's our human biases that often bring out racist, sexist, and classist social hierarchies and what we think we see in facial expressions and people's general appearance that help us categorize them; in turn, they also influence who we hire. Our own internal biased preconceptions, which I am sure feel intuitive and right to many, are not necessarily correct.

"While we form impressions almost reflexively from facial appearance," Agüera y Arcas and his coauthors state, "this does not imply that these impressions are accurate. The evidence suggests that they are not."[9]

It's not clear whether AI tools actually find information of significance; many researchers use deep neural networks to build their algorithms, where the "learning" and predicting happen in hidden layers; so, the algorithms are, essentially, black boxes. This practice has led to problems and misfires in algorithms. Using this kind of technology also makes it hard for humans to understand exactly what the difference is that the AI has predicted upon and whether the difference is actually meaningful.

An easy way to illustrate an AI tool misfiring is the wolf and husky example: researchers programmed an AI to learn what wolves and huskies look like using labeled photos of the animals. The AI trained itself and identified huskies and wolves correctly in new photos fed into the system—until the tool got it wrong.

The researchers, looking closer, checked the software to reveal what in the photos the tool had made its predictions on. From this analysis, the researchers determined that the AI hadn't, in fact, learned what huskies and wolves looked like; the software was predicting whether a photo showed a husky or a wolf based on something in the background: snow. The software noticed a pattern in its training photos that the pictures of wolves had snow in the background and the photos of huskies didn't. But then a new photo of a husky with snow in the background tripped up the system, making it clear that the AI had not "learned" the difference between a husky and a wolf after all.

The same problem, which researchers call "overfitting," may have happened with the "gaydar" process. The computer taught itself to solve a problem the researchers gave it. Michal Kosinski and Yilun Wang might not even know themselves why the computer classified someone as "gay looking." As discussed in the previous chapter, HireVue, one of the one-way video interview market leaders in hiring and other vendors in the HR world, used deep neural networks for facial movement analysis in its tools, and this could have led to similar overfitting issues. (HireVue says that it uses several practices to reduce overfitting.)

Overfitting is why a computer may find patterns of criminality in people's faces when there are none—it picks up random patterns in the data set that may have no meaning, but look convincing to the researchers. "Machine learning does not distinguish between correlations that are causally meaningful and ones that are incidental. . . . Deep learning can't extract information that isn't there, and we should be suspicious of claims that it can reliably extract hidden meaning from images that eludes human judges."[10] Agüera y Arcas and colleagues also note that "it is worth emphasizing that there is no superhuman magic in this (or any) application of machine learning."

If we don't double-check the results of AI systems, run many tests, and take a deeper look at the outcomes, these kinds of mistakes can easily slip through. With huskies and wolves, the stakes are low, but if a flawed tool is used in an employment setting, it can cost people their livelihoods and future opportunities. In addition, if we don't critically examine the process of training an algorithm, the results can easily feel like objective science even if the tool just found meaningless correlations.

THE ART OF GRAPHOLOGY

In the past, hiring managers have been prone to believe in pseudoscience, such as handwriting analysis (graphology), which a couple of decades ago was still popular in hiring in France. Pseudoscientific methods usually feel intuitively right: every individual's handwriting is different; ergo, it must reveal at least some of our "essence."

In 2004, psychologist Mike Millard said, "All recruiters are looking for the Holy Grail on how to get the best people for their companies. Everyone wants a quick fix."[11] Graphologists in France have defended using handwriting analysis in hiring because, they say, job applicants can embellish their résumés, train to give the right answers in job interviews and on personality tests, but handwriting is unique and the act of writing reveals our personality, the real "you" that can't be faked. They maintain that because handwriting is an expression of personality, a systematic analysis of how the words and letters are formed can reveal personality traits.

"When used correctly, graphology can give a good indication of a person's personality structure, their abilities, ability to grow and develop, and perhaps most importantly, their integrity," said graphologist Margaret White, who uses her skills to assess job applicants for recruiters.[12]

"For example, size of letters indicates confidence, slant is linked to spontaneity and pressure is associated with energy," wrote the *Financial Times* in 2001.[13]

Some graphologists analyze handwriting samples from a company's top performers to find dominant personality traits among executives. Then they examine job applicants' handwriting samples looking for the same personality traits.

This sounds similar to how AI technologies are described today. For example, vendors suggest personality analysis based on someone's social media feeds, which would be hard for a candidate to fake, will give a quick look under the hood. Many AI gaming companies use these same methods, having current employees play the games to find the "right" personality traits. But unless the vendors do a job analysis, there is no evidence that any of the personality traits allegedly found by the tools are related to job-relevant skills.

There is also no evidence that graphology works. "Graphology is a pseudoscience that claims to be a quick and easy way of saying how someone's wired, but there's no evidence that this is encoded in handwriting," stated Barry Beyerstein, a former professor of biological psychology at Simon Fraser University in British Columbia and coauthor of *The Write Stuff: Evaluations of Graphology—the Study of Handwriting Analysis*.[14] Rowan Bayne, a psychologist who tested top graphologists against their claims, says the practice is "useless . . . absolutely hopeless."[15]

"Lots of studies over the years have shown that it is all a load of rubbish and not fit for use in any professional setting," said psychology professor Laurent Bègue, who works at the University of Grenoble in France. "If you ask a group of graphologists to study the same piece of handwriting, they all come out with different interpretations. It's no different from astrology or numerology."[16] The same goes for blood type analysis, which was used widely in Japan to understand whether someone was a good fit for a job. There is no scientific evidence that our blood type is related to our personality.[17]

I am sure a lot of these tests and the underlying assumption that almost all our outward expressions reveal our inner "essential" self would be fun games to play at parties or as self-discovery exercises, but most are without scientific evidence, and we shouldn't be using them in high-stakes decision-making like hiring—not in traditional tests and not in AI. Again and again.

CHAPTER 6

Does One Size Really Fit All?

On the Bias Against Disabilities

We have heard a few times now that AI vendors market their tools as objective, unbiased, and fair and say that they democratize hiring. Everyone is finally getting a chance, these vendors say; the computer is not doing cheap or biased shortcuts that human hiring managers have done in the past; their tools analyze and assess every applicant the same way.

Vendors confidently declare that AI-based video interviews and AI games will work for (almost) anyone. That's one reason these tools appeal to employers—one algorithm sets productivity rates for all workers or one employment test analyzes all job applicants. But when it comes to people with disabilities, will the tools work fairly?

About 10 to 25 percent of the US population have a disability, including mental and physical disabilities ranging from cerebral palsy to depression, Crohn's disease, deafness, and long COVID.[1] The figure is similar in the UK, where government statistics indicate that roughly 24 percent of the population are living with some form of disability.[2] People with disabilities have not fared well in the workplace with humans doing the hiring—the unemployment rate for people with disabilities is roughly double the unemployment rate for people with no disabilities in the US, and 20 to 30 percentage points higher in the UK.

In this chapter, we will be looking not at a particular AI strategy but at one of the main problems many of the strategies share, a one-size-fits-all approach, which is perpetuating bias against a vulnerable population instead of overcoming it.

I wanted to find out what kind of pitfalls people with disabilities might encounter when they are asked to complete some of these AI-based assessments. I asked Henry Claypool, a disability policy analyst and visiting scientist at Brandeis University in Massachusetts, to assess different AI hiring tools with me.

TO DISCLOSE OR NOT TO DISCLOSE

Henry Claypool, a white man in his fifties, is himself disabled. He sustained a spinal cord injury in a skiing accident during his college years that left him paralyzed in two legs and one arm. But this hasn't held back his career. Claypool worked in the Obama administration and he helps companies with their disability policies.

He is looking at one of the opening screens of Pymetrics' suite of games. It asks players to select whether they want to play a version of the games that's modified for color blindness, ADHD, or dyslexia or a non-modified version. Claypool isn't so sure what to do.

"I think I do have a form of one of these things, but I don't have any diagnosis or anything like that," he shares with me. He says he feels uneasy about disclosing a disability to a potential employer so early on, although employers by law must offer reasonable accommodations to job applicants.

"You are putting the applicant on the horns of a dilemma, right? Do I choose to disclose and seek an accommodation or do I just push through?" he asks. "The fear is that if I click one of these, I'll disclose something that will disqualify me for the job. And if I don't click on, say, dyslexia, or whatever it is, I'll be at a disadvantage to other people that read and process information more quickly. Therefore, I'm going to fail either way."

He is afraid that disclosing a disability would essentially route his application in a "Pile B" that hiring managers may not want to touch. By law, a job candidate can ask for reasonable accommodation during the hiring process, but exactly like Claypool says, many candidates are afraid to ask because a potential employer might conclude that the applicant has a disability and ignore their application.

I brought this concern up with Frida Polli, the former CEO of Pymetrics. She said that Pymetrics did not tell employers which applicants requested in-game accommodations during the hiring process, which should have helped prevent employers from discriminating against people with certain disabilities.

She added that, in response to my reporting, the company will make this information clearer to applicants so they know that their need for an in-game accommodation is private and confidential. (I do not have access to Pymetrics' games anymore.)

But beyond the in-game accommodations offered for dyslexia, ADHD, and color blindness, job applicants with other disabilities may not know what they will encounter in these games—how would they know if they need accommodation before they get started? (Pymetrics, now Harver, said it clearly stated it can accommodate three conditions—ADHD, dyslexia, and color blindness. For all other disabilities, employers using Pymetrics were required to provide an alternate pathway, and this was clearly stated in the Pymetrics instructions.)

"Either way, now my anxiety is heightened because I know I'm probably at a disadvantage," Claypool says.

POOR PERFORMANCE OR BIASED TESTING?

He is playing the same suite of games I played. It starts with the one where you get money for pumping up balloons. He has to bank the money before a balloon pops. He pumps and pumps thirty-nine balloons with his mouse.

"Okay. Now carpal tunnel is setting in," he says.

A few minutes later, he is starting to question himself, just like I did.

"I really hate that game," he says. "I don't see any logic in there at all. Knowing that I'm being tested by something that doesn't want me to understand what it's testing for makes me try to think through what it's anticipating."

In other words, he has the same meta dialogue going in his head that I had, trying to figure out what the system might want from him. And that distracts him from playing because he begins to fear he might not be doing well.

He then moves on to the game where numbers quickly flash on the screen and you have to recall the sequence. "This raises my anxiety," Claypool says.

"Why?" I ask.

"It's difficult for me to recall a sequence of numbers. Whenever I get the six-digit code for my authentication, I have to look at it twice and make sure I got it right."

Claypool's paralysis results in a trunk instability which makes it difficult to use a traditional keyboard, which makes it harder for him to fulfill this specific task.

As mentioned earlier, I got ahold of some internal Pymetrics documents that describe this game. Supposedly, the faster the applicant hits the space bar, the higher their processing speed and the more intelligent and creative they are.

But if someone has a motor disability, their brain might function well, but their hands may not function as fast; presumably, they would score lower on this game, which may mean to Pymetrics that they have below-average intelligence and creativity.

Claypool has another question: "What is the connection between pushing on buttons on a keyboard and how one performs the essential functions of a job?"

I've wondered this myself. Assessments should be checking whether job applicants can fulfill the essential functions of a job and not focus on other traits or tasks, which could be arbitrary and may have nothing to do with the role. For Claypool, it's not clear how a job and pushing the spacebar on a keyboard as fast as one can are related.

After he finishes playing all the games, I ask him what he thinks.

"The main takeaway was that it was really stressful and that it was very impersonal. I wasn't able to pick anything up off of an interviewer like, 'Where are we going with this? Why are we doing this?'" he says. "Human interaction is kind of essential to me in terms of knowing what we are supposed to be doing in a particular situation. My ability to process information is slower than average and therefore I'm at a distinct disadvantage and I think it shows up in the test results."

The idea that he and his peers may have to play these games to get a job doesn't sit right with him.

In a webinar on AI hiring tools and the impact on people with disabilities, Maria Town, the president and CEO of the American Association of People with Disabilities, said she was worried that facial expression and voice analysis in job interviews could negatively affect people with disabilities like her.

"You might be seeing me getting very nervous. I have cerebral palsy, a disability that often makes me spastic and unable to control my own movement. It's likely that if I were subjected to one of these tests, it would deem me unqualified for any job and I would not advance in the process."[3]

The problem, she said, is that there is so little transparency about how decisions are made. And technology may have become a fig leaf for companies to hide behind.

"Technology, in many cases, has enabled the removal of direct accountability, putting distance between human decision-makers and the outcomes of these hiring processes and other HR processes."[4]

THE NEED FOR BETTER REGULATIONS

In the webinar, Maria Town pleaded for the Equal Employment Opportunity Commission (EEOC), one of the regulators of the world of work in the United States, to start acting: "It's for this reason that we encourage guidance to say that job seekers and others whose outcome decisions will be directly impacted by AI be informed of these processes and provide active consent for the use of these tools."

Henry Claypool would like to see more regulation as well. He also hopes that companies will rethink using some AI tools, including these games. He is especially worried about people with disabilities who will try their best to play these games but might not be able to, and the company will miss out on their talent.

"This just makes me mad to think that people have to go through this to get an actual interview because you could get started out here because you're not processing information the right way. And they're going to miss out on a diverse applicant pool because of it."

A one-size-fits-all algorithm like Pymetrics' looks for statistical patterns in the "high-performing" employees category, which often lacks game training data from people with disabilities since they are underrepresented in the workforce as a result of historical human bias. In addition, people with disabilities experience and express their disability individually and on a spectrum and in all likelihood their data would fall outside of statistical patterns because of this variability.

Claypool believes it will be harder for those with disabilities to get hired if almost all personal interaction early in the hiring process is replaced with AI-based tools, which is rapidly increasing. "It is too bad that we've lost that human touch. Is there a way to use the merits of these analytic tools without leaving people feeling so vulnerable? I feel almost scared," he says. "And a little bit violated that I have been probed in ways that I don't really understand. And that feels pretty bad."

He is not the only one who has had unpleasant experiences with automatic hiring tools.

NOT HEARING DEAF AND HARD OF HEARING PEOPLE

Sophie Powell is a Black vocational counselor in Rochester, New York. She is in her early thirties and worked with mostly Deaf and Hard of Hearing folks between August 2018 and December 2020 for a state-sponsored program called ACCES-VR. (She still works with Deaf and Hard of Hearing people, but in a slightly different capacity at another organization.)

Powell's job was to help people with disabilities find employment. She has assisted people in a variety of settings to get jobs—from retail to a professorship at the University of Rochester. Most people she worked with applied for hourly jobs in hospitality and retail, where AI hiring tools are ubiquitous.

For those with disabilities, even applying for jobs can be a struggle. Powell said that job applications on Indeed.com were especially difficult for her Deaf and Hard of Hearing clients because they assessed applicants in English, which is a second language for many. In fact, some assessments were even hard for her to make sense of and English is her first language.

Powell, who knows American Sign Language (ASL), would sign her understanding of a behavioral question to her client, for example, "What would you do if a coworker did X?" "But the Deaf person would be like, 'I don't get that,'" Powell recalled. "And it could be from a cultural perspective; they don't just imagine situations like that and how they would respond, or it could be the language."

English and ASL, which many Deaf and Hard of Hearing people learn first, are separate and distinct languages. Powell said that sometimes even a professional sign language interpreter can be puzzled about how to explain a particular concept in a job assessment to a Deaf client.

In English, meaning comes from words placed one after another; for example, "a car hitting a tree." In American Sign Language, one would show with their hands how a car hits a tree.

Other vocational counselors shared with me that nuances in English, for example, personality tests asking if someone "agrees," "strongly agrees," "disagrees," or "strongly disagrees," make little sense in American Sign

Language. So for many Deaf and Hard of Hearing people, although they might be able to read English, they might not understand these concepts.

Another problem Powell encountered, on top of the comprehension and translation issues, was that the tests are typically timed. There often wasn't enough time for her to read or listen to the question, understand it, sign it to her Deaf or Hard of Hearing client, have the client sign their answer back to Powell, and for her to translate it into English. She estimated that, if an assessment had ten questions, she and her client often made it to only the third or maybe the fourth question in the time allotted. One problem was that Powell and her clients didn't know if an assessment was timed before starting it, so they might click and begin and then run out of time, which made it hard to get an accommodation afterward.

This was frustrating for Powell, who knew that some clients worked hard to even get to their hour-long appointments with her. Many had saved up gas money and arranged childcare. She didn't want them to waste an entire hour on an assessment they were doomed to fail because they had a disability.

Video interviews from vendors like HireVue didn't work at all for her clients because many Deaf and Hard of Hearing people she worked with didn't use their voices. Powell would request accommodation for her clients when they encountered video interviews, which most employers are required by law to offer.

I was surprised to learn what happened when she would request accommodation: "Never got responses. Ever," she said. She asked for at least twenty accommodations.

In the United States, companies with more than fifteen employees must offer accommodations, according to the Americans with Disabilities Act.[5] Sadly, Sophie Powell is not the only person who has had this experience.

Patti Sanchez is an outspoken, middle-aged New Yorker who

relocated to Tampa, Florida, where she now works as an employment specialist at the MacDonald Training Center. Sanchez is Latina, originally from Puerto Rico, and she is Deaf. She mainly works with job seekers who are Deaf or Hard of Hearing. She fights for every one of her clients to get a job and she doesn't care if she ruffles any feathers doing it. Like Sophie Powell, she has been frustrated by AI tools used in hiring.

A few years back, one of Sanchez's clients applied for a job at Amazon that required a video interview through HireVue. Sanchez wanted to request accommodation. "So I called [the number] and the mailbox was full."

She then took to Twitter to air her grievances: "@AmznFulfillment Interview for the #Deaf is getting more difficult if using #hirevue for the last step prior to the hiring event. Is there someone to understand the #SignLanguage? And the disability accommodations mailbox is FULL and unable to leave messages."

Her outspokenness has earned her a special nickname in Tampa: "They call me the Whip," she said, laughing.

But even the Whip didn't hear back in this particular case. Instead, she brought her client and a sign language interpreter to the job site, where applicants were interviewed in person after passing the HireVue interview. She persuaded the hiring managers there to interview her client.

Her strategy worked. Amazon hired her client, but Sanchez said that issues like these are common when navigating automated systems. It makes her sad to know how many employers are missing out on talented and dedicated employees who just happen to have a disability but can still do the job and are highly motivated to work.

Sanchez said that often folks with disabilities are not even considered by companies: "Sometimes, when I give a presentation to a company on why they should hire a Deaf and Hard of Hearing person," she said, "I notice so many CEOs and managers, they're like, 'ohh, I didn't think of that,' and I'm like, that's the problem: you don't think outside the box, because you're just focused on one way."

This attitude extends to the people who build the technology used in hiring, Sanchez said. These technologies are often designed and produced without people with disabilities in mind.

Even when companies try to bolster accessibility, the efforts may fall short. Sophie Powell recalled that some companies started to use closed captioning in video assessments, but doing so sometimes created another challenge because the captions ran too fast to read. "They have to keep in mind that the closed captioning is trying to follow along with the voice, but not everyone reads at the same pace."

Many companies use AI tools to make hiring easier and ensure that the tools screen every applicant, but they may underestimate how much harder these tests and assessments (and lack of accommodations) make it for people with disabilities.

Patti Sanchez recalled one assessment that asked about two hundred personality-focused questions—too many for her and her client to translate back and forth from English to sign language. It took forever and Sanchez didn't even understand what the questions had to do with the job because many of her clients apply for manual labor or janitorial positions. "This has to do nothing with cleaning toilet bowls, and so what's the point to use this?" she said. "It's a real waste of time and it's frustrating for people who really want a job so badly."

This particular personality test frustrated her so much that she decided she was done. "I want to cry and that's where I'm like, 'I'm not wasting time anymore, because it's ridiculous,'" she said. Sanchez decided to take a radical step for many of her clients when they encounter assessments: "I do it for them." She feels that the tests don't have much to do with the job anyway and are just an unrelated obstacle.

Thousands of miles away, Sophie Powell, the vocational counselor in Rochester, New York, came to the same conclusion: "I got so frustrated for the people I was serving that honestly sometimes I would just do it for them because I knew that those tests were not representing them as a person," she said.

RELUCTANT ACCOMMODATIONS

Patti Sanchez is pretty familiar with these digital tests her clients encounter all the time: she does "market research" by randomly applying for jobs to understand how the process works so she can better assist her clients. Some of the assessments, she said, are obscure and hard to understand, even for her—and she has a bachelor's and a master's degree and speaks English.

For Sanchez, having her clients meet with hiring managers in person used to make all the difference because many hiring managers understood that people with disabilities were human beings, often hungry to work, and could do the job. She laments that human interaction is essentially gone in the age of AI hiring, especially for the blue-collar and hourly jobs, which most of her clients apply for. "That's going to be one big challenge I'm going to have to face in the twenty-first century," she said.

Both Patti Sanchez's and Sophie Powell's frustration was palpable. "It almost made me want to figure out if I need to go back to school to study law or something, because this is ridiculous. I wanted to do something about it," Powell said.

But she had only limited time with her clients: "I couldn't focus on that because I just have to keep going on to the next one because I'm trying to help them get employed, so I couldn't put too much time into that frustration and trying to resolve that."

Like Sanchez, Sophie Powell just wanted her clients to meet with a real person and convince that person of their abilities, not a computer, which wouldn't understand them.

Another part of Powell's responsibilities was following up with hiring managers to see whether they had any questions about her clients' applications. She remembers one call specifically in which she talked to an HR manager and inquired if they had received her client's application materials: "They saw their education history, that they went to a Deaf school, and immediately over the phone this HR person tells me, 'Well, they have to hear. And if they don't, then we can't hire them.'"

Powell was shocked. She replied: "'Okay, I'm aware of that, but are you aware of the ADA [Americans with Disabilities Act]? And perhaps there is an accommodation available? How about we just schedule the interview first and then we can go from there?' Nope. Click."

Before they hung up, the HR manager told Powell why she needed someone who could hear: "It was a loading dock kind of position and it was because of danger, so if they don't hear trucks coming or something like that. . . . I'm like, 'If it's in a warehouse, you can install a light,'" she recalled.

If a blinking light could be a reasonable accommodation, then a company in all likelihood would have had to install that under the Americans with Disabilities Act. But disability discrimination claims are hard to prove for folks who often already struggle with day-to-day activities such as securing transportation and childcare.

All these frustrations with companies not following what is set out in the ADA led Sophie Powell to a sobering conclusion: "Apparently, it's the law by choice. It is a law that you can buy into by choice."

IN SEARCH OF FAIRNESS

The Americans with Disabilities Act, the UK Equality Act 2010 and other similar anti-discrimination laws around the world exist because it matters that hiring is fair; it matters that everyone gets a chance to have a paying job and put food on the table.

"This is the gateway to opportunity for so many people. It's a huge part of not only economic stability but also personal identity for people," Alexandra Reeve Givens said. She is the CEO of the Center for Democracy and Technology, a nonprofit that advocates for using technology to increase equality and promote human rights. (Full disclosure: She and I authored a *New York Times* opinion article together in 2021 about a new AI hiring law that was being debated in New York City.)[6]

"The risk that new tools are being deployed that are throwing up artificial barriers in a space that already has challenges with access is really troubling," she said.

Givens and her team study the potential impacts of hiring algorithms on people with disabilities and other marginalized people. She thinks the marketing language of some AI vendors is designed to make us believe that their technologies are the answer to all our hiring problems and don't need any further scrutiny.

"You hear people saying, 'Well, this is the move toward future equality,' right? HR run by humans is inherently flawed. People are going to judge you based on your hairstyle or your skin color or whether you look like their friends or not their friends and so let's move to gamified tests," said Givens, who is the daughter of the late Christopher Reeve, best known for his film roles as Superman. In 1995, he was paralyzed in a horseback riding accident.

She doesn't buy this positive narrative the vendors put out: "We want to see this optimistic story around the use of AI and employers are buying into that without realizing all of the ways in which these tools really can entrench discrimination and in a way even worse than human decision-making because they're doing it at scale and they're doing it in a way that's harder to detect than individualized human bias, because it's hidden behind the decision-making of the machine."

I am lucky to be one of the few people who got a peek into these AI games. I described the spacebar game to Givens. She wasn't impressed and shared her concern: the game might screen out people with motor impairments, maybe even people who are older. She had another concern: Does this test check for a skill that's required for the job? "They're trying to use this as a proxy, but is that proxy a fair predictor of the skills required for the job? And I would say here, the answer is no for a certain percentage of the population. And indeed, the way in which they're choosing to test this is affirmatively going to screen out a bunch of people across the population in a way that's deeply unfair."

One concern that comes up again and again in discussions around AI at work is the lack of representation of people with disabilities in the training data of these algorithms.

"One of the main ways in which an algorithmic hiring tool 'learns' is by looking at a group of employees and figuring out what are the common traits that they share and how do we screen future candidates for those traits?" Givens said. People with disabilities have historically faced discrimination in finding jobs and are more often underemployed and underrepresented in companies. "You're going to automatically be perpetuating the exclusion that we know already exists in the labor force."

Others agree. "The more general challenge for the AI community is how to handle outliers, because machine learning systems, they learn norms, they optimize for norms and don't treat outliers in any special way. But oftentimes people with disabilities don't fit the norm," said Shari Trewin, former researcher in the IBM Accessibility group in an interview for *MIT Technology Review.* "If you don't have enough gender diversity in your data set, you can fix that. It's not so easy to fix disability diversity."[7]

"What do you do when an entire system is set up not to account for statistical outliers and not only not to account for them, but to end up intentionally excluding them because they don't look like the statistical median that you're gathering around?" Givens asked.

Vendors stipulate that they do bias audits, but those don't usually include people with disabilities either. In fact, that would be almost impossible because disabilities are expressed so individually.

"We know for a fact that people with disabilities aren't being considered," Givens said. "The reason I can say that with such certainty is that these vendors are very often saying we've audited our platforms for bias. And what they mean by that is that they've done a statistical audit for race and gender bias. And that's it. That's what tells me that they are not thinking about disability."

Shari Trewin echoed these sentiments. "A lot of systems will model race or gender as a simple variable with a small number of possible values. But when it comes to disability, there are so many different forms and different levels of severity. Some of them are permanent, some are temporary. Any one of us might join or leave this category at any time in our lives. It's a dynamic thing," she said.[8] And people with disabilities may not look like the current employees, but nevertheless might still be able to do the job.

The requirement in the Americans with Disabilities Act is that job applicants must be able to perform the essential functions of the job with accommodations if they need them. "That precludes you doing some big statistical analysis and saying, 'Oh, well, that person kind of falls outside,'" Givens said. "No, you need to look at their individual circumstances and see: Are you testing them based on their ability to perform the job and could they do so in the workplace? So the law has something to say about this, and it's asking more of employers than just following basic correlation."

Understanding that an applicant might need accommodations often requires a conversation with a human, not a machine. But the problem is that many companies use machines to make the first round of rejections, so many applicants don't even get to speak to a human until they are in the final rounds of hiring.

"The test isn't letting somebody get through to that level, to be able to have the nuanced conversation with the employer about what their abilities are and how they would perform in the role. So you're being screened out before you even get to have the conversation about how you would perform in the role. And that's the part that I think is really troubling," Givens said.

She advocates for companies to also route some percentage of applicants without a need for an accommodation to whatever accommodation the company provides job applicants with disabilities, for example, offering a job interview with a human hiring manager instead of playing AI games. This way employers have an incentive to check out the job applicants in "Pile B," the folks who requested an accommodation.

But neither Alexandra Givens nor Roland Behm, a lawyer turned AI and hiring activist, believe that many companies will implement such an approach. Instead, they have experienced careless attitudes from employers that use these kinds of AI tools.

"In my conversations with many major employers, the general response to my questions asking about their validation and selection process is that they didn't do any. That basically they go in there and they say, 'This is being used by seventy out of the Fortune 250,'" Behm recalled in his testimony to the EEOC in February 2022.[9] He described a herd mentality by company executives: "Why would we spend any money validating that? Because you've just told us that it's being used by all of these companies, so, ergo, it must be okay."

He also said he has encountered a grave naivete in regard to an employer's liability if these tools are proven to be faulty or discriminatory. "If this [test] is an illegal preemployment medical examination, every person who takes that assessment has a potential claim against the employer. And when we're talking about major employers who are screening ten million people a year, we're talking about a potentially significant liability that I don't think many employers are understanding or are aware of," Behm said.

He is also wary of companies pulling the innovation card, basically saying that all innovation is progress: "This laundering of human prejudice through computer algorithms can make those biases appear to be justified objectively. And while it may be innovative, the world doesn't need more innovative ways to discriminate against persons with disabilities."

He wishes all employers would think through the possible ramifications of using a technology before utilizing it. "Just because you can, doesn't mean you should. And maybe that should be inscribed on a plaque and given to all the employers, or at least all the providers of automated decision-making systems that use AI," Behm said.

Alex Givens says that companies need to do better than just following the law. Companies need to demand from vendors that accessibility is built into the products and that these tools are tested on people with disabilities to ensure that the tools are not biased or discriminatory.

She believes companies have a duty to better society, including making sure they have inclusive hiring practices and offering fair accommodations, processes that often get lost when companies introduce AI screens: "What you are losing is the nuance that you can pick up on in a more human interaction or a place where there is space for there to be dialogue for a person to be appreciated as they are and for what they bring to the table—as opposed to how they stack up against this false statistical representation that's created by the model."

The same ethical considerations should be applied not only to AI-based hiring tools but also to algorithms that are used to monitor productivity, for example, in warehouses. These AI-based productivity rates could lead to exhaustion, and some workers might even be injured or become disabled because of productivity rates. Amazon warehouses are infamous for their productivity rates, and their workers suffer almost twice as many injuries compared to similar companies, according to a study by the Strategic Organizing Center.[10]

Experts call Amazon's warehouses where algorithmic tracking is used "digital sweatshops" and are afraid this one-size-fits-all model could be illegal and might harm especially vulnerable employees.

Some workers who can do the job but who may need temporary accommodation—because they are pregnant, for example, and need to sit down for a minute or need more bathroom breaks—could have lower productivity rates. The same might happen to those who develop a disability and need accommodation. Reprimanding or firing them for needing accommodations might be illegal, said Charlotte Burrows, chair of the Equal Employment Opportunity Commission. "An overly rigid application of a productivity algorithm will result in unlawful treatment."

For Givens and others, the lack of accommodations and even thought for people with disabilities is one of the big civil rights questions of our day: "Thinking through how technology is transforming people's access to opportunity and where it's perpetuating discrimination," she said. "It's a moral failing."

And this does not apply only to people with disabilities or older people.

"This is a question about the functioning of our society," she said. If we don't get this right, discrimination will just continue and may even get worse.

A CASE STUDY OF CHANGE

After these sobering conversations about how AI affects people with disabilities, I wanted to have a longer talk with the EEOC, which is tasked with enforcing fair and equal access to employment across the United States. We know about all of these problems with AI tools; why is the EEOC doing so little?

I was the first reporter to interview EEOC commissioner Keith Sonderling in 2021 on AI. He is a former employment lawyer who was appointed to the EEOC by the Trump administration and sworn in in September 2020. During his confirmation hearings, he said that again and again he'd heard concerns about AI tools and decided to make this topic one of his signature projects.

Sonderling (which means "unworldly eccentric" in German and doesn't fit the commissioner's temperament and demeanor at all) assured me that, by law, employers must offer an accommodation if job applicants cannot take a test because of a disability, but, as I learned, that doesn't always happen.

"Disability discrimination, year after year, is one of the highest-filed claims. For the EEOC, disability discrimination is extremely serious," he said. "We need a workplace that is completely free and fair, and that there's no discrimination happening while you're at work."

I was surprised that he still viewed AI as this breakthrough technology that would solve a lot of problems. "There's unlimited benefits here," he said. "[AI] is an excellent way to eliminate bias in recruiting and promotion, but also, more importantly, it's going to help employers find the right candidates who will have high-level job satisfaction. And for the employees, too, they will find the jobs that are right for them. So essentially, it's a wonderful matchmaking service if it's properly designed and implemented."

He did bring up some caveats: "Although artificial intelligence can help employers find the right employees quickly and can help employees thrive in the workplace by doing the tasks and jobs that they're most adept to at the same time, it could potentially discriminate worse than some of the original discriminations you could think of," Sonderling said.

What's important to understand is that the commission mainly goes after two types of discrimination. It sues employers that intentionally discriminate, for example, by not hiring people over fifty or by laying off an employee because they got pregnant. That's intentional discrimination and unlawful.

The commission also goes after employers that might have had the best intentions but used tests or other tools that unintentionally have discriminatory effects against "protected groups," which is the EEOC terminology for discrimination based on race, color, religion, sex, sexual orientation, pregnancy, national origin, age, disability, or genetic information.

The unintentional discrimination statute, which would most likely be applied to AI tools, goes back to a landmark 1971 Supreme Court decision called *Griggs v. Duke Power*. "In that case, Willie Griggs and twelve other African American employees sued their employer, alleging that the company was violating the law by requiring employees to either have a high school degree or pass a general intelligence test to qualify for a higher-paying position," Sonderling explained. The employees argued that the degree and the general intelligence test requirements weren't relevant to the job and filtered out more African American employees than white ones.

Duke Power disagreed and argued that requiring a high school degree or a passing score on a general intelligence test were nondiscriminatory because these requirements applied to all employees equally. (And as laypeople, that probably seems reasonable to many of us. Everyone gets a chance to go to high school and can pass a general intelligence test, right?)

But at the time in North Carolina, African Americans were less likely to have a high school education than white Americans. And the tests were also unequal: "The pass rate for the general intelligence test that the company wanted to require was 58 percent for white workers and 6 percent for African American workers," Sonderling added.

The Supreme Court sided with the African American workers and declared assessment tools that passed applicants from different races at widely different rates to be unlawful, unless the company can make a case that the assessment is testing for specific job requirements, which was not the case in *Griggs v. Duke Power.*

There is one crucial difference between the assessments of the past and those of today. Employees, up until very recently, knew which tests they would have to pass to get a higher-paying job at a company, but with AI, folks often don't even know that they are being tested or assessed or on what basis an AI tool makes decisions. Because of this lack of knowledge today, many won't be able to file a discrimination claim. In the *Griggs* case and in countless other assessment challenges, employees and job applicants were able to bring a case because they knew they were tested, they knew what the test entailed, and they could make an argument about why it was potentially discriminatory.

Even if job applicants or employees know that an AI games tool, for example, is assessing them for a job, they do not know how they were analyzed and scored or whether their rejection was based on merit or on a faulty algorithm. There is no transparency.

That has consequences for everyone, but especially for people with disabilities. For example, in AI-based video interviews: "If the software cannot understand the interviewee because of a disability, such as a speech impediment, the program will automatically score them lower than someone without a disability, even though they are the most qualified applicant," Sonderling said. But, so far, no one has been able to show any evidence that the tools work or don't work for applicants with speech impairments, because overwhelmingly AI-based video interviews are black boxes.

I spoke to Lindsey Zuloaga, the chief data scientist at HireVue, about this in June 2023 and she told me that the company has thought extensively about this problem and that AI-based speech-to-text transcription tools are getting more accurate for English speakers with accents.

When I asked her about individuals with speech impairments and how different speech disabilities could lead to higher error rates in speech-to-text transcription, which the AI uses to score job applicants, she acknowledged a problem: "This is a whole interesting area because it's so hard to find enough data on that," she said. So she built her own data set: "One afternoon, I did my own little study on stuttering."

Zuloaga created a data corpus for some ad hoc testing: "I took some transcripts and manually messed with them to make it look like people are stuttering."

Most forms of stuttering, such as when applicants stop their speech stream or repeat the beginning of a word, do not induce problems in the AI's transcriptions and predictions. But she found one problem: when applicants repeat whole strings of words. "That long string repetition can hurt your score," Zuloaga said. She described her test cases as extreme cases of stuttering and wondered how humans would also judge them. She would love to work with a disability rights organization to obtain more data to study this area in more depth.

In regard to AI games, EEOC commissioner Keith Sonderling and the chair of the commission Charlotte Burrows (whom I interviewed a few months later) believe that asking someone to press the spacebar on the keyboard as fast as they can, as Pymetrics does in its suite of AI games, might be questionable. "Someone who maybe has a disability that affects their ability to use a keyboard will take that differently and could be disadvantaged, not for anything to do with the particular job, but solely because they are in the position of having to have less dexterity in their use of that keyboard," Burrows said. "If that's not a problem that will be ever relevant in the job, that could be a violation of our laws."

Another issue is that applicants don't know how the data collected on them is used and why they have been rejected for an opportunity. Without having concrete evidence of harm (Did the key-pressing game result in them being rejected? Did an applicant's stutter lead to the wrong prediction?), which is almost impossible to get in the age of AI, it is challenging to file a case in a US court that will stick.

Some experts, including Ifeoma Ajunwa, the law professor at Emory University, have argued that we need to change our laws to adjust to this new reality. Job applicants should be able to file a case "per se," which means "on its face," without having concrete evidence of harm. For example, someone with a motor disability who plays an AI game in which they are asked to press the spacebar as fast as they can would have an option to file a lawsuit: "When a plaintiff using a hiring platform encounters a problematic design feature—like platforms that check for gaps in employment—she should be able to bring a lawsuit on the basis of discrimination per se and the employer would then be required to provide statistical proof from internal and external audits to show that its hiring platform is not unlawfully discriminating against certain groups," Ajunwa wrote in a *New York Times* opinion piece.[11]

A change in the law could give people the right to challenge the design of these tools and make the company responsible for showing that its tool is not harmful. This could also help the EEOC start an investigation. Keith Sonderling said that the EEOC's hands are tied until someone comes forward with evidence. But in this new world of AI, the evidence usually stays with the company.

"A big reason why you haven't seen more litigation in this area or more federal enforcement in this area is that the employee may not know that they were discriminated against by a computer, by a person—whether it's intentionally or through the results of a skewed test," Sonderling said. "But as far as the EEOC authority to investigate AI and hiring claims, all EEOC cases have to start with an employee."

I could tell that Sonderling was frustrated by the lack of enforcement or any kind of communication from the EEOC in regard to companies using AI: "There have been no guidelines. There's been nothing specific to the use of artificial intelligence, whether it is résumé screening, whether it's targeting job ads or facial recognition or voice recognition, there have been no new guidelines from the EEOC since the technology has been created," he told me.

I interviewed Keith Sonderling in early July 2021. The podcast and print series on the subject were published later that month in *MIT Technology Review*.[12] Following is a timeline of events that contributed to the EEOC waking up and looking into AI at work.

DECEMBER 2020

In December 2020, eleven Democratic senators wrote a letter to the US Equal Employment Opportunity Commission expressing concerns about the use of hiring technologies: "While hiring technologies can sometimes reduce the role of individual hiring managers' biases, they can also reproduce and deepen systemic patterns of discrimination reflected in today's workforce data."[13]

The senators basically reminded the EEOC to be an enforcement agency. "Job applicants and employers depend on the Commission to conduct robust research and oversight of the industry and provide appropriate guidance." The letter asked specifically whether the agency had the authority and capabilities to investigate whether these tools discriminate. "We request information about the Commission's authority and capacity to conduct the necessary research and oversight to ensure equitable hiring."

JANUARY 2021

The EEOC responded with a letter in January 2021 that was leaked to me and was published in an article in *MIT Technology Review*.[14] In the letter, the commission acknowledged that it was not investigating any AI tools at the time: "To our knowledge, the Commission has not received a charge of discrimination from a complainant alleging discrimination based on the use of such technologies, and the Commission has not conducted enforcement proceedings alleging such discrimination."[15] The EEOC stated that the commission would likely encounter hesitance from the industry to share data and that AI tools calibrated to different companies' software would prevent the EEOC from instituting any broad policies.

"I was surprised and disappointed when I saw the response," said Roland Behm, the lawyer and advocate for people with behavioral health issues. "The whole tenor of that letter seemed to make the EEOC seem like more of a passive bystander rather than an enforcement agency."[16]

At the time, the EEOC was run by Janet Dhillon, who had been nominated by Donald Trump. What's interesting, though, is that the Department of Justice has taken a much more proactive role. When I filed a Freedom of Information request with Atlanta Public Schools (APS), which has used HireVue's AI-based hiring system, I came across some interesting information. Apparently, the Department of Justice started an inquiry into APS's usage of HireVue.

The EEOC's oversight is often reactive, but because it's so hard for applicants to prove discrimination, the industry is basically untouched by one of the most important agencies tasked with overseeing hiring in the United States. In a report on the subject, the authors at the not-for-profit organization Upturn stated: "In practice, most employers face too little pressure from enforcers to meaningfully evaluate their selection devices and consider less discriminatory alternatives."[17]

OCTOBER 2021

A few months after my *MIT Technology Review* stories were published, in which I called out the EEOC for not reacting to evidence of discrimination in AI tools, especially for people with disabilities, the EEOC announced that it was launching an AI task force.

Task forces sound great—action is taken—but they could also just make it look to the outside world that an agency is doing something, when really they are doing nothing. I wasn't on the edge of my seat about this development.

FEBRUARY 2022

In February 2022, the EEOC offered me an interview with the chair of the commission, Charlotte Burrows.

I reiterated my concerns and we talked about specific examples of AI tools not working. She promised me that her agency was looking into AI being used to make decisions in the workplace: "It's really important for us at the EEOC and other law enforcement agencies to be thinking about how AI is really fundamentally changing employment practices," she said. "We have to make sure that [AI tools] don't become a high-tech pathway to discrimination."

To her, looking at AI is at the core of the EEOC's mission: "I really see our agency as essential to ensuring that everyone has the opportunity to enjoy what is the basic agreement of this nation, which is equality and justice for all."

MAY 2022

In May 2022, I got a heads-up on some interesting news: the EEOC, together with the Department of Justice, finally released its first-ever publication on AI and hiring—a technical guidance document,[18] so it's not holding anyone accountable or enforcing the law against a case of discrimination, but it lets companies know the EEOC is watching them and they are on the hook if the commission finds out that the technologies used are discriminating against people with disabilities.

In a media call, Kristen Clarke, the assistant attorney general for civil rights at the Department of Justice, didn't mince words: "Today we are sounding an alarm regarding the dangers tied to blind reliance on AI and other technologies that we are seeing increasingly used by employers," she said.[19] She also asked employers to be transparent about the technologies they are using.

Although the document the EEOC and DOJ released was meant to be a guide on how to use AI tools, it was forthcoming. "The use of these tools may disadvantage job applicants and employees with disabilities. When this occurs, employers may risk violating federal Equal Employment Opportunity ('EEO') laws that protect individuals with disabilities."

Sometimes it's hard to do this kind of journalistic work. We find wrongdoing after wrongdoing, but it feels like nothing will ever change. But every now and then, there *is* a little bit of change, and this publication seemed like the first step by the EEOC toward acknowledging that there is a problem with these automated systems. A small win. Now more than ever, I believe that change is possible. (I am not per se against AI tools; I just want to make sure that the tools pick the best candidates and that they don't discriminate.)

I was surprised how broadly the EEOC and DOJ announcement took the idea of discrimination. Under the question "How could an employer's use of algorithmic decision-making tools violate the ADA?" the EEOC and DOJ wrote: "The employer relies on an algorithmic decision-making tool that intentionally or unintentionally 'screens out' an individual with a disability, even though that individual is able to do the job with a reasonable accommodation."

I am not a lawyer, but that sounds like almost anyone with a disability could ask for EEOC enforcement if they were rejected for a job, even in one of the first hiring rounds, given they could do the job with reasonable accommodation.

Here is a critical paragraph that I think might turn out to be problematic for employers that use tools like Pymetrics' or Plum's AI games and personality tests: "If an open position requires the ability to write reports, the employer may wish to avoid algorithmic decision-making tools that rate this ability by measuring the similarity between an applicant's personality and the typical personality for currently successful report writers. By doing so, the employer lessens the likelihood of rejecting someone who is good at writing reports, but whose personality, because of a disability, is uncommon among successful report writers," wrote the EEOC.

A BETTER FUTURE

My hope is that the EEOC and DOJ will go after broad enforcement goals because the use of personality tests is so ubiquitous, especially for hourly workers.

It's a step in the right direction to warn the industry, but experts I have spoken to want more. As a first step, the industry needs more transparency. Applicants and employees must know when they are being analyzed. We also need to know how individuals are being assessed.

Other critics are tired of the proprietary algorithm argument that many vendors utilize to avoid scrutiny: "We have a secret sauce that we can't disclose to you," Frank Pasquale said, characterizing what these firms sound like. Pasquale is a professor at Brooklyn Law School and an expert in algorithmic accountability.

He and others would like more accountability and independent audits of these tools, but not by private companies because payment for audits can easily lead to conflicts of interest, which I found when reporting on two audits in the AI hiring space for *MIT Technology Review*.[20]

The two audits in question, one paid for by Pymetrics, the other paid for by HireVue, showcased how conflicts of interest can creep in. The "independent audits" could have been used to hide controversial practices behind the auditors' stamp of approval. Both vendors used the audits for marketing purposes.

What struck me about the HireVue audit was that it was basically a roundtable discussion and the auditors highlighted potential problems stakeholders had mentioned. The auditors did not access HireVue's data or algorithms. Nevertheless, HireVue issued a press release declaring that "HireVue Leads the Industry with Commitment to Transparent and Ethical Use of AI in Hiring" and that HireVue "assessments work as advertised with regard to fairness and bias issues,"[21] although the auditors didn't actually get to audit the training data, the algorithmic processes, or the results on a technical level. Additionally, anyone who wanted to download the report from HireVue's website was required to sign a quasi nondisclosure agreement, which is highly unusual. (Hire-Vue says that audits have been an opportunity to share the company's approach and their science to stakeholders.)

For the other audit, of Pymetrics' suite of games, the vendor paid two computer science professors from Northeastern University, Christo Wilson and Alan Mislove, and their graduate students to test the fairness of the Pymetrics models.[22] This audit was criticized for crediting four members of Pymetrics as coauthors of the report, which calls into question the very idea that this report was editorially independent.[23] In addition, the company declared its product "independently audited" in its marketing materials.

The researchers did access the data, the models, and the source code but didn't test whether the tools picked the most qualified applicants: "We are not looking at whether these games actually measure people's ability to do work in the real world," Wilson said. Instead, the team tested whether the tools abide by the quasi industry standard of "fairness" called the four-fifths rule.

According to the four-fifths rule, hiring screens should select roughly the same proportion of men and women and of people from different racial groups: so, for example, if 1,000 men apply and 800 make it through the assessment, that is an 80 percent passing rate for men. If 100 women also apply, for the assessment to be considered "fair" under the four-fifths rule by the EEOC, then at least 64 women need to pass the assessment because that is a passing rate for women of 64 percent (four-fifths of 80 percent). Of course, a pass rate of 80 percent for women would be precisely fair, being the same rate as men, but the four-fifths rule allows for some wiggle room.

It's kind of a minimum federal standard, and the Pymetrics algorithm passed: "The big takeaway is that Pymetrics is actually doing a really good job," Wilson said.

But others disagreed: "It effectively felt like the question being asked was more 'Is Pymetrics doing what they say they do?' as opposed to 'Are they doing the correct or right thing?'" said Manish Raghavan, a professor at MIT Sloan School of Management who has published extensively on artificial intelligence and hiring.

And that idea of doing the right thing came up in my conversations with Christo Wilson in regard to intersectional fairness. Instead of just checking the "passing rates" of men versus women and Asian versus Black versus white versus Native American, and so forth, as the EEOC suggests, Wilson's team also tested whether the model allows for intersectional fairness, meaning that passing rates might be in the acceptable range for women overall, but would Black women or Asian American women, who sit at the intersection of two factors, also pass at acceptable rates?

This was a problem in the Gender Shades study in which MIT researcher Joy Buolamwini found that three face detection tools had an accuracy rate between 92 percent and 98 percent overall for all women in her data set, but only a 65–79 percent accuracy rate for Black women.[24]

"We know that it is typically an issue," Christo Wilson said. "Lo and behold, it's an issue."

Wilson's team looked at intersections of race and gender in Pymetrics' AI tool and found that in some instances intersectional groups including Black women did not pass the four-fifths rule compared to white men, for example. He shared this information with me during an interview before the final report was published.

But before publication of the report, Pymetrics convinced Wilson and his team to leave their testing of intersectional fairness out of the final audit report because Pymetrics told the researchers that it couldn't implement intersectional fairness because of the EEOC guidelines and case law, Wilson recalled. "It would be unfair for us to say that Pymetrics failed at this thing if they couldn't actually correct it" was how Wilson described the reason for why this was left out of the final report. (Harver, the company which acquired Pymetrics in 2022, declined to comment.)

I believe it was important that Wilson and his team did the additional checks, even though they were not part of the final report. We should test for intersectional fairness even though the EEOC did not explicitly require it at the time. (Experts I talked to believe that the EEOC has always allowed more testing, for example, on intersectionality.)

In May 2023, two years and change after the Pymetrics audit, the EEOC issued technical assistance guidelines on its website asking companies formally to actually check for intersectional fairness.[25]

So, instead of relying on private audits paid for by product vendors that raise conflicts of interest, many experts want the government to test these tools before they come on the market: "There should be a preemptive regulation so that before you use any of these systems, the Equal

Employment Opportunity Commission should need to review it and then license it," Frank Pasquale said.

The Food and Drug Administration is a good model here, he said. Instead of allowing any kind of AI hiring tools on the market, vendors would have to go through a preapproval process similar to how new medications are approved by the FDA. Instead of just assuring customers that their AI tools don't cause harm, vendors would have to prove it to the government first in double- or triple-blind tests just like pharmaceutical manufacturers have to do, because the stakes in the employment arena are high. It would be a costly process, but it might be necessary to ensure that these tools don't harm job applicants.

For that to happen, Congress would need to change the law and give the Equal Employment Opportunity Commission the power to proactively regulate the field instead of only going after employers once an individual has complained.

It's on us to be aware of these developments and to try to influence lawmakers to change the rules. We do not have to passively accept this new world that is being thrust upon us.

CHAPTER 7

Finding Hidden Gems

On Predictive Analytics and Quiet Hiring

We are entering an era of mostly unlimited measurement options with artificial intelligence. We now have the means to record keystrokes and track website visits, emails, Slack messages, company reviews—almost anything. But do the signals that AI systems capture reveal anything meaningful? Many people in HR think they do. In this chapter, we pivot from exploring how AI is used in hiring to how AI can be used for monitoring and evaluating employees.

Two dominant strains of monitoring occur in many workplaces. One is top-down surveillance: monitoring every move an employee makes in the workplace (and after hours), which I tackle in the next chapter. The other is predictive analytics: analyzing signals to understand workers' skills in order to build career paths and learn as much as possible about employees to benefit the business (and the employee).

It's a relatively new application of technology and mostly used in internal company systems. Unfortunately, there is not a lot of public knowledge and critical scholarship yet. But it's still to me important to show what is happening inside many large companies.

HR AS A SCOUTING OPERATION

In the past, most companies have seen their employees as cost centers—the largest one by far for many organizations. Human resources was viewed as the company police who made sure everyone behaved as a way to protect the organization. Now, HR is becoming a critical part of the business.

"If we want to really grow as a company without HR, it just wouldn't happen," said Marc Starfield, the former head of HR technology for Vodafone, a telecommunications company.

Especially in the United States, in the past companies would simply lay off employees who had outdated or undesired skills and hire new ones with the desired skills. But that is no longer a sustainable long-term option for most businesses since there are more open positions than skilled unemployed workers to hire.[1]

Companies are now turning to their own employees to find "hidden gems." HR uses predictive analytics tools to try to understand a company's own people and discover previously invisible talents and new leaders inside the organization. Some researchers call this trend "quiet hiring."

Several AI vendors, mainly Eightfold, Gloat, and Fuel50, came onto the scene a few years ago. These companies use artificial intelligence in interesting ways: for example, to create an internal marketplace for employees to help them learn new skills and apply for internal positions.

Hundreds if not thousands of companies and government agencies are now using these tools, including the State of New York. Eightfold has become a unicorn company and was valued at $2.1 billion in 2021.[2]

AI is changing how companies hire and promote internal candidates by relying less on credentials and degrees and more on skills. From what we have covered so far about the use of AI in HR, this is a positive development.

"If you go back in time, it used to be 'What college did you go to? What was your GPA? Where did you work? Oh, you worked at IBM? You must be good,'" said Josh Bersin, an industry analyst of the HR technology market. "Now we're in a world where we're saying, 'Let's do some work to figure out what the skills are. Now let's go out and find people that fit that.'"

Eightfold runs a platform where employees can use their LinkedIn account or their résumé to build a quick profile. The AI then pulls out an employee's skills, infers skills they might not have listed, and recommends appropriate jobs. The company offers similar technology for hiring.

Marc Starfield is a fan of Eightfold's software. When we spoke in late 2022, he was in charge of all technology that supports the roughly one hundred thousand Vodafone employees and any programs that help the company's HR strategy. He has worked in HR technology for more than twenty years, based in London, and is originally from South Africa.

We met in Las Vegas at HR Tech, one of the largest HR technology expos in the world. He told me that Vodafone has a big goal and that's why it decided to bring in Eightfold: Vodafone wants to move from being a telecommunications company to being a technology and communications company—a move that many companies in other sectors are doing as well. For example, many banks don't want to just be banks anymore; they want to be technology companies that happen to be in banking.

But tech talent is in high demand and this convergence of businesses toward technology makes it easier for employees to change jobs. Many have done so.

Looking at last year, "a third of employees changed jobs in the United States; 45 percent of them changed industries," Josh Bersin, the industry analyst, said. "The amount of mobility between companies, between industries, skyrocketed." This trend is partially driven by remote work possibilities but also because workers can more easily transfer their skills. Employee skill transfer, in turn, makes it harder for companies to attract and retain talent when their employees can easily move from banking to tech to telecommunications.

Eightfold's AI helps employers push against this trend: it promises to match applicants and employees to jobs on the basis of their skills and to find employees who could learn a couple new skills, which could help them futureproof their jobs or slide into new jobs, a process called "upskilling." *Reskilling* and *upskilling* are some of the latest HR buzzwords, but skills are changing rapidly and jobs are changing faster than ever before.

According to the 2020 World Economic Forum's *Future of Jobs Report*, core skills will change for 40 percent of all workers by 2025, and 50 percent of all employees will need reskilling or upskilling.[3]

Vodafone wants to hire at least seven thousand software developers, but because there are not enough people with these new skills on the open job market, it is turning inward to develop its own employees. Or more specifically, the ones who want to learn, Starfield said. He categorizes employees into roughly three groups: "One group will make the shift to the new skills and behaviors we need. One group is still deciding. One group will never."

With this HR initiative, he is trying to activate the middle still-deciding group. He describes the initiative as "democratization" and giving everybody a chance to "grow in our organization." He hopes that employees will want to stay with Vodafone and will feel valued by getting this personalized career advice. Another upside of Eightfold's tool is that Vodafone can make long-term plans for its workforce, something that has been nearly impossible to do before the advent of big data, Starfield said.

AI AS CAREER COACH

Marc Starfield and his team studied the market and decided on Eightfold as their vendor in 2021. The tool went live in January 2022.

Eightfold operates in over 140 countries and has more than two billion data sets of employees, about half of the world's workforce. The software can predict with 90 percent accuracy the next two roles of an employee over the next five years, said Kamal Ahluwalia, Eightfold's former president, who recently transitioned to an advisor role. (There has been no independent testing done on these claims, so this high accuracy number is difficult to verify.)

The system can also predict an individual's potential to acquire new skills, something that makes executives' hearts beat faster because many want agile employees.

Eightfold's AI engine learned from the sea of data that employees who know Python often also know other programming languages that people might not list on their profiles. Inferring skills based on other people's résumés helps more modest résumé writers, who are mostly women, not fall behind—the AI just adds these presumed skills.

"We've had people who got hired where their validated skill was one, then there were eleven inferred skills, and that person got hired,"

Ahluwalia said. Inferred skills have helped the companies Eightfold works with, such as Micron, to increase diversity. "They've hired more women, more Black Americans, more veterans, more people with disabilities with Eightfold."

Because many applicants can't decipher job descriptions, Eightfold's AI also helps the 80 percent of workers who apply to the wrong job, according to Ahluwalia. Job descriptions may be too long and include too many preferred skills and capabilities because hiring managers keep adding more and more requirements to existing job descriptions. Hiring managers may also include internal job classifications that make no sense to applicants, hence the high number of applicants applying for the wrong opportunities, according to Ahluwalia.

When job descriptions become too long and include too many skills, Eightfold reveals to hiring managers the limited talent pool. "What it shows is, if this is what you're asking for, this is what the talent pool looks like right there: twelve people, one woman, all others men," Ahluwalia said in a hypothetical example. This transparency helps managers to act. "What we help customers do is see what is really required, because now you can see the impact on your talent pool. What's the pipeline? What is nice to have? How much experience makes sense? So each of these things you start to see in real time what the impact is."

On a so-called capability matrix, the AI shows the employees with the skills that a manager is looking for, but it also shows the employees who could learn the required skills in three to six months, which helps managers find the right people internally to train for the opportunity.

With these insights, managers often opt to lower their expectations and refocus on just the core skills of the job instead of asking for a laundry list of skills and capabilities.

Another helpful Eightfold feature is suggested skills adjacencies—for example, the AI suggests that a graphic designer at Invisalign who helps with building retainers might be a good graphic designer for a gaming company.

When I spoke with the former CEO of the job portal CareerBuilder, Irina Novoselsky, she explained that hiring based on skills adjacencies will become the new normal in hiring because there are too few people for the most sought-after jobs. CareerBuilder rejiggered its algorithm a few years back to focus on skills. Its AI now matches people to jobs on the basis of their transferable skill set. "I like to say, it's not what you've done, but can you do it?" Novoselsky said.

It's all about potential and transferring a skill set from one industry to another. During COVID, many flight attendants were out of a job, but their skills were suitable for customer service roles: "They are dealing with problems, their communication skills, they are logistic handlers, they are project managers, and so when you look at that high customer satisfaction and customer interaction skill set, they were a perfect match," Novoselsky said.

As the world needs fewer bank tellers, they might be a good fit for the empty seats in customer support, too. But some skill matches are more surprising than others.

"Prison guards, when you look at their underlying skill sets, are a huge match for veterinary technicians. Empathy, communication, strength, being able to manage difficult situations," Novoselsky said. "Pest control has a really huge match with meter readers."

She also said this skills-based hiring approach is the secret sauce to increasing diversity. "The by-product of this is increased diversity, because you are now not looking for the same type of person that you have been looking for that has that experience. You are widening your net and you are able to get a very different type of person into that role.

We have seen that play out where our clients have been able to get a much more diverse skill set using our tools."

Another by-product is that companies may find people who don't have a college degree but have the right skills for the job. Too often, experts say, companies require college degrees, which excludes about 60 percent of working Americans who don't have a bachelor's degree but might have the right skill set.

Large sets of data make other kinds of analysis possible. Ahluwalia estimated that Eightfold probably has data on 70 to 80 percent of all knowledge workers: "It's simply a matter of what they're saying, what words they're using, what skill they're using in what context." The data is "time stamped," showing what people did at certain points in their career and what their next steps were, which essentially provides a career path. The AI tool can recognize this and recommend it to others.

The Eightfold tool also shows managers if an employee is climbing up the career ladder faster than others in the organization. "That's also a mark that this person has been working really hard and progressing faster than their peers," Ahluwalia said.

It could be a signal. But we all know that promotions are not necessarily based on folks doing their best work. And what does this mean for employees who are on a slower trajectory, for example, employees (let's face it, mostly women) who take time off or work part-time to care for their children or elderly relatives? Or those who have a disability or are struggling with a chronic illness?

This is the other side of pattern recognition. The AI notes what's "normal," which means that individuals who don't follow one of the normal paths might be penalized or flagged as unusual—although they may have perfectly fine reasons for why their path is different. I asked

Ahluwalia about this. What happens when someone is flagged as very slow moving up the career ladder?

"What we do is transparency and it's both ways," he said. "Whatever the employer is seeing, show the same information to the person as well."

But I'm not sure how that solves the problem, since it doesn't leave room for context or explanations, but at least the employee knows what information managers are seeing about them.

EMPLOYEE COMPLIANCE

What's surprising is that the biggest challenge for many HR teams is not whether the new technology works or creates bias (although this should be a priority) but its adoption among employees. Employee uptake is a metric often used to evaluate HR investments and it's a tricky one. Will employees use the system? Many of us hate learning new technology programs, especially if it's unclear how they benefit us.

Eightfold has a high adoption rate at Vodafone and other companies for a reason: it's pretty clear what's in it for employees. Many people are pretty bad at long-term, strategic career planning, and Eightfold tells people where their career could go by showing where others have gone. It's not necessarily a career ladder but more like a lattice that reveals different options; for example, how a software developer could become senior software developer, then director, then vice president of technology.

The platform helps employees understand which skills they have today and which skills are required for different roles they aspire to. The tool also shows employees roles within their current employer that they are qualified for or are almost ready to apply for. And crucially, Eightfold shows employees not only which skills they need for the next role but also how to obtain them—linking to learning libraries like LinkedIn Learning or Udemy.

"I sometimes joke about having a 'Vodafone Me' brand, which is saying I know exactly where I am in my career," Marc Starfield said. He described how Eightfold can help Vodafone employees. Once an individual uploads their résumé, "It immediately then gives them this 'You are a strong match for these roles.' I think that gives people confidence to say, 'Let me go and have a look at that role,' and think, 'Wow, I didn't realize that, and if I only had these two or three things, I could go into a different career path.'"

The incentives for the company and the employees to use this upskilling system are aligned: what helps an employee's bottom line also helps the company's bottom line.

The next challenge for Marc Starfield is to figure out how the ambitions of his employees might be harvested for Vodafone's wants and needs, especially if they are at odds. For example, say he wanted to become an academic; on its face, that wouldn't help Vodafone. "Can the organization say, 'Okay, that's interesting, we really want to get much more data insights. You are not a data scientist, but your interest in research kind of combines those two things,'" Starfield speculated, trying to build a use case for Vodafone.

However, employees should make no mistake—the advice this tool gives can be incredibly helpful, but the way employees use it is also recorded. The AI might notice that you don't engage in any of the learning opportunities (might that mean that you are not agile and not a go-getter?) and it points out if users are slower to move up the ranks in a company than others.

(Recently, LinkedIn asked if I was still an assistant professor of journalism at New York University. This is the sixth year I have worked at NYU, and usually in their sixth year, assistant professors go up for tenure. But I was on maternity leave, and when the pandemic hit, I received more time on tenure track. But maybe LinkedIn's algorithm noticed that most assistant professors become associate professors in year six and has now categorized me as "slow"? Or maybe most people switch jobs after so many years? I will probably never know what signal was derived from this automated question.)

Some critics believe that allowing AI to rely on résumés is not a great idea. "We believe the résumé is the root of the whole problem," said Josh Millet, the CEO of Criteria Corporation, a hiring assessment firm. "Hiring is a big prediction business. We're all trying to predict outcomes, one way or another, and the outcomes we're trying to predict are job performance." Vendors need to use the most predictive data, not the easiest available data, like résumés, he said.

"For us, it's sort of a garbage in, garbage out scenario. What you're getting from a résumé essentially is two things: you are getting some sense of the educational background and then you are getting some sense of the amount of relevant experience. All the science shows that those two things are pretty weak signals in terms of predicting job outcomes."

Weak signal, lots of noise. Millet asked, "Is seventeen years in sales predictive of greater success than eight years? It's not at all." Who knows if someone who has seventeen years of experience in sales is really good at it? They may have struggled for those years, going from one job to another.

An AI skills-matching tool that is based on analyzing résumés won't understand whether someone is really good at their job. The only information it gets is that the person had this or that experience.

"We know there are better signals out there that aren't based on experience and educational background: work ethic, problem-solving, critical thinking—those we know are highly linked to outcomes," Millet said.

Other critics of skills-matching technologies à la Eightfold find the matching too basic. They believe that these AI tools reduce humans to just a few keywords on a résumé, that the tools don't understand potential. Still, with improvements, skills matching promises to be a powerful asset for employees who want to move up in their careers.

Vodafone only lets employees match their profiles to in-house jobs. Companies like Unilever have taken this technology one step further. They have opened an internal marketplace where employees can apply to different projects within the company—working for different teams and learning new skills a few hours a week while still working in their old jobs. Employees learn new skills and get to meet new colleagues inside the company. Some are eventually able to find new jobs.

If done well, these marketplaces can save companies real money because they don't have to hire outside workers; instead, managers find the talent they need internally. Unilever used the AI system built by the Israeli company Gloat. In an earnings call, the former Unilever CEO Alan Jope praised the tool: "We've also unlocked 300,000 hours of people's time to our internal digital talent marketplace. . . . And what that does is it matches employees who have capacity with projects and opportunities to do interesting new types of work."

Three hundred thousand hours probably equals millions of dollars in savings for a large corporation.

MEASURING BURNOUT AND FLIGHT RISK

But data from employees can be used in many other ways as well. Vendors take in all kinds of "people data" from benefits, annual reviews, emails, calendars, contacts, résumés, and so forth, to understand who is at risk of leaving the company in the next year, who is "quiet quitting" (that is, just doing what they are being asked to do), and who is at risk for burnout.

In the fall of 2022, workers were still resigning at an all-time high and many companies worried about the flight risk of their current employees, so predictive analytics was all the rage at HR Tech in November.

One of the most interesting perspectives was shared by Nydia Serna, a veteran HR manager at PepsiCo. At the time she was the head HR operations director based in New York and her work bridged the gap between HR and IT. She'd come to HR in a roundabout way: "I started my computer science degree and I didn't like it. I was the worst coder you'll ever meet, but I understood the system. So when it was time to take an internship, I was very interested in HR," she said on a panel at the conference.

To her, data gives managers a much better grounding when making decisions; whereas before most managers relied on intuition or incomplete data, now they can make more complex business decisions based on people data. This is the strength she brings from IT to HR.

"One of the most powerful things we've done is introduce analytics, because it surfaces up to the entire organization where we have gaps in data quality, where we need to push more and transform this data into actual information that's going to change the way we work," she said.

For managers, easy dashboard access to interact with this data is important in understanding their own employees: "We're very interested in understanding attrition, identifying very early where we might be experiencing quiet quitting. Where do we have those gender gaps?"

But these kinds of systems can cause harm if the data fed into them is incorrect. "We need to be very careful about what we do, where do we send the data and how accurate it is. And sometimes it is not as accurate as one hopes. I review this on my very own self," she said. When Serna checked the system, she had a 3 percent chance of quitting in the next twelve months.

PepsiCo had also started a campaign for employees to self-identify and Serna found out she was misclassified. She started at PepsiCo in Mexico, where no one describes themselves as Latina. When she moved to the United States to take another position with the company, she was misclassified as white/Caucasian/non-Hispanic.

"So when I went in and changed that information, the entire communications approach that PepsiCo has towards me, not as a HR operations director, but as the employee of the company, started changing," she recalled. "I had more notifications about targeting my gender, targeting my ethnicity, targeting my development, and so I can see how it's important for the company to have the right information."

For their predictive analytics needs, PepsiCo just started using Visier. Serna was eager to find out what the AI would uncover—for example, which of her team members might be quiet quitters.

Visier is a start-up that has risen like a phoenix out of the ashes. In 2022 it raised $125 million with Goldman Sachs Asset Management, which valued the company at $1 billion.[4] Visier's customers include Experian, one of the three leading credit reporting agencies in the United States; Uber; Adobe; and Snap, the parent company of Snapchat.

I spoke with the vice president of research and strategy, Ian Cook, who also demonstrated the tool for me. He said Visier's predictive analytics answers a lot of the questions that Eightfold leaves open.

Eightfold solves a very specific problem, which is matching people to work, either internally or externally. What its AI doesn't solve for is this: "So what?" Cook said. "They just said, 'Ian can do this and the job needs to get done—we will help Ian and the job get together.'" Cook says with

Visier's AI he can find out if "Ian" succeeded at the new job and how he feels about the new job.

Visier tries to intake as much data as companies have—from business data to people data. If possible, Visier will also take performance data from employees, engagement data from surveys, and AI-based sentiment analysis, which rates email and other written communication as positive, negative, or neutral.

Cook thinks that passively monitoring all emails gives a more accurate picture of employees' feelings than asking someone once or twice a year via survey how they are feeling does.

"People aren't always really good at telling you how they feel. They don't often know. And it varies depending on if they just had a coffee or if they had just had a bad conversation with their boss. Detecting [employees' sentiments] passively from the tone of communication, style of communication gives you a cleaner signal around what's happening," he said. He emphasized that sentiment is only sampled at a group or team level, not from individuals, to ensure people cannot be identified.

At the same time, the more granular and individualized data from employees that Visier gets, the better the predictions. "The volume and the flow of data is quite extraordinary. Massive," Cook said. He estimates that Visier processes about ten thousand signals per employee.

So once Visier has a massive data lake, what insights can it draw from it? Cook said most companies ask the same question. "Do I have enough heads? Do I have the right heads? Am I paying too much for the people I have? When we get more sophisticated clients, that starts to go to, 'Do we have management that is helping people be committed and perform well?' They start to look at that next layer in terms of 'Are we helping people work?'"

Cook gave an example where Visier's tool might excel: if a company promotes an employee to a new position, Visier can find out whether the person has stayed in that position and whether this move has helped the business.

For Cook, everything goes back to business decisions for companies and that's how he pitches Visier. The software can help with employee retention, which saves money in hiring. But other benefits are a two-step process: if you help employees not burn out, then you also save money.

"We've got a decent amount of proof that using data makes better decisions. Better decisions make better returns," Cook said. True, that is, if the data is meaningful and drives thoughtful decision-making.

"We've done the background that says those of our clients who have more data being given to more users outperform their peers on profitability and return on assets. There is an association between sophisticated use of people data and business outcomes. It's not finally proven without a doubt in terms of causation, but the association is becoming clearer."

So it's not proven yet, but it appeals to common sense: more data equals better decisions.

Then Ian Cook showed me how companies can make sense of their own data with Visier: "I can bring in headcount. I can bring in applicant ratios for how many women are applying for certain jobs. I can look at cost components all together," he said. "We can tell you your gender pay gap straight away."

Managers can drill down to the individual level and fact-check whether the data is correct for members on their teams. The tool also does a network analysis of all the employees on a given team. "It can show them who they are talking with," Cook said. The software also delivers recommendations based on other people's data: "I see you talking to Jane. People who talk to Jane also talk to Brian. Have you thought about connecting with Brian?"

The software can detect potential burnout over time by recording any changes in employee behavior; for example, someone not responding as often and as fast as they used to. He suggests that for someone who used to go above and beyond, work twelve-hour days, fire off messages left and right and who is now in quiet quitting mode, the algorithm would detect this work pattern change and this employee would show up as being at risk of burnout.

Visier identified burnout in numerous hospital groups and the data helped the nursing and finance departments greenlight more hires. One hospital ended up not spending any more money but improved the process and had fewer absences. Cook said the data made the difference in moving the needle: "When you don't know, you're just arguing about people's perceptions and what somebody said in the corridor. When you have the data, you can address it as a material business problem and solve it."

He argues that Visier's algorithm can also predict, to a certain degree, which employee will leave in the next twelve months by calculating a flight risk score. The algorithm is trained on the data of employees who left. The algorithm tries to find patterns that people who left have in common and predicts which current employees have similar risk patterns.

This kind of flight risk software typically measures such factors as engagement level, absenteeism, changes in performance review ratings, time since last promotion, and even data like commute time and activity on LinkedIn, according to the HR organization SHRM.

Cook said that calculating who will leave is not an exact science because human behavior can vary so much: "You can make a space rocket hit an asteroid eleven million miles away; that's easier than predicting if someone's going to leave." At one company, Visier predicted nine out of sixteen resignations of senior-level executives and got the contract.

Other people, such as Enpei Lam, the former global head of people analytics and planning at Cushman & Wakefield, a large multinational real estate firm, have also analyzed why employees are leaving. Lam and his team built the algorithm at Cushman & Wakefield from scratch.

When he started at the company in 2021, the great resignation was in full swing and the company was losing people left and right. "They want to figure out 'why are people leaving?' Is this just because of the pay? Is it because they're not happy with their bosses? Is it because they're not happy with their work? What is going on?" Lam said. His bosses also wanted to know how they could stop the resignations. The executives thought that Lam and his team could tell them exactly when someone would leave. "They look at us like we are psychic."

Lam and his team incorporated over 130 attributes about employees, including demographic data (gender, ethnicity, disability), promotion, performance, manager's gender and ethnicity, tenure and reimbursement, base pay increases, commute time, engagement survey data, workplace analytics data (daily working hours, daily focus hours, number of daily meetings, percentage of external network contacts), and many more from 2020 and 2021 into their model to understand the most important factors driving people out the door.

Lam said the model was 80 percent to 90 percent accurate on a very broad group level: "We can't really predict down to the individual level," he said. "That's where the model starts to fall apart." The accuracy of the mode for individuals can fall below 50 percent, which means it is less predictive than a coin toss.

Lam and his team found the five most important factors connected with people leaving the organization were internal mobility, the number of daily meetings, pay, performance, and manager tenure. "Internal mobility continues to show up as the number one reason why people are leaving," Lam said. "If a person has continued to do the same thing for two years, that person's likelihood to leave is going to be higher—a lot higher—than those who have switched roles during the past two years."

To me, these findings were hardly surprising. People who have been stagnant at a job and overlooked for promotions and better pay would be unhappy. But maybe that is the beauty of data science. It helps us find solid evidence for things we suspected or knew through qualitative analysis all along.

The team's analysis was based on the 130 attributes they fed into the model. What the team didn't investigate were the other reasons why employees may leave because there wasn't any data available. In surveys and studies, employees at all different kinds of companies have expressed that they left because of a toxic work culture or "bad managers."

"Bad managers" is an amorphous data point and probably not available in an official data set, but Enpei Lam told me that other proxies, including manager tenure, manager performance rating, relationship with manager, and manager gender, were fed into the model. "Our employees have a pretty good relationship with their managers," he said. "What came up is that the longer a manager is in a job, the happier employees are."

I always wondered what companies do with the information once they have flight risk scores for individual employees or specific teams. Do they give folks instant promotions? Start monitoring them more closely?

Ian Cook from Visier said the first question many managers ask is if the person flagged is a high or low performer. "There could be people on the top of the list: 'Oh, thank goodness, my communication about their lack of contribution has been working. They've decided to take themselves out. Excellent.' That is a legitimate strategy," Cook said. If the person is a high performer, managers and HR will in all likelihood discuss options on what they could offer to retain this employee.

But some question whether flight risk predictions work at all. Thomas Otter is a former product manager in the HR space and now works as a venture capitalist. He is deeply troubled by flight risk predictors and thinks they are at best nonsense, at worst discriminatory. He believes that flight risk predictions are often incorrect because they are not based on solid science and they have the wrong input data.

"If you could really measure the things that determine flight risk, it wouldn't be really fair to be measuring it," because a lot of factors outside of work play a role in people's decision-making, Otter said. If someone is taking care of their parents, their flight risk is reduced. If someone has a trust fund and is independently wealthy, their flight risk is higher. If someone is in a long-distance relationship, their flight risk is higher.

"The biggest impact on flight risk are things that are outside the data sets that HR departments should ethically be holding," he said. So, flight risk predictions made on the existing data are vague and often of low value.

Another problem is how companies use the flight risk predictions. Some managers might prepare for the exit of an employee and limit that person's promotions, training opportunities, and compensation and reward people on the team who are likely to stay. "A manager can never unknow that information or unsee it," said Helen Poitevin, a Paris-based vice president and analyst who covers HCM technologies for research and advisory firm Gartner, to SHRM.org. "Will having that information now influence every decision or interaction they have with employees who are deemed flight risks?"[5]

Other managers might decide to pay someone that the system said is at risk of flight more money to entice them to stay, but because most managers have limited funds, other people on the team would get less compensation for the wrong reasons.

"Young, single white males have a higher flight risk than married females," Otter said. "If you're going to do flight risk correctly from a corporate perspective, at an individual level, it's going to be, by definition, discriminatory."

Flight risk scores that do not take into account external data but analyze only internal data are also problematic, said Matthew Stevenson, a partner and coleader of the workforce strategy and analytics practice at the consulting firm Mercer in Washington, DC. "Many of the data sets only contain information about what's happening internally with employees and say nothing about what the competition is doing, what the market pay rates are for similar jobs or external labor market data like the unemployment rate."[6]

In Nydia Serna's case, the flight risk predictor was wrong. In 2022, when she tested it against herself the system predicted that she had a 0.03 chance of quitting in the next twelve months. In early 2023, she left PepsiCo.

TOXIC TEAMS

In our conversation, I asked Ian Cook whether the software could be used to find toxic teams and toxic managers. Wouldn't a toxic manager have a high number of employees leaving? Cook said yes, but that data can also show us that one manager has a high number of people leaving for a different reason. "There's a huge risk to say, 'Manager A is toxic.' No, Manager A is hiring A-class talent, which then is going somewhere else in the business."

He learned from a client that one particular department at their organization had the highest resignation rate. When they looked deeper, they found something surprising: The manager was doing an amazing job. Many folks joined their department and then got a job in a different department within six to seven months because the manager had an open transfer policy. This was an excellent manager, although the data at first glance might have suggested otherwise.

To Cook, this is why AI is only one part of the puzzle: "So it's very hard to say there is one reason why things are happening, which is an absolute pain to people, because they really just want you to solve the problem," he said. "I can't solve the problem without all of this additional context."

When managers only take in the data and stop thinking critically, this is where decisions might become unfair, because they're not considering the context.

And, unfortunately, context often gets lost. At HR Tech in 2022 I met a similar service provider, SplashBI. I talked to the CEO Naveen Miglani and he told me that SplashBI pulls in many data points on employees, including about their personal life (for example, benefits data, which shows if someone added or dropped a spouse from their healthcare plan or had a child), performance reviews, pay grade, and, interestingly enough, commuting distance.

I asked him how he makes sure that the data is not leading to bias, for example, because commuting distance is highly correlated with race and socioeconomic status in the United States as a result of historical redlining. He told me that he trusts his data people, but the fact that commuting time is even part of the data set shows me that there may be a lack of critical analysis.

As we have seen before, trust in data scientists is not enough to root out bias in AI, especially when this technology is most often used on rank-and-file employees without their knowledge.

CHAPTER 8

We Are Watching (and Measuring)

On Surveillance at Work

Emily Smith is a blonde woman in her late thirties. She lives north of Albany in New York with her young son and works as a medical coder. She was laid off at the start of the pandemic in May 2020, and four months later she found a new medical coder position at an insurance company working fully remote, which she preferred.

Her job was to analyze patient charts, copy medical codes, and add Medicare reimbursements. She didn't work directly for the insurance company; she worked for a staffing agency that "lent" her to a hospital, which meant almost no benefits, no paid time off, no vacation time for the first year, no paid holidays, and lots of surveillance, which left her shaken.

The new company didn't beat around the bush about the surveillance and certainly didn't keep it a secret. She got a full introduction on day two: she was told that her supervisors checked how many charts she read to make sure she was meeting her goal of at least five charts per hour.

On top of that, she learned that the system also tracked the status of her computer and sent reports to her supervisors: "It shows how much time is work time, how much time the computer is locked, and then how much time is idle time," she said.

If she didn't move her mouse for sixty seconds or tap a key on her keyboard, the clock for idle time started running.

"The managers check it. Supervisors check it every day. And if your ratio of work to lock to idle is not where they want it to be, you get a, 'Hey, what's up?'" Smith said.

One time she forgot to lock her computer when she went on a fifteen-minute (unpaid) break. Her supervisor pinged her wanting to know why her computer was idle for so long. When she explained that she had forgotten to lock her computer, they were understanding but asked her to make sure it wouldn't happen again.

Even while she was doing productive work, like reading a chart, she had to do busywork of hitting keys on her keyboard or moving her mouse so the system wouldn't record her as idle. "It's like, well, if I'm making my goals, what does it matter if my mouse isn't moving while I read a chart? But that's what I had to do. I had to just move my mouse while I was reading so that I didn't get dinged," she said.

The company also tracked every website she visited and flagged in daily reports if she visited an unauthorized site.

She'd set a timer for two minutes when she went to the bathroom so she wouldn't have her computer sit on idle for too long and wouldn't exceed her total thirty-minute break time.

Emily described the monitoring as extremely stressful: "I was afraid to go to the bathroom. How many minutes is that going to take? Am I going to be able to make myself a snack after? Or what if I am not feeling good?"

But the software wasn't programmed to care that humans have human needs and may need a slightly longer bathroom break. On top of monitoring every minute of her work, each day her supervisors sent out an email ranking the more than twenty workers on her team from "most productive" to "least productive."

"It felt demeaning," Smith said. She still checked every day to make sure she was at least not listed as the worst.

And over time, she learned simple hacks to trick the system. Her supervisor told her that if she had a chart that was eight thousand pages and she obviously wouldn't be able to analyze at least five charts per hour because of it, she should go back to shorter charts from other days to bring up her hourly count for that day and make her load look more balanced.

And even on days when no charts were assigned to her, she had to jiggle her mouse for eight hours to get a paycheck.

Despite feeling like every one of her moves was tracked, there were reports to complete: "On top of that, we had to fill out a form at the end of the day: the amount of time we spend on break, the amount of time you spend in charts, and then the amount of time spent in meetings."

While she was working at the company, her stepmother died suddenly, and it was heartbreaking to her that she didn't get any paid leave and had to calculate how many days she could afford to take off unpaid to help her dad. She could afford three days off.

Emily Smith lasted a little over a year in the heavily surveilled job and found a new one in late 2021.

But the experience left her with self-diagnosed "surveillance PTSD."

In her new job, there is no surveillance and Smith is asked to track her own hours. She said her boss is a human without any micromanaging tendencies.

Once, when a coworker of Smith stressed over clocking in two minutes late at her new job, their manager didn't care at all. In fact, their supervisor said she didn't need to know when someone was going to take a bathroom break. "She says stuff like, 'You're an adult—as long as you get your work done, I don't care how many times you go.'"

The lack of monitoring and a human boss made her new job a hundred times better than her old one: "It's so much more chill and I'm not worried. And they listen to me when I say something."

SECRET AGENT LEVELS OF SURVEILLANCE

In the last chapter we covered how companies are surveilling employees to measure abilities and potential for future promotion. In this chapter we cover the broader category of how companies monitor employees in general. The trends reveal a potentially troubling future.

One benefit of working in a physical office has always been that managers can make sure employees are working. But surveillance at the office was limited. Workers might be sitting at their desks but choosing to do nothing or to surf the web or to doodle in charts. But we are entering a new era of monitoring.

"This is secret agent levels of surveillance," said Matthew Scherer, the former employment lawyer and senior policy counsel at the Center for Democracy and Technology. "It's never been practical before for an employer to have a physical supervisor attached to your hip every second of every day monitoring what you are doing." But that is essentially what these surveillance programs are doing. They are also used for remote workers.

"It really is a different level of intrusiveness that we haven't seen in workplaces, at least the vast, vast majority of workplaces before," Scherer said.

The numbers back him up: "Eight of the 10 largest private U.S. employers track the productivity metrics of individual workers, many in real time," according to an examination by the *New York Times*.[1]

In 2020, at the height of the COVID-19 pandemic, a *Times* reporter spoke with Chris Heuwetter, who was running a marketing company in Jupiter, Florida.[2] Heuwetter told the reporter that work hours had collapsed after his twenty employees started working from home, with some not responding to messages until ten o'clock in the morning. He was also facing a drop in sales, and customer response times had slowed.

He began using a surveillance tool called Hubstaff, and employees' productivity levels rose "immediately," Heuwetter said.

I couldn't resist and contacted a company to get a productivity tracking tool on my computer. I used it for a few weeks. It literally tracked how I spent every second on my computer. It recorded every website I visited and classified them as productive and unproductive, which could be adjusted by individual managers. It felt kind of weird to know that everything I did was being recorded.

The tool didn't record the full scope of my tasks, of course, because outlines I wrote on paper, time spent on phone calls, and other noncomputer tasks weren't recorded and I couldn't find a way to manually input them. But if an employer was using this kind of monitoring software, it would probably lead me to adapt my habits: start making outlines on my computer, use an app on my computer to make calls, keep moving my mouse while on the phone to generate activity.

Matthew Scherer and others say that this kind of all-out surveillance, especially if employees are reprimanded for taking breaks that are too long or not doing tasks fast enough, has negative effects on our mental and physical health.

And surveillance may not always stop during work hours. Recently, Microsoft filed for a patent to track whether employees are working outside their designated working hours. The filing states that the app can be used to track who is working after hours so companies can put a stop to that. But a log like this could also help employers understand who is putting a lot of time in for the company.

IS SURVEILLANCE WORTH IT?

For years, drivers, warehouse workers, and call center employees have been monitored and now the technology is moving into white-collar professions, including for contract lawyers, healthcare workers, bankers, and employees working from home.

But maybe it's worth it for employers. I spoke about this with Tara Behrend, a professor at Michigan State University's School of Human Resources and Labor Relations. She teaches management psychology and is an expert in technology used in the workplace.

She and her team surveyed workers about their attitudes toward being monitored at work. They also analyzed seventy-six studies that covered digital performance monitoring. The studies in the meta-analysis included more than twenty-one thousand participants.

The increase in monitoring at work was striking. Behrend said that surveillance has gone up by over 600 percent. "It's because everyone who has suddenly been classified as a remote worker, their bosses don't know how to manage their performance remotely, and so they lean too heavily on these surveillance tools," she said. "They think, 'If I can't see the person working, I cannot give them effective feedback, and so I need some sort of technological solution to find out what they're doing when I'm not physically present.'"

Supervisors can choose from many different technologies, including tracking and analyzing someone's voice or location monitoring through GPS. Managers can also remotely access computers and record every keystroke and take photos of workers. Surveillance can even involve physiological sensors that track heart rate and eye movements.

In her survey, Behrend was surprised to find a very nuanced take of what workers think of monitoring at work. "They're not categorically rejecting this. They're not categorically accepting it. They're saying that it is sometimes acceptable depending on the purpose, depending on the context, and that their attitudes are very based on the technology involved," Behrend said. "A technology like tracking your heart rate, generally people feel that that is not warranted as a part of work performance."

But cases in which monitoring bodily functions is used to keep workers safe—for example, monitoring radiation exposure or cameras that track truck drivers' eyes and warn them when they are falling asleep—are generally more accepted.

Many workers judged surveillance that tracked which files were downloaded from the company's computer network to be either always or sometimes acceptable. "The rationale is that this might involve security for the company or it's clearly work-related. And so it's acceptable," Behrend said. Generally, "people find monitoring acceptable when they can give consent, when it's clearly job relevant, and when the target is about behavior."

If monitoring happens without employees' consent, it can become a serious source of stress. Many employees will start trying to game the system to maximize their performance rating. A whole niche industry caters to them: there are devices for sale that help folks keep their computer on "active" status—from mouse wigglers to USB sticks that simulate movement. In TikTok videos, people have connected their computer mouse to a robot vacuum cleaner and other devices.

But the surveillance points to a worrisome trend, Behrend said. "Worker privacy is already well on its way to becoming a luxury good unless it's regulated and protected—and in the US, it is not at all." US companies can basically do whatever they want on computers they own and give to employees.

There is more regulation in Europe and especially in Germany and Austria. As soon as a company has five workers, the employees can vote for a works council, an internal employee representation group. In paragraph 87, number 6, of the German works council law, it states that the works council has to agree to technologies that monitor the behavior or performance of employees.

Works councils in Germany have been able to force some of the largest tech companies in the world to prevent or abolish individual surveillance and productivity rates, thanks to this one sentence in the law. In the world of worker surveillance, Germany is terra incognita.

DOES SURVEILLANCE INCREASE PERFORMANCE?

Tara Behrend and her team tried to answer the question of whether surveillance increases performance in their meta-analysis of seventy-six studies. They found that surveillance has the opposite effect of what many executives hope it accomplishes.

"Being monitored for your performance does increase your stress, does increase your negative attitudes, but it doesn't accomplish the goal that it is meant to accomplish, which is to improve your performance," Behrend said. In fact, the more intense the monitoring, the more performance goes down. Monitoring also leads to higher burnout rates and people like Emily Smith leaving their jobs.

What's even more mind-boggling is that the vendors of surveillance tools themselves say that monitoring workers has negative effects, but they still offer the tools.

Microsoft released a report in September 2022 that "surveyed 20,000 people in 11 countries and analyzed trillions of Microsoft 365 productivity signals."[3] The authors of the report found that tracking "productivity" was counterproductive: "As some organizations use technology to track activity rather than impact, employees lack context on how and why they're being tracked, which can undermine trust."

It also leads to "productivity theater," which means that some workers are doing things for the sole purpose of signaling to their boss that they are working, including moving their mouse (or using an automatic mouse "jiggler"), emailing coworkers so their status light is green or active, checking in early on Slack to show they're working at early hours, or even showing up to meetings that have nothing to do with their work just to show they are present.

Workers in the Microsoft report said they spent about an hour each day on such shenanigans, an hour that could have been used to get actual work done.

"People just stopped caring [about the job]," one surveilled employee shared with the *Washington Post*.[4] Microsoft has said again and again that tracking activity is not a good way to understand whether workers are productive.

"At Microsoft, we believe that using technology to spy on people at work is not the answer and our technology is not designed for that purpose. Measuring productivity with mouse movements is like using a sundial as a stopwatch. And surveillance doesn't just lead to bad data—it undermines trust, a critical factor in organizational success that, once lost, is incredibly difficult to regain," said Microsoft's Jared Spataro, the corporate vice president of modern work, in an op-ed piece in *Fortune* in September 2022.[5]

What's interesting and ironic is that part of the data in the report came from Microsoft's own software tools, a vast ecosystem from Microsoft Teams meetings, emails in Outlook, Word, Excel, PowerPoint, and many other applications, which track how employees use these tools. In product descriptions, Microsoft states that "the data covers how workers communicate, collaborate, and manage their time across all the applications and services in Microsoft."[6]

Although Spataro believes employers should restrain their surveillance, the software Microsoft has been selling to other companies over the past few years has pushed into the employee monitoring space. It seems that companies want to keep quiet about the capabilities that are built into these tools, because when something leaks out, there have been public outcries.

In 2020, Zoom introduced "attention tracking" during video calls, which showed managers if participants were opening other tabs or were solely looking at the Zoom meeting. After a public backlash, Zoom deactivated the feature.[7]

Microsoft encountered public pushback when it unveiled a productivity score in 2019.[8] The software tracked individual employees' activity levels in Microsoft applications and gave every worker an overall productivity score.

Even the term "productivity score" seems odd here because the tool only tracked activity in Microsoft tools and the benchmark for good productivity was undisclosed. Maybe someone was reading a report, but not while using a Microsoft tool. Maybe they wrote an email in Gmail or used another non-Microsoft application to get work done or made a phone call? Or they were in an in-person meeting?

Productivity scores are a tough benchmark, because it's hard for companies to clearly know which tasks that can be tracked make an employee productive or high performing: Is it when they send out a ton of emails? Go to every meeting? Or attend almost no meetings? Are they productive when they do some deep thinking, which would probably generate very little data? Or when they have long in-person meetings? This probably changes from job to job and from individual to individual. Since we don't really know what most of this data means, these kinds of productivity or performance scores are arbitrary because there are no established benchmarks for productivity markers in any given job, but they could potentially get workers in trouble if people don't score high enough.

After a public outcry, in late 2020, Microsoft backpedaled and said that the productivity score would not be available as a measure of individual productivity anymore but only show the adoption of Microsoft tools at an organizational level, which doesn't make individuals' scores and activity levels available anymore.

"Going forward, the communications, meetings, content collaboration, teamwork, and mobility measures in Productivity Score will only aggregate data at the organization level—providing a clear measure of organization-level adoption of key features," Jared Spataro wrote in a blog post.[9] "No one in the organization will be able to use Productivity Score to access data about how an individual user is using apps and services in Microsoft 365."

Since 2020, the productivity score function, which is now called adoption score, was disabled and data analysis should be available only on a team level.

But it turns out that monitoring in Microsoft applications is still possible if a company chooses those functions—at least for investigators, HR, legal, and other administrators. In the fall of 2022, I went down the Microsoft rabbit hole on YouTube and watched videos in which Microsoft engineers explain how companies can track employees and where potential threats come from.

In one video, the Microsoft hosts even make the argument that, because nearly 50 percent of employees in 2022 were looking to change jobs over the next year, companies should really consider any of their workers a threat to the organization. "Insider risk management should really be part of a 'zero trust' approach for the protection of your data and communications," says Talhah Mir, the principal project manager of Insider Risk Solutions at Microsoft. "We're used to thinking about data exposure caused by external threats from cyber attacks or insider threats from rogue admins, but less so about insider risks introduced by everyday employees. And this is an expanding problem that most organizations are worried about."[10]

Then the video takes a bizarre turn and suddenly "insider attacks" become all-encompassing and extend to all employee communications. "When you look at things like burnout, which is an underlying reason why somebody leaves an organization, what you find is that there's a direct correlation to somebody's venting in the communication platform, which then in turn leads to things like an unhealthy or toxic workplace. Or worse—can lead to workplace harassment," Mir says.

Notice the twisted logic used here to justify surveillance: people at risk of burnout should be monitored because they are more likely to leave and more likely to vent in internal messages, and venting can lead to a toxic workplace or workplace harassment. Remember that Microsoft also reported that individual monitoring can create a stressful or toxic work environment. To the public at large the company says it's not helpful to monitor individual workers, but to IT (and HR) teams it claims Microsoft products can monitor all communications and allegedly detect harassment, profanity, and discrimination in messages.

Is there any data or science backing this up? I am sure there is a correlation somewhere between burnout risk and venting, but how does that lead to a toxic work environment and even to harassment?

In my opinion, it is likely that burnout risk or even people leaving an organization is also correlated with toxic or bad managers. Because we know for a fact that many employees leave because of terrible managers, should we now monitor all managers and find the toxic ones? The two Microsoft employees in the video don't address this, but they are addressing why companies should monitor all communications: "This could play a key part in your overall strategy to maintain a healthy work environment," Mir says.

The software scans individual user behavior, including files copied to USB drives and emails sent outside the organization. In the videos, Microsoft employees emphasize that the data is anonymized. But in the software, any "risk signals" are connected to "pivotal events," such as an employee's resignation. At this point, most anyone would be able to decipher which employee is being surveilled—in most companies, there aren't thousands of people resigning on a given day.

Anyway, in reality, the data isn't really anonymized at all. In fact, the whole system can be set up so that certain admins can see all employee names at all times. The admins can see the number of messages with targeted harassment, profanity, and discrimination the algorithm claimed it found. The software is capable of scanning every piece of communication. Microsoft said that Purview is built on a privacy-first approach, incorporating multiple privacy protections to ensure customers can effectively mitigate insider risk without compromising users' privacy. Auditable records ensure that any access of insider risk incident information (including an employee's name and underlying content) is logged and trackable.

I am not alone in finding these loopholes. Websites that give employers tips on how to surveil their workers also describe ways to monitor employees using Microsoft Teams, and in these tutorials, they include exact screenshots on what options to set up in the tool.

Microsoft does not seem to limit how employers can use these auditing and analytics programs. In the United States, many workers don't need to be informed that the technology is being used on them. (Deep in Microsoft's privacy policy, I am sure employees are informed that the software can access and process all data, but when I start a new job, I don't really have a choice but to agree to a company's and a software's privacy policy because I will most likely have to use company servers and certain software products for work.)

THE PROBLEM WITH ALGORITHMIC PRODUCTIVITY SCORES

If you are an employee, I would recommend that you assume your employer has a "zero trust" policy toward their workers and is monitoring everything.

Because companies are tracking our behavior, some employees might decide to change their behavior to try to rig the metrics: "No one is stopping a worker from setting up automatic emails to themselves or setting up 'fake' meetings with like-minded colleagues in order to increase their performance statistics," writes Privacy International, a nonprofit based in the United Kingdom, in a report on Microsoft's capabilities.[11]

This would probably render the productivity signals meaningless, but experts in the field have called productivity signals largely meaningless anyway.

Particularly in knowledge work, there's no definition of productivity, there's no definition of performance, said Ryan Fuller, the former vice president for workplace intelligence at Microsoft. "How do you evaluate the output of a marketing team? A legal team, an R&D team? That's not a technology problem, it's a human problem. We just don't really know," Fuller said. "Knowledge work is the team; it's more than one person. It's a collective effort and it's something about the individuals and how they function with the team and how well the team is aligned against goals. There are just so many dimensions to it," he said. Not all of these dimensions can be covered by an algorithm.

Although we are at the beginning of a time of algorithms ruling our lives, there is some history here. More than a decade ago, school districts in New York City, Houston, and Florida used algorithms to score teacher performance. A teacher's pay and promotions could be affected by their performance scores, and some teachers were fired based on the scoring system. But the secretive algorithms received a lot of pushback.

In 2014, the Houston Federation of Teachers filed a lawsuit against the algorithm used by the Houston Independent School District. "The teachers say, among other allegations, that they are being evaluated on the scores of tests that do not assess the curriculum they are supposed to teach, that the formulas are incomprehensible, and that their Constitutional rights to due process are being violated because teachers cannot challenge the results," wrote the *Washington Post*.[12]

One of the teachers in the lawsuit, Andrew Dewey, was scored as the "most effective" teacher one year. The next year, he was scored as making "no detectable difference" in his students' education.

The teacher evaluation algorithms did not use AI based on deep neural networks, but the idea behind them was the same as today's AI: the algorithm will help employers find an employee's "objective performance." That was at least the hope.

Gayle Fallon, president of the Houston Federation of Teachers, said that the algorithm wasn't accurate and that the lack of transparency was hurting teachers: "The test scores are plugged into a black box where no teacher can either calculate or try and refute the number that comes out that tells if they are a good teacher."

In the related lawsuits, the courts often sided with the teachers. One judge called the New York State teacher rating system "arbitrary" and "capricious."

In 2017, the Houston Independent School District settled the lawsuit and agreed to stop using the controversial teacher evaluation system.

Since those landmark decisions, these kinds of teacher performance algorithms have fallen out of favor, but that doesn't mean that private companies are steering away from trying to measure their employees' performance.

PROTECTING THE RIGHT TO UNIONIZE

The data that companies collect may not work for productivity scoring, but once data is available, it can easily be misused, said Brian Kropp, former managing director at Accenture, where he covers human resources.

One company he worked with used swipe-in data (when employees clocked in) to identify high performers based on the hours they spent at their desk—a poor proxy for productivity because some people might sit at their desk and not be productive, running down the hours.

When the same company was faced with layoffs during the pandemic, executives tried to use the same data that supposedly identified high performers to identify low performers and lay off those employees.

"We get a lot of data, we get a lot of information, we get a lot of analysis, but what decisions we're making with that are really questionable in some cases," Kropp said. "The technology is outpacing our knowledge on how to use the technology, in a lot of cases, when it comes to managing our employees."

But soon companies might face pushback on all-out surveillance from a government agency. In the fall of 2022, the general counsel of the National Labor Relations Board, Jennifer Abruzzo, wrote an enforcement memo saying that she will litigate against employers who use surveillance in cases where it could interfere with their employees' rights to unionize. This could actually mean a broad stop to surveillance, because many kinds of employee communication and even social media feeds might include unionizing efforts.

"Close, constant surveillance and management through electronic means threaten employees' basic ability to exercise their rights," Abruzzo wrote.

It is well documented that employers are increasingly using new technologies to closely monitor and manage employees. In warehouses, for example, some employers record workers' conversations and track their movements using wearable devices, security cameras, and radio-frequency identification badges. On the road, some employers keep tabs on drivers using GPS tracking devices and cameras. And some employers monitor employees who work on computers—whether in call centers, offices, or at home—using keyloggers and software that takes screenshots, webcam photos, or audio recordings throughout the day. Electronic monitoring and automated management are not always limited to working time. After the workday ends, some employers continue to track employees' whereabouts and communications using employer-issued phones or wearable devices, or apps installed on workers' own devices. And even before the employment relationship begins, some employers pry into job applicants' private lives by conducting personality tests and scrutinizing applicants' social media accounts.[13]

Abruzzo believes that this kind of omnipresent surveillance could interfere with lawful union activity because employees are allowed to work together to build a union and workplace surveillance may uncover those activities. She said that she wants the NLRB to force employers to disclose what surveillance they engage in and how the data is used beforehand so employees can then decide whether it interferes with their rights to organize.

If these new steps can be implemented, which would probably take years to wind through the court system if employers sue, a new era of transparency could help employees understand what surveillance they are subjected to. Forced to be transparent, many companies would likely shy away from using the most aggressive technologies because executives probably understand that finding out how much surveillance goes on during and after work hours would upset their employees.

But this might just be a pipe dream written in a memo.

CHAPTER 9

We're Ready to Help

On Our Health Data at Work

The COVID-19 pandemic brought mental health struggles to the forefront, especially at work. Buzz phrases like "bring your whole self to work" acknowledge all of the human messiness that we bring to the table. And many companies are now trying to help their employees with their physical and mental health.

That is hitting another cultural force: improving and optimizing ourselves is also part of the zeitgeist, which resonates with many folks, especially those in white-collar professions. I have read many articles on how I can bolster my productivity and find more time to work out. I also know folks who track their sleep patterns and number of steps. Some even track their brain activity. We love to optimize ourselves, so that's probably why many of us are open to employers helping us in this endeavor.

But what many are not aware of is that the technology being used to help us live healthier and more productive lives in all likelihood includes a built-in surveillance element that could be used against us.

In this chapter, we will focus on how AI is used regarding our physical and mental health.

PHYSICAL HEALTH

The rise of health data technology at work started a few years back with fitness trackers, which many of us willingly put on our wrists. A lot of companies noted this trend and started giving employees reimbursements when they went to the gym, held walking meetings, or tracked their steps.

The underlying idea is that healthy companies are made of healthy employees and employees need to take their health into their own hands (with a little nudge from their employer). There is the added benefit that employers might save money on health insurance premiums.

Wayne Gono is a fitness tracking devotee. He is the chief networking officer and former CEO of his family-owned company, Regal Plastics Supply, in Texas, which has about 115 employees.

A few years back, the company's health insurance supplier, United Healthcare, approached them. Would Regal Plastics want to offer fitness trackers to employees? The incentive was that, if employees met their fitness goals, they could get back modest amounts of money from their health insurance.

Wayne Gono and his family, the leadership team at Regal Plastics, didn't hesitate: "We like the idea of what it would do as far as challenging our staff to exercise," Gono said. He added that his family cares deeply about their employees.

At Regal Plastics, signing up was voluntary. About fifty employees started tracking their fitness, including Gono, who loves friendly competition. "Being the oldest one in the company, I always wanted to be the one that had the most steps in the day. And then I would challenge people: 'Well, you know what, Craig, I'm twice your age, I am getting eighteen thousand steps a day, you are barely getting in five.'"

One day, Gono checked the stats and called Chris Zubko, an employee who had just returned three weeks after a heart attack and triple bypass surgery. Gono congratulated him on his progress: "Man! I noticed your steps have picked up," Gono said.[1] "You used to be under 2,000, now you're over 6,000. Two times you worked out this week. Good!"[2]

Chris Zubko appreciated his boss cheering him on, although if I were in his place, it would personally have felt a bit invasive. But total transparency is central to Regal Plastics' mission: "We drive competitiveness within the company, because we have flat-screen TVs in every one of our offices, and they're all over our offices. They just got real-time sales numbers. And real-time projections. Everything is real time," Gono said in an interview with me.

His employees loved it as well, he said, because leadership didn't penalize people at the bottom of the list. "We are people before profits," he said. "We're not worried about degrees. We are not looking at pedigree. All we look at is, do they line up with our values? If they line up with our core values, they can get taught the plastics business."

On Glassdoor, the company has forty-four reviews and an average rating of 4.4 out of 5. People praise the company's culture and the relationship employees have with their colleagues: "Could Not be better fit! Amazing Autonomy. Unmatched Company Culture. They give you the freedom to succeed!" wrote one anonymous reviewer.[3]

It's been a few years since the company started fitness tracking. In a recent conversation, Wayne Gono said he still loves getting a maximum of three dollars back per day from his health insurance company for reaching his goals, but the company's health premiums have only gone up, not down.

Some companies use this kind of surveillance data in benevolent ways, including Regal Plastics, but once the data is collected, it could easily be misused: for example, the company that used employee swipe card data to find "high" performers for promotions also wanted to use the same data to fire "low" performers.

When a company has to do layoffs, some executives might want to fire the employees with the lowest Fitbit numbers since they might be perceived as "lazy" or "overweight" and will cost the company money in health insurance premiums. Like I said, once data is collected, it's hard to put it back in the box and make sure it's not being misused.[4]

Me collecting data related to my fitness or bodily functions to track my health feels completely different from when my employer wants me to do it. A few years back, the *Wall Street Journal* reported that one vendor's software tried to predict pregnancies on the basis of the insurance claims of women who stopped filling birth control prescriptions.[5] That feels invasive and could have unintended consequences. The software might predict that a certain percentage of female employees will get pregnant soon, so a manager might not put female employees up for leadership positions if they are worried that the women will go on maternity leave.

Many employees may not know that in the United States their employers are free to sell their data: "All the data that's being collected as part of workplace performance programs through wearable tech," professor of law Ifeoma Ajunwa said, "can be sold without the knowledge or consent of the worker."

A fitness tracker and other wellness devices that check vital statistics such as heart rate could also inadvertently disclose to an employer that an employee has a disability, which might be illegal under the Americans with Disabilities Act.

For some privacy scholars, it's a great irony that law enforcement can't search our emails or health insurance claims without a court order, but no such protections exist in the workplace.

PREDICTING HEALTH

It's surprising what can be predicted about us from the data many of us share routinely with our employers.

At one of the largest HR tech conferences in the world in Las Vegas in the fall of 2022, I stumbled upon a company called Alight, which draws conclusions about what employees might be going through from basic employment and benefits data: for example, an employee dropping a spouse from their health insurance plan indicates a divorce and possibly a need for mental health services.

Alight's pitch is that its software personalizes benefits and helps employees find the right benefits to improve personal well-being. Sounds like a great idea on paper.

Craig Rosenberg, a white man in his fifties who is the vice president of health solutions at Alight, told me that many companies offer a lot of benefits, but that "people don't know about them. And even if they do know about them, they don't remember them when they need them and then it's hard to engage with them."

Alight says that its personalization tool, which is used by around one thousand clients, including 70 percent of the Fortune 100, helps to get the right information to employees at the right time. Because when an employee is in a crisis, they don't want to do research and wade through all the benefits a company offers.

At the beginning of the demo, Rosenberg showed me a few different fictional employees and how the Alight Workforce tool could help them.

His first example was a middle-aged man named "Aiden." The Alight software "knew" that Aiden was recently divorced because he'd dropped his spouse from his health insurance. "We see from the HR system that he hasn't taken any vacation in six months and we see on the 401(k) side that he took two 401(k) loans out in the past year," Rosenberg said. "There's something going on here that he is dealing with."

The tool then makes personalized recommendations for Aiden. "It's going to prioritize mental health. Emotional well-being for him is the top thing we want to engage him on. And then maybe the second priority is financial—connect him to a financial advisor."

My ears were ringing as he was telling me this. It felt kind of creepy. I would absolutely feel weird if my employer gave a third-party company access to my personal benefits data, which might put them in a position to predict such intimate details about my life as a divorce—even if it's to help me.

In a webinar, which I had to sign up to watch, one Alight employee even acknowledged this: "We have to constantly walk the line between the personalization that will bring that value versus feeling creepy," said Kellee Eavenson, vice president of information technology.

The next example that Craig Rosenberg shared also became creepy fast. "Ellen" is a fictional female employee who, the system learned, just had knee surgery and an MRI, and the AI tools predict that she is a new parent. "Think about someone where they just added a baby to their medical plan. Well, that's a trigger for us to say 'Hey, here are all the things that we can help with.'"

I am sure options for childcare paid for by the employer would be helpful. But the tool can do much more, including suggesting the best doctors for Ellen to see, promised Rosenberg.

But in an Alight webinar geared toward HR managers, I learned something slightly different. The web presenters said that all the medical recommendations were optimized for care quality *and* cost. In Rosenberg's demo with me, he said that Alight suggests the best doctors to employees. He didn't mention that costs are a criterion in the recommendations. (Alight said that the medical recommendations are optimized first for quality and then for cost.)

Alight built a feedback loop into the product that automatically updates the software if an employee uses the recommended health providers. "Ellen had a knee issue," Rosenberg said. "I promote [a health care provider] to Ellen. I can tell whether she clicked on our promos or not. And then I can get data back from [the provider] and say, did she use [them] or not?"

I asked Rosenberg where Alight got the information that Ellen had knee surgery and an MRI. How could Alight know such specific medical data? Was this pulled directly from her health insurance? "We can pull in health claims data; we can pull in wealth data; we can pull in data from the HR system," he said. Plus the company pulls in search data from their platform.

After the demo, I reached out to him again and asked specifically whether Alight has access to employees' medical records: "We obtain health and provider data from a combination of health insurance carriers, public and commercial sources, and run it through proprietary algorithms."

Somehow health insurance data is being traded among companies. I wonder what might happen if the tool "learns" that an employee has a sexually transmitted disease? Or someone had an abortion? What would the tool suggest?

We share some of our most intimate health details with our providers. In fact, the Health Insurance Portability and Accountability Act of 1996 (HIPAA) is a federal law that protects sensitive patient health information from being disclosed without the patient's consent or knowledge. I have always assumed this meant that my health data would stay private, but I guess I was wrong.

My expectation of privacy is not the reality in the United States. Employers can share data, and apparently there are whole data lakes out there. "We have a proprietary data set that has data on a hundred million Americans, over thirty-three billion data points," Rosenberg said. The company also "interacts" with about thirty-six million people, which Alight caters to directly. These interactions generate hundreds of millions of more data points per year.

Rosenberg insisted that having access to all this data was not a problem because Alight wouldn't disclose the names of employees targeted by Alight's campaigns: "We do protect privacy. You, as an HR person, would never be able to see that Ellen has an issue," Rosenberg said. "So you would know that we have engaged fifty people who have musculoskeletal issues and they used [a specific provider] to help or not, but obviously you wouldn't be able to see that 'Ellen' had an MRI."

But security breaches at Alight could happen, and we know from other research that even anonymized data can easily be de-anonymized.

There is a lack of ethical considerations in regard to data sharing among vendors and employers. To some HR managers, I am sure some of these products seem like must-haves. They don't think about what all that data might mean and the downstream consequences of having all this data out there. (Alight said that clients can determine which level of personalization the companies would like for their employees.)

When I asked Rosenberg if some employees were creeped out by Alight's services, he said that most would never find out how much information Alight has on them because the software's messaging is subtle. "Think of these as nudges. You'll never see something like, 'Hey, I saw you got divorced and we can help you with mental health issues.' You might see a message of, 'Wow, sometimes life is hard, we can help.'"

The convenience of these recommendations trumps privacy concerns, Rosenberg said, speaking for employees. He added that folks are already used to recommendation systems like Netflix, Hulu, and Spotify.

(I am not convinced Netflix's model works all that well for me. But that is about the consumption of TV shows—the stakes are very low and that data is about me watching TV, not if I have a chronic illness.)

What Alight uses for these recommendations is my personal data. I wouldn't want that data to be traded, sold, or used by third-party vendors so that just anyone can piece together my medical and mental health challenges. I want to trust my employer and the healthcare company my employer has contracted with to not share this private health data with any third-party vendor that might sell it to Alight and other companies. We have seen too many data and security breaches. It's also infuriating that, no matter how hard I try to safeguard my information online, the company I work for or my health care provider might just share this intimate data with third-party vendors like Alight.

In fact, a number of lawsuits against Alight alleging cybersecurity breaches are pending and the Department of Labor has opened an investigation. (Alight said it is "steadfastly committed to providing our clients with the confidence they need to ensure their employee's assets and information are protected," and that it is "typical for an organization of the size and complexity of Alight to manage a range of claims and litigation.")

The company continues to pitch its services, saying it is changing how employees see their employers: "It's not just, 'I have my medical insurance through them or life insurance.' It's like, 'This employer is really supporting me,'" Rosenberg said.

Alight is determined to do more with the data to predict medical issues earlier: "We're going to be continuing to push really hard into the analytics space," Rosenberg said. "Who's at risk of musculoskeletal [problems] before we even see it in a claim? Or what events could happen to someone that is a mental health risk before it even happens? So we might say something like, 'Hey, we looked at a hundred thousand people like you and this is a pattern. This means that you might be at risk.'"

But company wellness programs could easily fall short and some employees might think that their company is just putting lipstick on a pig, since they are not tackling broader, underlying problems at companies that may contribute to employees' problems. "If you are not managing the company to be healthy, you're not going to be able to undo that by giving people a yoga class," Josh Bersin, the industry analyst, said.

It's just not believable that a company cares about its employees' mental health when it creates the problem in the first place, for example, by not dealing with incompetent managers or a toxic work environment. Over 40 percent of American workers are afraid to go to work, said Josh Bersin.

Data analysis, personalization, and surveillance software that checks for employee health issues and whether they are using the recommended services feels like work paternalism: an employer making sure their employees are healthy and productive, but in a new and very invasive way.

To a certain degree, employers have always tried to control their employees: After the Industrial Revolution, some employers built factory towns so they had oversight over their employees' physical whereabouts. Some required their employees to go to church and live a "moral life." Other factory towns had private schools that educated children to have viewpoints favorable to the factory owners.

Generous philanthropy and dependency on one company as a savior was common in those towns. The employer might have donated a library, an ice rink, or housing to the town in order to win favor with residents. A common critique of the so-called robber barons at the end of the nineteenth century was that, with their donations, they wanted to buy people's appreciation and build what they deemed important. If they wanted to improve lives, they could have paid their employees more, but chose not to.

Maybe it's a stretch, but it feels like companies today are doing similar things. Before the pandemic, Meta and other large tech companies basically built new company towns on their campuses: giving employees free access to hair stylists, gyms, massages, dry cleaners, food, and therapists. Like the industrial factory towns from earlier centuries, everything is in one place.

Now that many people are working from home, these perks are less meaningful. But financial and health perks and benefits can be delivered through personalization platforms and they can also make sure employees are making the "right" choices in life that employers want them to make.

OFFERING MENTAL HEALTH HELP

Some companies, including Google, offer mental health services to employees directly (in addition to health insurance benefits), and employees can get help right away and do not have to pay co-pays and other insurance fees. But this has backfired and created conflicts of interest, said former Google employee Chelsey Glasson. She used to work as a user researcher and witnessed discriminatory behavior against a pregnant person who she was supervising at Google. According to company policy, she reported the allegations to HR. Glasson said that the retaliation started after she made the complaint and continued when she herself got pregnant. She brought her concerns to HR and they suggested she speak to a third-party counselor paid for by Google.

"What a great resource, of course I'm going to take advantage of this," Glasson said to the *New York Times*. "I was naively grateful that the EAP [Employee Assistance Program] counselor was at least one person I could talk to freely."

When Glasson filed a lawsuit against Google a year later, her therapist told her that she was "really nervous and uncomfortable" meeting with Glasson after her legal team asked for the records of their sessions together. Her therapist hadn't been in touch with her since, and Glasson felt abandoned. "I believe she was worried that affiliating with me would compromise her relationship with Google," Glasson wrote.[6] She believes there is a conflict of interest at the heart of these mental health counseling services when employers directly pay for the services.

Based on her experience, she is advocating for new laws and mandatory transparency when companies suggest employees see counselors through their employee assistance programs (EAPs): "None of these things will likely happen until legislation is passed to regulate and monitor EAPs, and the appropriate government agencies investigate how companies like Google use EAPs, and whether they cause further harm to victims of workplace misconduct." She is also worried that many HR managers might suggest counseling sessions to employees who complain about discrimination, which can send the message that the employee is the problem, and that no one is taking a look at the wider systemic problem.

Glasson settled her lawsuit with Google last year. Her experience may be a cautionary tale for employees using these services.

At the same time, employers are also starting to question how helpful employee health programs really are: "This costs a massive amount, and CEOs know this needs to be tackled," said Gordon Watson, the CEO of Asia and Africa for the global insurance company AXA. "But it's like a slippery fish that we can't get our hands around. You have meditation apps and apps to sleep better, but no real integrated approach. Are we doing well? We don't know. How do we measure progress? How are we compared to our competitors? So we had the idea to make that visible and tangible."[7]

Large employers, including Bank of America and AXA, have formed the nonprofit OneMind at Work that will score the effectiveness of an organization's mental health programs. Data sharing and ethical considerations around these programs are not on the nonprofit's agenda.[8]

SURVEILLANCE IN THE NAME OF SAFETY

A less contested area in which health surveillance is thriving is safety precautions.

Some organizations go even further than Alight: instead of personalizing benefits and tracking our movements à la Fitbits and walking meetings, some companies are now going directly to the source—tracking our brains.

In education, at work, and in health care, there is a movement to get under the hood, to know what moves us and drives us before we ourselves might be aware of it.

One big push is tracking brains for safety. For example, SmartCap in Australia built a cap that records brain activity via electroencephalogram (commonly called EEG). The company says its tool can track truck drivers' alertness and fatigue. When the cap detects fatigue, it sends a visual and audio signal to the driver to prevent them from falling asleep at the wheel. The company also advertises the cap for miners. Every worker's brain waves are stored in the cloud, which SmartCap claims makes compliance and auditing easier for the company using the tool.

In China, brain wave detection tools are used in factories and in transportation, reports the *South China Morning Post*: "Concealed in regular safety helmets or uniform hats, these lightweight, wireless sensors constantly monitor the wearer's brainwaves and stream the data to computers that use artificial intelligence algorithms to detect emotional spikes such as depression, anxiety or rage. The technology is in widespread use around the world, but China has applied it on an unprecedented scale in factories, public transport, state-owned companies and the military to increase the competitiveness of its manufacturing industry and to maintain social stability."[9]

Also in China, brain wave–sensing headbands are being used on schoolchildren to check their attention levels during instruction time, according to a video report in the *Wall Street Journal*. The data and a ranking of the kids are then shared with teachers, parents, and the scientists studying the headbands.[10]

In the United States and Europe, EEG-based headbands as a consumer technology are marketed directly to users who want to track and optimize their brain function during meditation and sleep. Some headband makers also advertise that their technology can strengthen the wearer's focus and mental resilience.

Vendors are also building headphones, such as one called MN8, with EEG capabilities for companies to use on their workers: "Sensors detect electrical activity across different areas of the brain, and the patterns in that activity can be broadly correlated with different feelings or physiological responses, such as stress, focus, or a reaction to external stimuli. These data can be exploited to make workers more efficient—and, proponents of the technology say, to make them happier," the IEEE (Institute of Electrical and Electronics Engineers) reported. "When a company uses the MN8 system, workers get insight into their individual levels of focus and stress, and managers get aggregated and anonymous data about their teams."[11]

With all of this new technology, I'm sure our brain data will be stored and used by developers to train new models and it may also be used in other ways. This technology is in use now, although there is scant evidence the products actually work.

DETECTING MENTAL HEALTH PROBLEMS IN OUR VOICES

Another way to try to improve our mental health and find out more about what is happening inside our brains is an emerging technology that could be applied almost everywhere, including in colleges and in the workplace, called vocal biomarkers. In fact, it was already used in at least one college in the United States and is accessible to anyone with a smartphone.

Vocal biomarker tools are based on the idea that AI can find signals of mental health problems in our voices. For example, instead of a psychiatrist diagnosing whether someone is bipolar, depressed, or anxious, an AI app can do it just by analyzing a snippet of that person's voice.

The technology mostly doesn't analyze the words patients say, but the underlying biological components of the voice tell an algorithm if someone is anxious or depressed. And because we use our voices every day, this technology has potentially wide applications: it could be used to analyze participants in Zoom meetings, on phone calls, or even in communication with smart speakers like Alexa.

If the technology works, its inventors say, it could alleviate a lot of suffering: "One out of five people in this country [the US], and in many countries around the world that ratio is even higher, suffer from symptoms of depression, anxiety, or even substance abuse disorder," said David Liu, CEO of Sonde Health, a vocal biomarker start-up based in Boston. "Those numbers have gone up in some cases to 33 percent or even higher in our adolescent population. It's an issue that we feel very passionate about because everyone is dealing with it." Even in developed countries, there aren't enough mental health providers to meet the need.

David Liu described poor mental health as a silent killer. Someone who's suffering from mental health issues may not be having direct physical symptoms, but the effects of depression and other mental illnesses can be catastrophic.

During the pandemic, mental health struggles came to the forefront, especially at colleges and universities but also in the workplace. At that time, a vocal biomarker start-up called Ellipsis Health approached Menlo College with the idea to test this kind of technology on the students. Menlo College is a small, private school based in Atherton, California, a town with one of the highest per capita incomes in the United States.

Lina Lakoczky-Torres, a business management major, was the wellness representative of the student government at the time and was brought into the conversations that administrators had with Ellipsis Health to discuss the collaboration and rollout.

Even before the pandemic, Silicon Valley and Menlo College were not easy places to be, Lakoczky-Torres said. "It is really overwhelming, fresh out of high school, going, 'Okay, now we're in a situation where twenty-one-year-olds have built unicorns. What are *you* going to do?' And it's like, I'm just trying to figure out how to exist as my own person."

As the wellness representative, she initially hoped to help students find in-person therapists at Menlo and to build an on-campus food pantry, but at the beginning of the pandemic, everyone was sent home. Lakoczky-Torres went back to live with her mother in Las Vegas.

"It was all online. How do you help everybody online?" Lakoczky-Torres asked. She needed to change goals and wanted to make sure that students could access virtual help. On top of that, she was struggling living back home with her family. "A lot of things come up. You're with your family. Family issues. You can't get away from it. You're with your mind, you don't realize how much you miss your social interactions," she said.

Therapy was needed by many people. Additionally, the pandemic brought unique challenges: Lakoczky-Torres had worked with a graduate student therapist in training via a free program at Menlo College before the pandemic started, but relocating out of state meant cutting the cord with her therapist because they were only allowed to work in California. "I was distraught. I'll be honest. I felt like I was breaking up with my therapist," she said. "It felt really abrupt, especially in the time that you need it the most."

Lakoczky-Torres wasn't the only student who was struggling, said the vice president for student success and strategic planning, Angela Schmiede. Just like Lakoczky-Torres, about half of the student body of Menlo College is not from California and all of a sudden couldn't access the college's mental health services when the need was greater than ever: "We did see an increase in mental health needs, and I think that's not true just at Menlo College but at colleges and universities around the country," Schmiede said.

At around this time, Ellipsis Health approached Menlo. The company pitched the college an AI tool that it said could assess different levels of anxiety and depression in students and prompt them to manage their feelings. Menlo College wouldn't have to pay a penny for students to use the app.

For Angela Schmiede, the Ellipsis software was another tool to help students. "If I've learned anything about students and their mental health over the last two years, it's that there's not a one-size-fits-all solution," she said. "You can offer face-to-face counseling and some students just won't take advantage of that. But if you can offer something where students are accessing it on their own and they can do it in real time and there's not a barrier associated with it, then some students will access that."

The tool was rolled out to the roughly eight hundred students at Menlo College in late 2020. Students who chose to use the app were asked to leave daily voice messages that were at least thirty seconds long in which they answered various questions. Ellipsis also utilized standardized depression and anxiety questionnaires that are used regularly in clinical settings.

Lina Lakoczky-Torres used the tool and answered questions such as: "'How's everything going at home?' And then I go for thirty to forty-five seconds: 'Hey, you know, things have been tough. I'm really stressed out. I'm feeling overwhelmed, I'm feeling like I'm being smothered,' etcetera. And then it would switch over to prompt me, 'How are you feeling lately or how is school going?'" she said.

"What Ellipsis Health has done," said Mainul Mondal, the CEO of the company, "is we've created vocal biomarkers to be able to understand stress, anxiety, depression at different severity levels so we can help providers and patients to have healthier lives." Spoken language provides that window into the mind, he said.

"What we do is we analyze human voices and deliver health insights from that analysis," said David Liu, CEO of Sonde Health.

The idea is that AI can find hidden information on depression and anxiety in our voice, and also if we suffer from Parkinson's or other diseases. The basic claim is that our voice is directly connected to the brain, and so with vocal biomarkers we can record the voice and reverse engineer what's going on in the brain.

This is a bold endeavor, because biomarkers are usually objective medical signs, something in our blood, spit, urine, or medical imaging that indicates a disease or medical condition. For example, high lead levels in blood can indicate kidney or brain damage. Or imaging of specific cells can suggest that someone has cancer. "Vocal biomarker" technology is still in its infancy.

Companies in the space say that, through analyzing voice recordings, they can objectively monitor patients, for example, if someone is sliding into depression or anxiety. They also say that their tools will eventually be able to diagnose mental illnesses and coach people to help themselves, which could be immensely helpful because there aren't enough mental health providers for all the people suffering.

"We are trying to find an equivalent of a blood pressure and heart rate monitor, the same kind of thing for psychiatry," Mainul Mondal said.

A technology like this, easily accessible on smartphones, could help solve several problems that occur in the traditional process of a doctor diagnosing a patient. A care provider might get the diagnosis wrong; presumably, the AI would not. Or folks who are depressed may not be aware of it or don't want to seek help because of shame, so they don't get diagnosed and treated, whereas with an app, especially with an AI tool running in the background, they could begin to assess and help themselves. These kinds of AI tools could also open diagnosis and treatments to many users around the world who don't have the means to pay for mental health consultations.

But because it's so easy to use, the software could be utilized without a person's permission, revealing mental health problems they might want to keep hidden. It could also be used and abused in workplaces. Vocal biomarker tools could be run on recordings of meetings, for example, and without employees' consent, companies could find employees who are anxious or depressed. They could intervene early so individuals can get help and stay productive (which is in the interest of the company). Or they could lay off people identified as anxious or depressed—all based on assessments by vocal biomarkers that have not been thoroughly validated in large studies.

A few researchers who contributed to the information these algorithms are grounded in decided to withhold some pertinent information: "I've done work on predicting depression and I intentionally did not include examples of the kinds of words that were used because then you have armchair clinicians like, 'Oh, well, they're using the word *ibuprofen* a lot and I heard *ibuprofen* was a signal of depression.' So now I'm going to be biased against this person in that way," said Margaret Mitchell, chief ethical scientist at AI firm Hugging Face, who has no commercial interests in the technology. She worked on developing vocal biomarkers at Oregon Health and Science University. "Even talking about this, it's a little bit worrying, but it is important for people to understand what's happening," she said.

Her own experience makes a case for why this kind of information can easily bias practitioners. After one of her colleagues went to a talk about signals of depression, Mitchell was frustrated about something and audibly sighed. Her colleague immediately asked: "Are you depressed? Depressed people sigh a lot!" Knowing this information, her colleague's impression of the world is fundamentally altered, Mitchell said. "Right now, she sees depression in people that she wouldn't have otherwise seen."

If someone is depressed, they might use a monotone voice. But if you are using a monotone voice, it doesn't mean you are depressed. "Understanding causality flow—if this, then that—is really critical and something that a lot of people mess up," she said. "Particularly if it ends up influencing people and people's impressions in situations like hiring, then it's a very serious concern."

AI tools, on the other hand, wouldn't just jump on one indicator. "It takes in six to thirty seconds of human voice and, from there, our algorithms and models, which have been trained on tens of thousands of people, both in the US and in Asia, are analyzing what I call the atomic level of your voice," said David Liu, CEO of Sonde Health. "We are analyzing the sound as you are going through and telling us about your day or telling us about how you feel in those thirty seconds and that's what's translated into these vocal feature scores," Liu described. The Sonde tool, for example, also measures pause duration. "What we look at is the time difference between when air is being pushed out of your mouth to when sound and voice are being detected. And so that time period, which is quite short, we can measure that."

In addition to pause durations, the tool also records the smoothness of the speaker's voice, control of vocal muscles, liveliness of the voice, energy range, clarity, crispness, and speech rate.

Claims about what the technology currently accomplishes differ according to the four start-ups that I talked to. Some say they can measure someone's depression and anxiety scores based on one short voice sample. Others, like Sonde Health, are more careful.

"The technology is at a point where we can now begin to understand things that are off-kilter," Liu said. Over a period of time the app can detect changes. He acknowledged that everyone has an off day, so an assessment can't be based on one voice analysis alone.

David Liu hopes that vocal biomarker technology can help us become more aware of our mental health issues: "Many of us are walking around suffering silently, right? And so part of this is the awareness, and I love what wearables have done for us, on the physical biomarker side of things. We just become more cognizant about even sleep cycles, whereas fifteen years ago, who the heck knew about any of this stuff? But now it's part of the common vernacular that we talk about," he said.

One day, he hopes, tracking our own mental health via these vocal biomarker scores will become the norm. Sonde Health is planning to build the technology passively into phones and wearable devices so that vocal biomarkers can be assessed from just speaking to your mom, say, when the biomarker technology is just "listening in."

David Liu assured me that Sonde Health plans to have users opt in to this technology and the analysis will not be passively running in the background without user consent.

JUST TALKING

Angela Schmiede, the administrator at Menlo College, tried the Ellipsis tool: "It's a little bit awkward because you're just sitting there and you're talking and you're not talking to anyone. So it's a little bit like talking to yourself and you do wonder, who's really going to listen to this?"

I tried out a similar tool from Sonde Health, which I downloaded on my phone. I recorded myself for thirty seconds multiple times a month. It was weird talking about myself to no one specific, but in a strange way, I always felt a little better after I recorded my messages.

I wasn't the only one who noticed that: "There is something therapeutic about just talking. I did find that to be the case," Schmiede said.

Lina Lakoczky-Torres and the other students started using the tool. Every time they used it, they were scored. Based on the range the score fell into, the tool gave students recommendations—from breathing exercises to a crisis helpline number for students in acute distress.

One student shared with Angela Schmiede that she felt empowered by the tool because she could use it anytime she wanted to and she didn't have to rely on a therapist's schedule. For Lakoczky-Torres, the suggestions the tool gave her weren't too helpful. When she was stressed out, she couldn't do the calming breathing exercises. She mostly used the tool to show her mom how stressed she was living at home: "Look, it's real. This is how I feel. You could see it. . . . There's data right there," she said.

Angela Schmiede noticed that the students weren't very concerned about the tool's accuracy: "They have a greater faith in technology than perhaps older generations do," she said.

Before rolling out the tool, the Menlo team and Ellipsis also discussed sharing crisis scores with the wellness center at the university but decided against it to protect students' privacy.

The trial petered out after a few months and the results at Menlo were mixed. "We had close to sixty participants in the study and some of them only used it once. Others used it multiple times," Schmiede said. About 75 percent of the users were female.

Reflecting on the pilot program, Lakoczky-Torres was happy with the process: "I thought it was pretty cool that this company cares about our data, how we were feeling. But also how we were feeling can reflect back on how they can improve it." She liked that she could track her scores over time and get a better feel for her mood: "If I take this during the peak of finals, what are my scores versus when I'm on spring break?" she asked herself. The tool, she thought, "is not the end all, be all, but it's definitely a step towards something."

How was the data the tool collected going to be used by Ellipsis Health? There wasn't a ton of concern, recalled Lakoczky-Torres. She just assumed that, apart from the engineers who tried to make sure the tool worked, no one from Ellipsis would have access to the data.

Even if they did, she wasn't concerned. "Privacy doesn't really exist anymore," she said. For her generation, sharing feelings was more important anyway: "If you feel some type of way, you're going to go onto your social media and put it on blast, you're going to tell your friends. It's not something you really want to keep to yourself," she said. She called the program a good social experiment. When I talked with Lakoczky-Torres, she didn't have access to the tool anymore.

I wondered if this whole endeavor had been worthwhile. Lakoczky-Torres thought it was, especially given the alternative: "Ellipsis ended up being a really big part of that, to at least feel like you've done something, accomplished something," she said. The tool also brought mental health to the forefront, she said.

She might be onto something here: Using the Ellipsis app prompted Menlo to rethink all of the college's mental health services. They are working on giving students access to more immediate help and providing a wider range of services, Schmiede said.

THE SCIENCE

There is no way to know if or how well this technology works because no company has done a double-blind, placebo-controlled study, which is the gold standard in testing medical products and devices, and no tool has gotten FDA approval.

Industry players assured me that vocal biomarkers exist and that they can diagnose health conditions, but the reality is a bit more complicated.

We may still be in the peak hype phase of this technology, and it's a bit uncertain how good it really is. While the technology is breaking into the market, there are very few safeguards for humans whose voices are used in this kind of testing.

Another threat to practicality of these tools is that AI-driven voice tools might soon enough be able to change our voices in real time, making them sound more monotone or happier, something the vocal biomarker community will have to grapple with as well as possibly HR managers if job applicants use the technology to make their voices sound more "upbeat."

In healthcare settings faulty vocal biomarkers could lead to misdiagnosis. Or the tools could work well on some data sets but not in the wild. These kinds of problems have happened before and could have life-threatening consequences.

Epic, a large healthcare software provider in the United States, built a proprietary Sepsis Prediction Model, which was used in over one hundred US hospitals. Sepsis is the body's extreme reaction to infection and is life-threatening. In fact, about 1.7 million Americans develop sepsis and around 350,000 adults in the United States die of sepsis in a given year, according to the Centers for Disease Control and Prevention. Sepsis is the leading cause of death in US hospitals, so it's of vital importance that doctors and nurses find the patients at risk of sepsis early.

A scientific analysis showed that the Epic algorithm performed worse than advertised. It had an overall accuracy rate of 63 percent—a little better than a coin toss.[12] After the study was published, many healthcare providers took a closer look.

So, should we build and use such new technology? We should of course try to help nurses and doctors find sick patients and make their lives easier, but we can't afford to use faulty technology in health care because patients could die.

In comparison, vocal biomarkers are a tricky technology to test. There is no concrete "ground truth" to check the algorithms against, like there is in the sepsis case—patients either developed sepsis or not, so the algorithm could be fact-checked. But it's difficult to check whether, for example, the Ellipsis Health vocal biomarker measure of depression and anxiety in students showed that these students actually had depression and anxiety because the students were not also evaluated by professional mental health practitioners whose scores the AI scores could have been checked against, and mental disorders are often misdiagnosed anyway.

To understand how far the science of vocal biomarkers has come and what its limitations are, I spoke to Bjoern Schuller, a professor of artificial intelligence at Imperial College London. He said that vocal biomarkers can most easily be used where doctors listen with a stethoscope—mainly in respiratory illnesses because these diseases cause audible changes in voice, breath, and cough. Other illnesses—for example, throat and neck cancer—change the voice as well and can be picked up by technology.

Bjoern Schuller said vocal biomarker technology "came from where people have been listened to and moved more and more into, 'Okay, let's think about what would make a change to your voice.' It's your cognition for speech production, it's your physiology, it's your motor system. If that is somehow affected, we should be able to hear it." He said that vocal biomarkers examining our speech can already accurately predict a person's height and even their heart rate from their voice.

But the vision is much larger than that. Schuller hopes that one day vocal biomarkers can help diagnose autism and other diseases very early on. "The idea is that you can have a baby phone with some smart ability that recognizes early warning signs of neurodevelopmental disorders like autism. Then one could say, 'Please go to a specialist,' and then have this [diagnosis] confirmed because the parents wouldn't notice that at month five or seven, but the baby phone would know."

Vocal biomarker technology could also make a huge difference in countries where medical care is hard to access. Instead of calling for the time, like people did decades ago, they could call a phone number, leave a voice sample, and the computer could tell them if they have dementia, throat or neck cancer, or another illness.

But the reality today is that diagnosing health conditions using vocal biomarkers is more muddled and complicated than many players make it out to be, Schuller said.

Because almost all vocal biomarkers are trained by deep neural networks, it's not always clear what the algorithm is detecting. For example, with COVID-19 coughing samples, a deep neural network would ingest the audio samples of people coughing and labels stating whether the coughing persons had COVID-19 or not. The software would then figure out on its own the differences between the COVID and non-COVID coughs. The hope is that the computer can detect differences between these types of coughs, but that's not always the case, Schuller said. The technology has misfired before.

"If you collect all the COVID people in the ICU and all the non-COVID people in the street, we're not picking up COVID or not, but the acoustics of ICU versus street," Schuller explained. An algorithm like that would be useless because it's just picking up different background sounds.

"There's a lot of people not fully revealing their test methods," Schuller said. Sometimes scientists can be biased to their own methods, and that's why Bjoern Schuller and his PhD student, Harry Coppock, want to replicate others' experiments to make sure they work. "It's so important for research groups to release their trained models and the code required to replicate these studies," Coppock said.

But that doesn't always happen, especially in the acoustic machine learning space. If an algorithm's training data consists of voice samples, that's personal data that in some cases can't be publicly released. And sometimes researchers and companies want to keep their algorithms shielded from the public because they regard them as their trade secrets.

But some studies are released without the underlying data, and scientists are asked to just believe the authors. That's why Schuller isn't a huge fan of companies releasing vocal biomarker technologies to the public yet, because the products have not been independently validated. He is afraid that vocal biomarker snake oil and the hype of the technology will make people turn away from it. (Full disclosure: Bjoern Schuller told me without prompting that he does own a commercial voice emotion detection company that sells to gaming companies. It does not try to diagnose health issues.)

It's a promising technology, but most voice biomarker applications have been not been independently validated or approved by the FDA. Many more studies are needed to prove that the technology works, and that's not easy because the ground truth for mental illnesses is not always objective like a blood test for many other illnesses is. Researchers must run large double-blind trials to find out if these technologies make a difference, but those tests and trials cost a lot of money.

Regardless of whether the technology works, people could utilize it in unintended ways: anyone could run a voice algorithm over samples of job seekers and not hire the applicants who are labeled anxious or depressed or as having schizophrenia or Parkinson's. In fact, I ran YouTube videos of random people speaking through Sonde Health's mobile app and got their "mental fitness scores," as the company calls them.

I wondered about other ethical questions I had never considered before: If a smart speaker like Alexa detects in my voice data that I am sliding into depression, should Amazon be obliged to tell me? Or what if Alexa discovers that our toddler has anxiety? Should Amazon tell me, the parent? If Alexa records an episode of domestic violence, are tech companies obligated to call the police or Child Protective Services?

This type of technology could also be used when people apply for disability insurance. Companies could use such tests to check whether a person is healthy or anxious or depressed to greenlight or deny coverage. This wouldn't be fair, but it doesn't mean that someone isn't contemplating using it.

Some law enforcement agencies across the United States are using a similar technology called Computer Voice Stress Analyzer, which, the vendor claims, can determine whether a suspect is lying by analyzing the stress levels in their voice.

I spoke to a company called Cogito, which analyzes conversations in call centers and gives real-time feedback to agents on what they need to change. The company said it can detect agitation and frustration in customers' voices. In late 2022, JPMorgan Chase filed a patent on a similar AI technology that can predict "dissatisfaction."

OUR PRIVACY IN THIS NEW WORLD

Vocal biomarkers are just one area where our privacy is threatened: at work, privacy is becoming a luxury good for many employees.

Warehouse and delivery workers have been subjected to surveillance of their movements for a long time, but now companies like Amazon are pushing the monitoring to the next level. In 2021, the company required delivery drivers working for Amazon to sign a consent form acknowledging that their movements, but also their biometric data, could be tracked and stored. New cameras inside the Amazon delivery vans can sense yawning and distracted driving and monitor drivers' body and facial movements, according to *Vice*.[13] Drivers fear that the recordings can also be shared with "third-party service providers," according to Thomson Reuters.[14] Albert Fox Cahn, the executive director of the Surveillance Technology Oversight Project, an advocacy group, said that Amazon can "do just about anything they want with this data."[15]

We are entering a new era where a lot of information, including indicators of mental illnesses, can be pulled out of our social media, our facial expressions, and our voices and could be used in work and educational settings. Wouldn't it make university administrators, students, and parents feel better if students were monitored constantly to predict which ones were falling into depression so a doctor could intervene ASAP? Would students consent to this kind of monitoring? Would *we* consent to this kind of monitoring?

Also, our facial expressions and voices are unique to us and, similar to facial recognition technology, we have very little control over how anyone uses this very personal information.

If companies start using these kinds of technologies, they could completely change the power balance at work and in our lives. The information they collect and predict upon could be used against us. And, of course, the technology might not work well at all, but that doesn't mean it won't get used.

Tech vendors are also trying to look into people's minds. Some background-checking companies now advertise that they can deduce from social media accounts whether people are prone to violence or self-harm. Lawyers I have spoken with believe this might be illegal because self-harm could point to a mental illness, something a company is not allowed to inquire about before making a job offer.

And as neuroscience swiftly progresses, so will tools that can record the electrical activity in our brain and measure focus or mind wandering. "Scientists have found various applications of in-ear EEG, including measuring employee attention in office settings," according to the 2022 *Tech Trends Report*. Another device, called AlterEgo, which was developed at the MIT Media Lab, can "speak out loud" the thoughts the headset's wearer is voicing in their head.

Companies are getting closer and closer to peeking into what is going on in our brains. To Nita Farahany, philosophy and law professor at Duke University, this is just the beginning of the information we can pull from our brains. "We can start to decode simple, simple things like simple numbers, words, things that a person is hearing, where their attention is focused, drowsiness."

She is worried that as the technology advances, the floodgates will open: "With our growing capabilities in neuroscience, artificial intelligence, and machine learning, we may soon know a lot more of what's happening in the human brain," she said. "But wasn't the brain the one area that you thought that you had some mental reprieve, the last bastion of freedom, the place that you thought you could have ideas and creativity, fantasize about something, have an absurd idea, have a brilliant idea. Is that the one space that you thought would always be secure?" Farahany asked.

It feels like we might all become guinea pigs in this gigantic data laboratory that is our lives. And once corporations (and governments) can read our thoughts, that will be the end of privacy and democracy as we know them. That is, unless we work now to write the laws needed to regulate use of these technologies.

CHAPTER 10

Fired by an Algorithm

On Trying to Find Problem Employees

Remember Lizzie* from the Prologue? She is the young makeup artist who worked at a MAC makeup counter in the UK when the COVID-19 pandemic hit. First she was furloughed and then the company announced layoffs. The termination decisions were based on previous performance, sales metrics, and a HireVue video interview.

When she was laid off because of her low scores in the HireVue assessment, Lizzie was livid, sad, and frustrated. Together with two other laid-off makeup artists, she found pro bono employment lawyers and challenged the decisions.

"We all believe that we'd lost our jobs unfairly," Lizzie said. And during the legal proceedings, when Lizzie got to review all the data her

---

* Lizzie asked to have her last name withheld for fear of retribution.

former employer had on her, she found on her HireVue results, she scored between 0 and 33 points out of 100. But the Rating and Recommendation sections were left blank, and under "Status," it said "further review."

To Lizzie, the "further review" meant that a technical error had occurred and the HR folks needed to take a second look at the interview and maybe have her redo it. She believes her managers misunderstood HireVue's results and interpreted it as her skills needed further review. She wonders why the Rating and Recommendation sections were blank, which indicated that something went wrong.

When she saw the HireVue result sheet, she felt relieved. She was a capable makeup artist after all: "It was refreshing to get the reassurance that my gut feeling about it was that something wasn't right with the situation."

She believes it's important for her to speak out about how AI technology was used on her. "How it reviews and how it's affecting people is quite scary, especially when we're not getting full transparency of how it's being used," Lizzie said. (HireVue's assessments are designed to be used as part of the hiring process. HireVue does not recommend use of these objective assessments when actual on-the-job performance data is available.)

How HR departments are using AI tools to determine who is being fired or laid off is the subject of this last chapter on AI surveillance. Whether we like it or not, layoffs and terminations are a fact of life. As Lizzie's example shows, AI is now playing a part in firings as more and more artificial intelligence-based tools penetrate the HR field.

Brian Westfall is an analyst at Capterra, a technology review and research company. He surveyed more than three hundred HR leaders in mostly midsize companies, and 98 percent of them said that they would rely on algorithms, HR software, and AI if they needed to make layoff decisions in 2023.

"Here is some evidence that companies out there are relying more and more on algorithmic tools to make these critical decisions," Westfall said.

But at the same time, many of the HR managers surveyed said that, although they will use tech to make layoff decisions, they don't trust these algorithms. Only 50 percent of the people surveyed were "completely confident" that algorithms or HR software would make unbiased recommendations.

These are similar attitudes to what Joe Fuller, the Harvard business professor, found in his survey of company executives discussed in an earlier chapter: the executives and managers his team surveyed overwhelmingly use algorithms in hiring, and even though these tech screens are cutting qualified candidates, they still rely on them. Same here: many HR managers don't trust algorithms, but almost all of them would use them to make layoff decisions.

Experts say leaders should exercise caution when using technology to decide who gets a pink slip. "There is a lot of danger there, obviously. If companies are not familiar with these tools and they are using bad data or they are using biased data and algorithms aren't going to be able to take that into account—they are going to end up making really poor decisions," Westfall said. "Like any tool, if you don't know what you're doing or you don't know how that works, something bad is going to happen. But if you do know how that tool works and you do know what you're doing, it can help you do your job."

It's not clear whether companies have a process for incorporating nonquantitative data into the layoff review procedure. For example, an exemplary employee might have an off year or an employee may constantly help others, which benefits many, but that may not be reflected in the employee's performance data.

THE HUNT FOR LOW PERFORMERS

For years, experts have predicted that human workers will be replaced by machines and artificial intelligence—humans will basically be put out to pasture. Some jobs have been automated, some jobs will change because of ChatGPT and other large language models, but many new jobs are being created that use human workers.

Algorithms are not going to replace us anytime soon, but what is changing is that algorithms and artificial intelligence–based tools are becoming the "bosses" of more and more workers. They check to make sure all tasks are done, rate employees' productivity, select employees for leadership training, and hire and fire people with very little or no human oversight.[1]

Warehouse workers and delivery drivers were on the forefront of workplace surveillance and algorithmic tracking. In fact, they are the canaries in the coal mine and show us what might lie ahead for workers in other industries.

One of these delivery drivers is Claire Grove, a white woman in her late forties. She lives in Worcester, England, and is the single mother of an adult autistic son. She joined the military at seventeen and became a pilot to make a point. "I was told, 'You can't do that because you are a girl,'" she said. "I think that's why I did it, just to impress my dad."

She resigned to get married, and after her divorce, she joined the reserves. In 2005, Grove had a skiing accident with her regiment. Her injury prevented her from carrying out her work, because she has a hard time sitting down for long, so she retired from her full-time job in the military reserves in 2006: "I've been very much a lost soul since then," she said.

In 2017, she needed an additional income stream after buying several rental properties and scrambling to pay the mortgages. That's when she decided to sign up with Amazon Flex. In addition to their regular van fleet contractors, Amazon also works with freelance drivers. They sign up for shifts and deliver overflow parcels in their private cars.

Grove regularly picked up shifts in the evenings delivering packages near her home while one of her lodgers, who was a teacher, could watch her son. She was embarrassed to take the job at first, she said, because she was overqualified. But it turned out she really liked it. "I would deliver to the farms and stroke the dogs and people would be like, 'Wow, you are delivering on Christmas Eve,' or 'You are so nice.' It was really enjoyable," she said.

Over the course of the day, Grove would check Amazon's app for shifts that suited her schedule. Most of the shifts in her area were for four hours and paid between 44 and 54 pounds (roughly $54 to $66) flat fee for her labor and the use of her car. Grove estimates she made about 800 pounds ($991) per month.

After she signed up for a shift, she had to get to the depot at least fifteen minutes before the start time, sign in, collect her parcels, and start her route. Her deliveries were tracked by an app.

When possible, she took a friend with her and paid them pocket change to guard her car when she had to double park. On occasion, traffic wardens would question whether she was making deliveries because her car didn't look like a delivery van. While driving, she and her friend would turn up the music and sing along, she recalled.

Grove was earning enough to make ends meet, so she decided to buy an electric car and make the monthly payments with her income from her Amazon Flex deliveries.

The things she didn't like about the job were most all related to management by algorithms. The drivers had to follow Amazon's GPS, and a few times, the system asked her to drive across rivers that had no bridge in sight or turn down nonexistent streets.

The GPS also meant that scanning packages was only possible in one exact spot, which the system designated. That could make things complicated in larger residential developments where mail rooms or individual buildings weren't exactly where the app told drivers to go. Grove remembered feeling embarrassed when she would be standing in front of a customer trying to hand over the package, but the app wouldn't let her scan it.

"You say, 'Sorry, I can't give you your parcel. I just need to ring up and say this is definitely the right address so they can move that dot to the correct place,'" Grove said. While they had to wait, some customers would get impatient, which made Grove nervous that they would rate the delivery as unsatisfactory, which would reflect poorly on her record. It also meant that she would lose precious time.

Another pain point was when the depot was running late, and drivers couldn't report to work on time. Amazon Flex drivers were afraid that the algorithm would register them as no-shows if they didn't scan in on time and this would hurt their standing. "Everyone's getting out of the car saying, 'I need to scan in, I am late.' And everyone's asking and people start piping their horns," Grove recalled.

Another time, she worried about her rating when she had a flat tire. She frantically tried to reach someone at the company, even sending photos of the tire and the recovery vehicle so Amazon wouldn't hold it against her when she was late to sign in for her shift. "You are desperately trying to get there and tell someone and then, well, it's too late. You missed your block," Grove said.

Many of her Amazon Flex colleagues were recent immigrants from India, Pakistan, and Eastern Europe, she said. Some struggled with speaking English and almost all of them couldn't afford to lose this gig. Grove was a bit of an outlier. She had no problem speaking up and advocating for herself and others.

For example, toward the end of a shift, when Grove was half an hour away from the depot and she still had a lot of packages to deliver, she would stop, drive back to the depot, and return parcels within the four hours allotted to her. The workers at the depot didn't like that. Sometimes they told her that the computer said that she could deliver all the packages within her shift, so she should have been able to.

Another time a worker told her: "Sometimes you'll work for three hours and you'll get paid for four. So the other times you should work for five hours and get paid for four. And I said, 'No, sorry, that's exploitation.' And they went, well, if you bring more than so many parcels back, you would get a threat to have your contract terminated," she recalled.

She doesn't know which occurrences left a black mark on her record. For some incidents she received an automated message:

Hello Claire,

Our records indicate that you did not complete all of your assigned deliveries on 3 February 2020. We expect you to attempt every package you pick up.

On rare occasions, we understand that attempting every package in your block might not be possible. Failing to attempt all your assigned packages will only affect your eligibility for Amazon Flex if it is a consistent problem.

If something unexpected prevented you from attempting all of your packages, please reply to this email with further information.

Your feedback is helping us build Earth's Most Customer-Centric Company.

Warmest regards,

Amazon.co.uk

Grove wrote back that a driver earlier in the day had already tried to deliver the parcels but wasn't able to, probably because it was really hard to find parking in the central business district of Worcester. She hadn't been able to find parking later in the day either, and she wasn't able to deliver the bigger packages on foot, so she returned several to the depot.

She suspected from experience that no Amazon worker would read her email explanation of why she had to return packages and that she would get dinged. Her frustrations with the largely automated systems shone through in her message: "I also expect from experience that you will not even read this email," she typed.

On February 13, 2020, Grove received an automated email from Amazon with her week's activity covering February 2 to February 8, 2020, which included the day she had to return lots of packages. According to the message, her record still showed a 100 percent reliability rate, a 99 percent delivery attempt rate, and a 100 percent on-time delivery/attempt rate.

Three days later, on February 16, 2020, Grove was fired from Amazon via email. The message with the subject line "Notice of Service Termination" addressed her simply as "Hello":

> Hello,
> Our records indicate that, on multiple occasions, you did not attempt all assigned deliveries. You should have received an e-mail alert for each of these occurrences.
>
> Due to these violations, we are terminating our agreement with you. Your account has been deactivated and you will no longer be able to participate in the Amazon Flex program.

Grove believes that she was terminated with the help of an algorithm.

She was upset when she read the email and worried that she wouldn't be able to make her car payments. She second-guessed herself, wondering if this would have happened if she didn't pick up that one shift or thinking maybe she should have worked extra hours. "You have this regret," Grove said. She tried to appeal the decision, but no luck. (Amazon said that it does not use automated systems or algorithms to fire delivery partners. The company said that humans on their teams determine all termination decisions and investigate all driver appeals.)

To this day, she doesn't know the exact reason why she was fired from Amazon. "You can't speak to a person over the phone ever. You never have a verbal conversation ever with Amazon HR."

Grove was terminated just as the pandemic started, which put her in a tough spot financially, especially when one of her tenants stopped paying rent. "I basically realized that I wasn't going to be able to make enough money to pay credit cards and mortgages and everything," she said. "I'm one month away from being homeless."

She stopped paying anything that she didn't need to pay to survive. She still owes money for her mortgage, her car, and her credit cards. "So I'm now in debt. My credit rating is shit, but I don't think I'm the only one in this economy that's in that position and I'm still alive," she said.

She's right: Claire Grove is not alone. At least not alone getting terminated by Amazon. Vicky Graham, a Black woman in her mid-twenties with red dreadlocks, is also a former Amazon Flex driver and believes she was fired by an automated system.

In 2020, during the height of the pandemic, she graduated college with a BFA in acting. "I was really looking for jobs that were flexible, that I was able to kind of create my own schedule while I was able to still look for other positions and audition whenever I needed to."

Safety was another concern, so Uber and Lyft were out of the question. "I didn't feel comfortable having other people in my car as a young female. I would much rather transport things instead of people," she said.

She started with food delivery apps like Postmates, then DoorDash, but it was stressful not having a consistent income and being dependent on strangers who may or may not want food delivered that day.

Then she heard about Amazon Flex: "Whereas Amazon, there were always shifts, there were always packages. Even if there weren't enough packages, you still had the opportunity to get paid anyway." Amazon paid between $18 and $21 per hour for package delivery near her former home in Columbia, Maryland, which is between Baltimore and Washington, DC.

"I was a little hesitant to apply and do it, because part of me was, I don't want to be part of the reason why Jeff Bezos gets even more money, but also I was getting paid and the hours and the pay were really good." She would make more money in less time working for Amazon than for food delivery apps. She tried to work around twenty-five hours per week for Amazon Flex.

Every connection an Amazon Flex driver has with Amazon is routed through one app, which Graham described as buggy from day one. She said it took her about a week to sign up. Even after she signed up, the app continued to malfunction. After the app directed her a few times to roads that didn't exist, she decided to run Google Maps simultaneously with the Amazon app.

In general, she enjoyed delivering packages: "I'm the kind of person who always watched HGTV [Home & Garden Television] since I was a child. So I really like driving through different neighborhoods and see-ing different houses," Graham said.

A frustrating part was the sign-in process at the pickup locations. It took about forty minutes of waiting almost every time she wanted to pick up packages at the different Amazon fulfillment centers she had signed up to. That time was unpaid.

On the flipside, sometimes the algorithmic flaws in the scheduling app worked in her favor. About every fifth pickup, Amazon scheduled too many Flex drivers and she either got only a couple of packages or none at all but would still be paid for her whole block.

She believes her ratings were high because she never had any issues with getting the job done.

But Vicky Graham thinks the buggy app caused her "mysterious termination" over a year after she started driving for Amazon Flex. She was trying to pick up packages at Amazon and she thought she had signed in via the app but got a notification that she was late to her shift. She spoke with different managers, who also tried to sign her in and assured her they had done so.

A few days later she lost access to the app.

"I was thinking it was a technical issue or I needed to update the app or I needed to delete it and redownload it. I did all of that multiple times. I was just expecting a technical error, because that was mostly my frustration with the app anyway. I didn't think I did anything wrong," she said.

She emailed technical support but was told to delete and redownload the app again, something she said she had done many times already. "I couldn't talk to a real person. That's ultimately what I wanted to do. But all of the phone numbers were automated and I couldn't even press the right number to get to a real person," Graham said.

Desperate, she called a phone number at Amazon in Seattle, but no one was able to help her and it made her feel helpless: "I just get frustrated with very greedy companies who automate everything because all they care about is the money that they're making. I feel like a lot of the actual personal connection and compassion and empathy is lost a lot of the time."

She found out she was fired when tech support emailed her stating that they did not have to disclose why someone was terminated. To this day, she does not know why she was terminated in February 2021. Afterward, she struggled with money and went back to DoorDash and other delivery services to pay her bills.

"I was just so surprised. I didn't know what to do. I just kind of gave up on the situation as a whole, because it's clear that there's just some automated program in this email that's just supposed to spit out these responses when they hear these keywords. So I'm not going to be able to talk to a person."

She decided to stop buying from Amazon for a while.

(Amazon stated that Graham and Grove were offboarded because they "repeatedly violated program policies.")

THE INSIDER VIEW

Cornell Causey is a Special Operations Forces veteran and a contractor in his forties. He left his job as a military contractor in 2019 because he wanted to stay stateside and spend time with his family. He worked as a supervisor in Amazon warehouses and got to see the other side—how managers were instructed to use algorithms and technology to keep track of, reprimand, and terminate Amazon warehouse workers.

His dream was to work for Amazon because even when he was stationed in remote and hazardous areas in Afghanistan and Niger as a soldier and then as a contractor, Amazon was always able to send him packages: "When you ordered it, it came," Causey said. "If you see some of the pictures of when we were in Afghanistan, if you look behind us, you'll see mountains of Amazon boxes from stuff that we had ordered."

Causey, who is a Black man with a salt-and-pepper beard, put his résumé on LinkedIn and almost immediately was approached by an Amazon recruiter. The company offered him $85,000 for a job as a manager at an Amazon fulfillment center in Miami, where he oversaw associates who picked the merchandise from mobile shelves and put it in boxes.

He loved the job, he loved Miami, and he admired how tightly Amazon ran the business. "Everything with Amazon is tracked digitally. Every single thing," he said. "The rate people work. How fast they get everything ready to go for delivery. How fast it takes drivers to scan their packages and put them in their van and get ready to go."

The work of so-called pickers, for example, is broken down into a few tasks that can be easily monitored: they have to pick an item off a mobile shelf, confirm that it's the correct one, and place it in a bin. Every picker has to do a certain number of these tasks (usually around 300 to 350) per hour to "make rate."[2]

Work under algorithmic rules basically means that humans have become more like robots: their work is broken down into just a few repetitive tasks that are overseen by algorithms that determine their fate based on productivity targets.

There were human managers, but they also had to abide by the rules. Tracking the associates working under him made Causey miserable, he said. When someone didn't "make rate," he had to go see the employee, find out what had happened, and read them a computer-generated warning.

Even when folks "made rate," but they were in the bottom percentage points, he had to go coach them. "At the end of the day, it's not about hitting a certain number," Causey said. "They just want you to work harder."

Workers could be reprimanded for problems with their productivity, behavior, or quality of their work. Causey didn't think that the automated decisions were always right. "I definitely saw a lot of things that I felt were unfair and people were treated less than human."

What may be surprising to some is that it wasn't the humans that most often caused the unfair treatment, Causey said. It was the machines.

"The managers who were over them had no choice; 'I know you were trying, but the computer is telling me that I need to coach you. I can't go against that as much as I like you and as much as I know you and I've seen you working hard. You somehow fell in the bottom 5 percent today and I have to coach you because if I don't, the computer is going to say I'm not doing my job,'" he recalled.

The only thing Cornell Causey was able to do was add a note that explained why someone may have underperformed that day. "'Oh, your father died today? I can put that in my note, but I don't know who's reading it,'" he said.

If workers accumulated too many warnings, they eventually would be let go. "If they weren't hitting their rates, they would basically just find a reason to terminate," Causey said. He himself was let go for an alleged safety violation he said.

AUTOMATICALLY FIRED

Amazon itself admitted that it had been terminating warehouse workers via algorithm. In documents Amazon filed with the National Labor Relations Board because of a labor dispute, first published by *The Verge*, a lawyer working on behalf of Amazon stated that the company was firing warehouse workers not because of union activities but because they were not meeting their "productivity rates," which are set by an algorithm.[3]

The lawyer also stated that the terminations were not initiated by human managers but by algorithms: "The criteria for receiving a production related notice is entirely objective—the production system generates all production related warning and termination notices automatically with no input from supervisors."[4]

I wonder if a one-size-fits-all method is the right way to monitor workers? Aren't we all different? Aren't some people stronger than others? Are some larger and some smaller? Maybe some folks have health conditions. Is a same-for-everyone approach fair, especially for people with disabilities?

"The use of these technologies is not only increasing employers' power, but it's decreasing their incentive to take into account individual variations and workers' circumstances or the reasons that different things happen in the workplace. It encourages them to take this rigid, one-size-fits-all approach to monitoring their workforce," said Matthew Scherer, senior policy counsel at the Center for Democracy and Technology.

In addition to the productivity rates, Amazon tracks how long employees are not doing their assigned tasks—it's called time off task (TOT). If someone has too many TOTs, they can be terminated. What's upsetting to many warehouse employees at Amazon besides algorithms tracking their time is that the algorithms still track TOT even when it's caused by mechanical failures that do not allow them to continue to work.[5]

There is an information and data imbalance. "The amount of information that employers collect about workers is dramatically greater than the information that workers have about how the employers are using that information and how they are being assessed," Scherer said. In many warehouses, workers are not allowed to bring their cell phones, so even if they wanted to document problems, they can't. Some warehouse workers document with pen and paper every time a conveyor belt breaks or a system is down so they can refute the algorithm's claim that they didn't make rate.

And even if a human manager is in the loop, it's hard to defy an algorithm, said Scherer. So, if an algorithm recommends that an HR manager fire someone, it's hard to override the recommendation. "What's going to be the easiest thing for them to do in that situation is to fire them. It's not going to be easy to argue with the machine and try to say, 'I'm going to override it and let this person keep working there,'" Scherer said.

"These technologies are potentially so all-encompassing in terms of their control over workers. I think the danger is that they are shutting off any sense, any opportunities for intervention or input or agency by workers. And that feels very different than a hundred years ago," said Annette Bernhardt, director of the Technology and Work Program at the University of California Berkeley Labor Center. (Amazon said that it is a common misconception that the company has fixed quotas. Instead, Amazon says that it assesses performance based on safe and achievable expectations that are based on time and tenure, peer performance, and adherence to safe work practices.)

The constant surveillance also plays a role in firings. Sommer Ketron is a consultant with Jumpstart:HR. She works with small to medium-size companies and helps them with their human resources needs.

She recalled that while she was working as in-house HR, there were a couple instances where monitoring the logs of employees' computers became the main evidence in their termination. From one of these logs she learned that one employee spent most of their workdays on the dating website Plenty of Fish. They were terminated. Another employee, who supervised minor employees, was watching porn at work and was also terminated. All of this was uncovered in computer logs from algorithms that recorded every website employees visited on work computers.

RULED BY ALGORITHMS

Most workers wouldn't know if an algorithm was involved in their hiring, promotion, or firing. That's why these AI tools have gotten way less attention than social media algorithms, Annette Bernhardt, believes. "It's so invisible, and right now, these systems are a black box to workers and to policymakers alike," she said.

Researchers have to do detective work to find out which surveillance tools employers use: "We are at this point largely reverse engineering the tech from the harms to workers," she said. And the public is seeing only the tip of the iceberg. "That is really an illustration of the lack of regulation or oversight," Bernhardt said.

There are few laws forbidding surveillance tech in the workplace in the United States. Some laws have been proposed over the years but have faced stiff hurdles.[6]

Simultaneously, as we have seen, more and more companies are now using surveillance systems: "We are in for a very steep, quickly escalating adoption phase," Bernhardt said. "In my mind, this is exactly the critical moment for us to start a robust discussion about whether and how much to regulate this technology, because if we wait till ten years from now, it's too late. The horse is out of the barn."

To Annette Bernhardt, our future looks dark with the knowledge we already have today. Change needs to happen now.

"The dystopian path here is literally that workers become basically robots in the flesh with almost no ability to make their own decisions, to question the decisions that are being made about them, either by the algorithm or by the employer or the two working together," Bernhardt said. "That is what feels different about this moment."

She wants workers to be at the table, deciding together with employers what technologies should be used in the workplace.

EPILOGUE

Living in a Predictive Society

I was so excited when I started this journey researching AI in the world of work. "Finally," I thought, "a solution to biased human hiring." But at the end of this journey, I feel a bit demoralized knowing that at least some of the tools people and companies use to make employment decisions do not work. At least some companies are basing high-stakes employment decisions on biased and junk algorithms, which cause real harm and prevent qualified people from getting jobs.

The corporations buying these tools from AI vendors must do a better job vetting the algorithms. "Companies should be concerned about that because when [the algorithms] don't work, they're paying millions of dollars for nothing, and complexity that they don't need and risk that they don't need. That's no good from a business perspective," said Eric Sydell, former executive vice president of Modern Hire, one of the largest AI hiring platform vendors in the United States. Modern Hire was bought by HireVue in May 2023. Sydell left the company after the merger.

Doing it the right way is hard work. Many people buying or overseeing these systems are not skeptical enough, are not asking the right questions, and are not demanding to see proof that these systems work probably because they are resorting to AI to make their lives easier, not harder.

The truth is coated in beautifully crafted marketing language and it's hard to break through that. But we have to do better. People's futures depend on this.

"My phone works because I can see that it works. I don't have to check it all the time to see if it works. It rings and I know it works. But algorithms aren't like that," Sydell said. It's hard to check algorithms because their calculations often are invisible. Many HR tools produce a ranking and decrease the applicant pool, so it looks like the system is doing well. But, as we have seen, that might not be the case.

"The vendor wants you to think that it works everywhere, of course," he said. "No, it doesn't. The demographics of the workforce, the applicant pool change, what good performance looks like changes over time, cultural things change, and demographics and geographical regions are different and have different norms; all kinds of things come into it and make algorithms work better or less well."

The technologies are essentially outpacing regulations, which many vendors use as a carte blanche to do what they want. "In the absence of clear guidelines, regulations, rules, there's nothing necessarily making them conform to any perfect, great high-standard way of doing things. If you are compliant in terms of bias and privacy, which you should be, obviously that doesn't mean the algorithm is any good," Sydell said.

Employers need to test that the AI tools will work for specific roles in their companies. "Before you use it, you need to validate it on your workforce. You can't just take their word for it that it's valid when hiring software engineers for another company because your software engineers do different things than the software engineers at that other company," said Matthew Scherer, senior policy counsel at the Center for Democracy and Technology. "The thing that I think is often missing for these employers is they don't try to think critically about 'is this test testing for the key things that make somebody successful at the job for which I'm using it?'"

For over three years prior to his current position, Matthew Scherer was a lawyer at the firm Littler Mendelson, which specializes in labor and employment law. His expertise was in algorithmic hiring tools and data analytics. Companies often came to him late in the game when they were ready to sign a contract with a vendor, which made his job harder, especially when he had to break the news that the tool wasn't very good. "Consistently, the tools were shitty. They weren't doing a very good job of identifying good candidates," he said.

"These tools don't work very well when you actually try to use them to predict success in a specific job; it's not doing much better than randomly picking a candidate's name out of a hat. They just aren't very accurate because they are so generic and so generalized."

So, trusting a vendor to critically audit its own product is not the answer. "What I've learned is you can't expect or rely on the vendor to necessarily do that," Eric Sydell said.

A first step could be to ask tough questions: "What data, what analytics? How are you making sure that it still works? How is it improving? How are you avoiding privacy concerns with the data you're collecting?" Sydell said. And if I was an HR manager, I would ask the question, "How did the vendor validate this tool for the roles we are hiring for?"

But Sydell also acknowledged how difficult it is for HR managers and even large companies to vet algorithms. "It's too hard because these algorithms are so complicated and nobody understands them," he said. "To really vet what those vendors are saying, it's a lot. You've got to look at studies; you've got to look at data; you've got to look at analytics; and you've got to see what techniques they used. Is the study design good? You have got to have multiple PhDs involved with different expertise to really do a good job. But who has that? Nobody."

One solution is to monitor the results of the algorithms. Are the results fair? Are the algorithms complying with fair hiring and work practices? And are they still functioning properly after being in use for some time? "What the solution is for all these things, in my opinion, is better monitoring—continual, better monitoring. The industry is not set up that way," said Sydell, who is in the process of starting his own auditing company. "The hiring industry, they don't want that. They want you to take on faith that the statistics they throw at you are what you will experience too, because they don't want things to be continually monitored. That's more work, that's more cost."

Sometimes, lawyers advise employer companies not to take a closer look at these AI tools or to collect any data because in a lawsuit they then might have to disclose their tests and their data. But, on the other hand, not doing anything to vet algorithms creates harm, experts say. "If you don't have the data and you're not looking at the data, guaranteed, you're doing it wrong—guaranteed. There's bias and lack of effectiveness," Sydell said. Regulation could help here by mandating continual monitoring by a third party.

These algorithms aren't going away, and researchers and journalists should not give up trying to investigate them from the outside to keep the industry accountable. I am all for innovation and new approaches, but they have to work and be fair.

I hope the science improves, independent researchers can reproduce the findings, and regulations ensure we are protected.

WHAT DOES OUR FUTURE LOOK LIKE?

Tomas Chamorro-Premuzic, the management psychologist and chief innovation officer at ManpowerGroup, paints a bleak picture of an AI-mediated future. He predicts that more and more of our data will be online and algorithms will get better at interpreting our "data exhaust," whether it's our buying patterns on Amazon, our temperature preferences on Nest thermostats, our music choices on Spotify, or our Twitter feeds. Everything will be fair game for the algorithm, and everything together will give AI a good sense of who we are.

"Life will seem like a never-ending job interview," he said. "Everything we do will be monitored by AI and algorithms and will be used to compute career potential and job potential." Eventually, we won't even need to apply for work, Chamorro-Premuzic said. In the future, algorithms will match us to jobs based on the data exhaust we leave behind.

And that would be the end of privacy as we know it.

We are in the early stages of this new era, yet some employers are already using automatic background checks to weed out job applicants who have sued their former employers. And others are using AI to find the right personalities for a job.

Vendors are discussing placing people's skills verifications and educational achievements on a blockchain server, which would make them easily accessible to recruiters and employers.

Other companies, such as Dice.com, have developed products that scrape social media websites and build skills profiles of people from their data exhaust. According to a class action lawsuit against the company, Dice's algorithm crawled dozens of social media sites and created employment profiles of people working in the tech industry. Recruiters then paid Dice for access to these profiles.

Many workers didn't know they were in the database, according to the lawsuit. Ian Douglas and other tech developers said that the website had incorrect information on them. When Douglas asked the company to delete his profile, which he hadn't set up, Dice refused. In 2019, Dice agreed to pay $1 million to settle the class action lawsuit and to substantially change its business practices by allowing consumers to access, request changes to, and even delete their Dice profiles.[1]

Another software company is trying to take this idea one step further. At a management psychology conference, I was approached by an entrepreneur who is trying to build a skill score system *about* workers—not *for* them. Like the now-defunct Klout score, which gave folks a score based on their online social influence, his company is attempting to build a skill score for everyone. He pitched it like a credit score, just for skills—he hopes that employers will pay his start-up to see the skills scores on potential employees. The workers being judged wouldn't necessarily have access to these scores.

I wondered how changes in skills or education level would be updated. Will we have a say whether our data is stored in these databases?

Ideas like this skill score system, plus dodgy instant personality tests and continuous background checks through our social feeds, are not far from China's much-criticized social credit score. One difference, of course, is that the Chinese government will score its own citizens. Certain infractions—jaywalking or not paying a court fine—could mean that the government will essentially blacklist a person and curtail their ability to participate in society, such as buying airplane or train tickets.[2]

That's probably not in the cards in Western democracies, although governments are also using AI-based surveillance tools to learn more about their own people. But a lot of power rests with private corporations, which have significantly less transparency than democratically elected governments.

What if I make a small mistake, like getting angry with someone on Twitter and answering a misogynist tweet with a swear word? What if a student leaves a negative review of me as their professor? Will an algorithm reject me for a job opportunity or will my university fire me?

Although personality traits are not very predictive of success on the job, as we have seen, employers are using these tests and AI to pull those traits out of our data exhaust.

This new era of surveillance by algorithm not only threatens our privacy but also threatens our idea of human sovereignty. It may take away our agency and free will to choose our career and who we want to be.

Should we really trust companies to build a human future for their job applicants and employees? Or do we need to start pressuring lawmakers to mandate transparency and regulate algorithms to make sure they work as advertised and help us build a future that preserves our will to act and keeps our humanity at the center of work and society?

I believe we need to act. Testing these tools shows how flawed some of the technologies are. I hope it brings about change and greater skepticism of vendors' claims.

Writing this book has shown me that we need to do more to fight off bad algorithms ruling our lives and making high-stakes decisions about us—many times without us ever knowing. What's problematic in the marketplace is that the vendors have very little incentive to make their products better or to monitor their algorithms over time because it would be costly.

The monetary pressure for start-ups to scale, sell their products, and get bought to give investors a payout is strong, preventing large parts of the market from regulating itself. The technology is too complicated for most people to understand. It is also to the benefit of vendors and their client companies for everyone to keep quiet about problems with the tools. The result is that many AI tool buyers and the general public do not know which tools are decent and which are junk.

One idea that came out of my journey writing this book is to take the monetary pressure off building AI tools. What if we could start a not-for-profit organization that will test and build AI tools in the public interest? I am working on that right now. Such a project would bring together researchers, computer scientists, social scientists, journalists, psychologists, project managers, data scientists, statisticians, and others to solve the problems with AI that we can foresee. For example, we could try to program a résumé screener that is unbiased and that works. We would carefully document every iteration and see at the end whether this is possible or not. All of that research would be available to anyone, and hopefully that would put pressure on companies to choose the right tools and not the ones that sound most magical. The same goes for chatbots, AI games, and other AI tools used for hiring. We could test and build them and show which methods are successful and which are not. We could also test whether they are accessible for people with disabilities and whether they are predictive.

If possible, we would run longitudinal studies to understand how assessments might predict a candidate's success on the job. We would obtain buy-in and legal clearance from employers in order to follow cohorts of new hires for two or three years or longer.

And maybe at the end, looking at the evidence we may or may not conclude that even the best AI tools are unable to predict what humans will do in the future, including being successful at a new job. A recent study showed that AI tools may not be very good at predicting the future.

DOES PREDICTING SOCIAL OUTCOMES WORK?

It turns out that predicting what I will have for lunch (probably some kind of salad with kale or salmon) is easy because I am the type of person who hates spending time on decision-making and just keeps ordering more or less the same thing. Predicting if I will be good at a job, however, is much harder to do.

People in charge of hiring have been trying to find the right people for the right jobs for decades. Judging by the number of people who quit or are fired after starting a new job, which is about 50 percent of employees after a year and a half, we are still not very good at matching people to positions. So maybe we should give AI a chance? But so far, the experiences with AI that I have chronicled are not encouraging.

Why is it so challenging to predict whether someone will be successful? In a work setting, most companies hire an individual and don't often think about the many other variables that go into hiring. What's the team like? Is the boss toxic? What are coworkers like? What is the company culture? And there are myriad ways a new employee's personal life can impact their performance—maybe they suddenly have to take care of a loved one. Or they develop a health condition. Or they are going through a divorce.

Predicting the future for hiring and other social outcomes, including forecasting whether a former convict will commit another crime, is very challenging because no one knows exactly what the future will hold. No human has been able to predict the future, but when it comes to artificial intelligence, we somehow believe that with access to thousands of data points a computer can do exactly that.

Even when we use thousands of data points and machine learning algorithms, there is evidence why predicting the future might be unreliable. Dozens of scientists worked together on a large study that was published in 2020. They asked 457 researchers (160 teams) to predict the individual social outcomes of more than four thousand families in the United States. The scientists had high-quality data on these families from an ongoing study that chronicled their lives from the time their children were born to fifteen years later (it's ongoing).[3]

The researchers asked participants to predict families' social outcomes in six categories: GPA, grit, material hardship, layoff, eviction, and job training. They asked questions like: Will a child's household face material hardship? Will the primary parent be laid off? What GPA will the child have? Will the child's household be evicted? Will the child have grit? Will a primary caregiver receive job training? The researchers didn't specifically ask about success at a job, but predicting these kinds of social outcomes is similar to predicting success in a given job, and traits like "grit" are in high demand in the workplace.

The great thing about this study was that the scientists had access to the outcomes already, so there was ground truth data. The prediction could be checked against the known social outcomes.

To answer the questions, the participating research teams received data for all 4,242 families in the Fragile Families study,* which tracked families from birth onward. The data from birth to nine years old is so rich that there were 12,942 variables per family, bringing the possible options to millions of possibilities.[4]

Such a mountain of data is something that machine learning folks would love to have to predict hiring outcomes. Most vendors in the space ask for more data, arguing it will increase accuracy.

In addition to the data of families from the birth to age nine of their child, the researchers were given access to the six outcomes for children at age fifteen for half of the families in the study. Because they knew what

---

* Since January 2023, the study is now called *The Future of Families and Child Wellbeing Study*.

happened to half of the families, could their algorithms predict the outcomes of the other half? When a child was around fifteen, what would their GPA be? Had there been an eviction in the household?

This seemed like a straightforward data science challenge. Lots of data and predicting social outcomes *should* be straightforward—AI vendors in hiring and people analytics do it every day.

It turned out that making these predictions wasn't easy at all. None of the machine learning submissions were rated very high for accuracy. There were 160 submissions, with a score of 1.0 indicating a 100 percent accurate prediction. Even the best submission scored only .23 in the category of Material Hardship. GPA prediction was at .19, and the best algorithms for grit, eviction, job training, and layoffs predicted future outcomes accurately at a .07 rate. Anything under .3 is considered a weak prediction in statistics.

"We discovered that even the best predictions were not very accurate. . . . Even though the Fragile Families data included thousands of variables collected to help scientists understand the lives of these families, participants were not able to make accurate predictions," wrote the researchers.

Here is what's striking: out of the 160 submissions, even the best machine learning algorithms didn't perform well in predicting how the futures of these children would unfold.

The scientists also wanted to see how the machine learning models compared to traditional predictive models. They worked with an expert and considered only four variables out of the thousands of data points: race/ethnicity of the mother (a questionable variable!); marital status of the parents at the birth of the child; education level; and one result when the child was nine.[5]

It turned out that the traditional predictive models that used only four variables were almost as good as the best machine learning algorithms. In fact, the traditional models outperformed many of the machine learning algorithms. But still, this study shows that neither machine learning algorithms nor traditional methods are very good at predicting the future.

In applied settings such as job searches, this means that the machine learning algorithms that data scientists use to predict job applicants' success could be underperforming when compared to traditional benchmarks. "For predicting social outcomes, AI is not substantially better than manual scoring using just a few features," said Arvind Narayanan, computer science professor at Princeton University.[6]

If companies need a method to select job applicants, manual scoring is preferable because the user can select features. Proxies for race, gender, or other demographic variables that might be biased and that are often hard to avoid in large data sets can be eliminated to the best of the users' knowledge. This matters because many AI experts ask for more and more data to improve their predictions. But as this study shows, more data might not be helpful if the data is being used to predict the future and what humans will do, but as we have seen throughout this book even a neutral-looking criterion like zip codes can result in racial discrimination in algorithms.

Additionally, many machine learning algorithms use deep neural networks, so the findings are often hard to explain, which makes the algorithms opaque even to developers. Independent auditors and researchers most likely can't verify or reproduce these findings even if they can examine the training data that was used to build the model.

Imagine a system like this: "Instead of points on a driver's license, every time you get pulled over, the police officer enters your data into a computer. Most times you get to go free, but at some point, the black box system tells you you're no longer allowed to drive.[7] Unfortunately, we have this kind of system today in many domains," Narayanan said. Including hiring.

That's why Narayanan and other experts suggest that vendors and data scientists should at least contemplate using traditional methods because they scored on par or better than AI methods in this large study but needed only a fraction of the data. What kind of data is used is also decided by the vendor, who can choose less discriminatory variables, so collecting less data usually causes fewer privacy, legal, and ethical problems and less discrimination.

As I described in Chapter 1, using first names to predict success in a job is obviously biased and unethical and should be made illegal, but because AI hiring algorithms are kept largely secret, not many folks find out what goes wrong inside these machines. Other methods like using Twitter feeds or assessing facial expressions to predict personality are invasive and not based on solid science.

CAN WE GO BACK?

So, why not just go back to regression analysis? For Arvind Narayanan, the problem with that idea is commercial interests. Vendors want to sell expensive AI products and they keep telling us that we need to use machine learning and lots and lots of data. But in most cases, he said, "manual scoring rules are just as accurate, far more transparent, and worth considering." But some are more labor intensive and often not as fast as AI-assisted decision-making.

Narayanan and his coauthors of the Fragile Family algorithm study are not the only ones who observed this problem. David Futrell was the director of selection and assessment at Walmart, which is the largest private employer in the United States. He and his team ran one of the largest hiring machines on the planet and assessed thousands of Walmart applicants every day.

He shared his experience with AI and machine learning tools on a panel at an industry conference in 2020: "I was very excited by these tools whenever I first started seeing them. So I've been doing a kind of traditional prediction using regression and correlation techniques for many years and a lot of these machine learning tools are just superfast and sophisticated ways to test all of the possible combinations."

Because Futrell's team assessed thousands of people a day, he had an abundance of data at his fingertips and didn't run into such problems as small sample size, which could skew results. He asked his team to test a lot of the new AI tools. And he was disappointed: "When we tested this and in practice, we didn't find the machine learning predictions to be substantially better than the old-fashioned way."

So, neither in computer labs nor in applied settings did AI outperform traditional statistical models. And neither method achieved much statistical relevance.

"These problems are hard because we can't predict the future," Arvind Narayanan said. "That should be common sense. But we seem to have decided to suspend common sense when AI is involved."

Humans can't predict how other humans will act in the future, nor can statistics or data science. In hiring, one of the best ways to understand whether someone is good at the job is to have them do the job, but that means companies might have to fire people shortly after hiring them, losing revenue in the process, since the process can be expensive. Job trials in virtual settings might give us more predictive answers in the near future, but no one can predict extraneous influences on someone's job performance. Some experts say that more can be done to take into account the candidate's team and managers during the hiring process.

Also, it might be helpful for employers to use more than one assessment to test candidates; they can assess on different aspects of the job requirements to get a better picture of the candidate. But, of course, that costs more money. Companies also should do a job analysis to find which skills are needed in a role, which is another extra cost and often gets shortchanged with AI tools.

To Arvind Narayanan, hiring is one of the worst areas to use machine learning algorithms because what the AI is predicting is unclear: "In algorithmic hiring, there are no clear prediction targets. We don't all agree on what it means for someone to be a good employee and so these systems are starting off with a very poorly defined task."

Companies want to hire "productive" or "good employees," but what does that mean? And how can we measure it? Employers don't even know how to quantify "productive" or "good," so how can they predict anything if the target of the prediction is fuzzy? "As far as I've seen, these companies are not really producing evidence that these systems are predicting some measurable future performance," Narayanan said.

That's harsh but true. After testing so many tools, I am also not sure what many companies are measuring exactly with their AI hiring and productivity tools. "I've called them elaborate random number generators and I'm sticking to that. I think they really accomplish nothing other than cost cutting," Narayanan said.

Many companies use AI tools to fill hourly positions, an area where HR managers receive lots of applications and regularly have to hire lots of people. "Companies are often using them for positions that are undervalued, and companies don't care about who they ultimately end up hiring," Narayanan said. "The imperative is to really make that process as efficient as possible. And so maybe from that perspective, it achieves their goals, but so would a random number generator. The idea that you can really quantify these things about job performance and then predict them—that's the part that I find incoherent. I think these systems are not really doing that at all."

He is not the only one who thinks this.

Because of financial pressures to sell products, making sure the tools work, which takes time, is not a priority for many vendors. "It's too easy to put stuff out that's not that great and to cheat and to short-circuit the scientific process," said Eric Sydell, formerly of Modern Hire. "Science doesn't sell."

To Arvind Narayanan, the burden of proof that these systems work should be on the vendor. Vendors should be able to show transparently that their system works and let others test it.

So, what's a better way? In medicine, doctors and patients tend to try less invasive surgeries first for logical reasons: there is less injury and loss, they cause less pain, and there are fewer complications. I suggest we use the same playbook for AI in hiring: let's use transparent algorithms, including traditional regression analysis, that are validated and fair and then mandate to test all AI-based algorithms.

In medicine and especially for new medications, manufacturers have to prove that a new medication works better than a placebo. To do that, companies run randomized controlled trials. "I think that needs to become standard in every domain of decision-making," Narayanan said.

In hiring it could look like this: Companies first would decide what constitutes success. Then, they would hire candidates who have been algorithmically labeled "successful" or "unsuccessful" through a third party, a not-for-profit research team, for example. (So the hiring company doesn't know how the candidates have been labeled.)

"So both of them get hired and then you compare their performance three years down the line and at a scale of hundreds or thousands of people," Narayanan said. If the folks labeled "successful" are truly more successful by a large statistical margin than the folks labeled "unsuccessful," it would prove that the algorithm worked.

We could also test AI tools by comparing them to random selections. For example, if a company is hiring truck drivers, a third party or nonprofit could use an AI tool to hire the most qualified folks the tool selects. At the same time, they would also hire candidates who have the minimum qualifications (like a commercial driver's license) but who are chosen at random. Which hiring method produces more successful employees three years down the road?

It's of course unheard of in hiring to do such a thing, but that's what's needed to prove whether these AI tools really work. "The knowledge that's going to be gained out of this is hopefully going to benefit billions of job seekers for a long time to come," Narayanan said.

In the meantime, I hope lawmakers will get wise to what's happening in the industry and start mandating transparency of training data and technical reports. It would be great if government agencies started testing these types of tools and even developed some sort of FDA-like entity for high-stakes AI decision tools used in such areas as policing, hiring, surveillance at work, credit rating, and criminal sentencing.

Right now, New York City, other municipalities, and states are working on making bias audits mandatory for vendors that sell hiring tools.[8] That's a laudable goal. I have dug deep into auditing and found that the two vendors that hired third-party companies to audit their AI tools both had controversial outcomes but used the audit to bolster their marketing. In short: hiring your own auditors creates conflicts of interest, and we have seen similar systems break down. In the lead-up to the financial crisis in 2008, for example, many banks and investment firms paid third parties to "audit" and rate their investment vehicles. Many subprime mortgages were bundled together and rated AAA.

An audit system that is solely focused on bias, which is now the law in New York City, would hopefully make sure that discriminatory algorithms disappear, but it wouldn't solve conflicts of interest and it wouldn't help the public understand if these algorithms actually work in picking the most qualified applicants or are just elaborate number generators.

A better system would be for an independent party or the government to set clear standards of transparency and effectiveness and test these tools for bias and validity before they are allowed on the market. Evidence that AI tools do not discriminate, including against people of color, people with disabilities, and people of a certain age, would have to be produced. This transparency would also help others, including researchers, journalists, and computer scientists, independently test these systems.

If the government is not willing to act, nonprofits and civil society stakeholders may be able to step in with enough funding to test and build AI tools in the public interest.

Another way to regulate the industry is giving employees more power and letting current employees have a say about which technologies are used on them and are used to hire applicants, similar to what works councils in Germany and Austria are doing.

That's how we could rein in junk algorithms and make sure they do no further or at least very little harm. But there is another area we need to watch: developments in neuroscience will soon have a profound impact on hiring and work. Scientists are getting closer to build tools that can read our thoughts, which has vast implications for technology used in the workplace and on us humans.

THE PRIVACY OF OUR
THOUGHTS IN THE FUTURE

Neuroscience is advancing at an incredible speed and we are in the early days of machines learning to read our thoughts.

I don't know why, but when I think of this dark Orwellian society we might be entering, with AI algorithms and neuroscience tools encroaching on our private brain space, I recall one of my favorite childhood songs that used to give me hope: *Die Gedanken sind frei*—"thoughts are free."

The song emerged sometime in the eighteenth century building on earlier versions, reflecting on life under oppressive rulers. (No idea why it resonated with me—I definitely wasn't thinking about oppressive regimes back in the 1990s when I was twelve.)

Die Gedanken sind frei, wer kann sie erraten,
Thoughts are free, who can guess them?

Sie fliegen vorbei wie nächtliche Schatten.
They fly by like nocturnal shadows.

Kein Mensch kann sie wissen,
No person can know them,

kein Jäger sie schießen mit Pulver und Blei
no hunter can shoot them with powder and lead.

Die Gedanken sind frei!
Thoughts are free!

"My thoughts freely flow. My thoughts give me power," sang Pete Seeger in his interpretation of "Die Gedanken sind frei" for his album *Dangerous Songs* (1966).[9] Even though we might live in an oppressive system, this song suggests our private thoughts are our own. But today, predictive analytics and neuroscience are challenging the very idea of us as autonomous individuals.

Makers of AI-based systems believe that, deep down, we are driven by patterns and that algorithms can find these patterns. We are still free to think what we want, but our thoughts, preferences, and behaviors can be predicted by artificial intelligence.

As predictive algorithms push into ever more sensitive and private aspects of our lives, other algorithms based on brain–computer interfaces now can literally read our thoughts and emotions.

A prototype of this technology exists: these neuroscience tools can extract simple words from our brains.[10]

Tomas Chamorro-Premuzic, the management psychologist, agrees that this paints a rather bleak scenario. "Are we going to engage in systematic social engineering and put people where they have to be? I often find that even though the questions scare us and shock people and they look very Orwellian and *1984*—we are trending in many ways toward that."

PREPARING FOR A SCARY FUTURE

It's a dark outlook—a system in which algorithms define who we are, where we excel, and where we struggle. What's at stake is the way we live. What if the algorithms get it wrong?

What if the algorithms take away human variability? A hiring system run by algorithms could prevent employers from finding candidates who can change the organization because a rigorous application of the algorithms keeps selection to a narrow, mainstream pool based on statistical analysis.

And what are the limits of what companies could and maybe should ask us to do?

"Could we also encourage individuals to start doing things like enhancing their brains? Could we ask them to take things like smart pills and smart medications? If you're drowsy while driving, should you take something like modafinil [a stimulant medication] in order to improve your wakefulness? If you're on a forty-eight-hour shift as a physician, should you take a wakefulness drug?" asked Nita Farahany, professor of law and philosophy at Duke University, where she investigates the social implications of emerging technologies.

Maybe in the near future, workplaces will send workers home who show less than stellar concentration or emotional agitation.

What if AI tools use vocal biomarkers at work or during the hiring process, for example, and infer that you have early dementia or cognitive decline? A company might not hire you, might ask you to retire early, or might fire you because you are too expensive to employ.

This idea of algorithms deciding our future counters the idea that we, as humans, can flourish and blossom and grow in a job, or outside of a job. What happened to giving humans a chance to grow with their job responsibilities and in their lives?

I believe that building a human future is still possible, starting with hiring and predictive analytics. It turns out that our traditional ways of hiring people and selecting them for promotions and leadership roles are riddled with bias and don't work well, either. (No idea why we thought automating a bad system would miraculously fix the problem humans haven't been able to solve.)

To build a future in which we all have a chance to succeed, we have to start regulating AI systems and make sure the neuroscience tools cannot be abused to read our innermost thoughts. Being free from these invasive tools must be considered a human right.

We also need to find a way back to our humanity. Humans are more than quantitative entities. We can exceed or fall below expectations. We can rise to the occasion, and we are more than our jobs and our skills.

I believe that with transparency about what is happening in the world of work and by pushing back against companies' and vendors' power by testing, auditing, and regulating algorithmic tools, AI can be helpful with some pattern recognition tasks to build a future with humans at the center.

This world needs to be open to us as humans, with our thoughts and creativity. We need to be given the chance to flourish and surprise others with our ingenuity—in our jobs and in our lives. But we need to fight for it. Starting now.

APPENDIX

Trying to Find a Job

We have dealt with the big-picture issues in the book, but here I would like to focus on specific strategies to use (1) when looking for a job in this new AI-driven environment and (2) when you think your company is tracking you.

JOB APPLICATION TIPS

- Instead of trying to stand out by choosing a unique design or color scheme, make your résumé machine-readable: no images, no two columns, no special characters such as ampersands or tildes—computers may not be able to correctly ingest that information.
- Use the most common template. Use short, crisp sentences: be declarative and quantify achievements where possible, said Ian Siegel, CEO of the job platform ZipRecruiter. (If you don't like the machine-readable version, consider having a second résumé geared toward humans that you can bring to job interviews, said Gracy Sarkissian, the executive director of the Wasserman Center for Career Development at NYU.)

- List licenses, including license number and certifications.

- Do not list your address or location, especially if you do not live near the worksite.

- List your skills in a separate section using bullet points so machines can easily ingest it.

- Make sure your résumé matches the keywords in the job description and compare your résumé to the job description using online résumé scanners (Jobscan and others) to see if you are a match for the role. (Aim for a 60–85 percent match because AI might filter out 100 percent matches, considering them a copy of the job description.)

- Companies that want to broaden their applicant pool may use AI to infer whether you are a woman and/or a person of color. Inferences are often made by pronouns and other breadcrumbs you leave in your résumé. For example, if you write that you are a member of the American Society of Hispanic Psychiatry, the AI will likely infer that you are Latinx. If someone lists that they are a member of African American Real Estate Professionals, the software would in all likelihood classify them as African American.

- Do not apply via job boards if you can avoid it. Recruiters have shared with me that the first résumés they check out are from candidates who applied directly via the company's website; if the candidate pool is insufficient, only then will they turn to candidates who applied via job platforms like Indeed, Monster, ZipRecruiter, and others.

- If possible, contact recruiters via LinkedIn after applying for a job.

- Engage with recruiters on job platforms. It will signal to the AI that you are actively looking for a job and will recommend you for more opportunities because most AI tools are optimized to find "qualified people likely to apply," said John Jersin, former vice president of product management at LinkedIn.

- Apply to jobs that require more experience than you have, as long as you meet some of the qualifications in the job description. "Let the algorithms decide whether or not you are a great match and they will sort you to the top or bottom," Ian Siegel said. This may also signal the AI to show you more senior jobs.

- If you have a profile on a job platform like LinkedIn, make sure to list all your skills because recruiters often search for candidates by location and skills.

- Network with folks in the industry and at companies you want to land in.

- For entry-level and administrative jobs, consider stating that you are competent in Microsoft Office Suite applications, even if it's not in the job description, said Harvard business professor Joe Fuller.

- Many job applicants now use ChatGPT and other large language models to write or polish their résumés and cover letters. Make sure you fact-check the results. You can also prompt ChatGPT for the most common interview questions and have it help you prepare answers in advance.

- And, most importantly: don't be discouraged! Many other job seekers are sending out hundreds of applications as well.

WHAT IF I AM BEING TRACKED?

Because there is very little transparency in surveillance at work, here is what I recommend to readers who suspect they are being tracked:

- Assume that everything on a work computer, tablet, and phone is monitored. Nothing is private, even private messages in Slack or Microsoft Teams. Everything can be accessed by an employer, including deleted messages. (According to the research firm Gartner, before the pandemic, around 10 percent of companies surveyed said they used this type of software, but since the pandemic, about 30 percent of companies purchased remote tracking software. *The New York Times* reported that eight of the ten largest private US employers use productivity monitoring.)
- Assume that every printout and every file you move off a work computer is tracked, as well.
- Use a second personal computer or your personal phone, if you can, to check your personal email or surf the web when you are at work.
- If you can avoid it, do not install company software on your phone.
- Check your emails for sentiment. Try to keep them upbeat and professional, since more and more companies are enabling "employee listening" tools, which may track sentiment in messages. The software can also track external signals like reviews and tweets.
- Keep your updates on LinkedIn steady and do not update everything at once because that can increase your flight risk score.

ACKNOWLEDGMENTS

This book is dedicated to my family and especially my daughter, Frieda. She is the light of my life. In the future, I hope that she and her peers will not be reduced to a number but will be recognized for their humanity.

First and foremost, I want to thank all my sources. Without them this project would not have been possible. Thank you for coming forward and sharing your experiences with me—I am so grateful for the trust you all put into me and the privilege of telling your stories!

I also want to thank my agent, Roger Freet, at Folio. Not only did he take a call from a first-time author and helped me in so many ways along the way, but he is also a wonderful human being.

My gratitude also belongs to Sam Raim, who acquired the book for Hachette and understood my vision. From there, Dan Ambrosio and his excellent team took over and made sure this book is the best version it can be. I want to especially thank copy editor Christina Palaia, production editor Seán Moreau, proofreaders Susan VanHecke and Erica Lawrence, and indexer Sherri Linsenbach who helped shape the final manuscript into this book. I also want to thank Amanda Kain for the fabulous cover.

I couldn't have written this book without limitless help from trusted experts in the field, including John Scott, Matthew Neale, and Fred

Oswald, who again and again took my calls and walked me through the ins and outs of industrial and organizational psychology research.

A special thanks goes to my research assistants, Victoria Albert, Priyanka Vora, Noah Daly, and especially Clara McMichael.

Additionally, I want to thank Lowri Daniels and Alice Milliken for helping me fact-check the manuscript.

I am grateful to all the amazing people surrounding me and my colleagues at NYU who took time out of their busy schedules to advise me and help me with this book. I have truly found a new intellectual home at the university and in the journalism department and I am grateful every day to work with such wonderful colleagues.

I also want to thank Mona Sloane for her unwavering support of this project and all of my other work.

I thank my friends and colleagues Rachel Swarns, Meredith Broussard, Sally Herships, Sayash Kapoor, Jennifer Strong, Mickey Maudlin, and Emma Cillekens for their support of my work. And my long-term mentors Jim Mintz and Sheila Coronel, who always have helpful advice. I also want to thank all the editors I have worked with at different publications. Your input and critical feedback were incredibly important!

I owe a lot of gratitude to my partner, Matt. He kept telling me how important this book is and made sure I had all the extra time that I needed to write it. Thank you!

I am also grateful for the fellowships and grants and invaluable support many organizations so generously provided: Deborah Blum and Ashley Smart at the MIT Knight Science Journalism Fellowship; Molly Rogers with the NYU Center for the Humanities; and Vilas Dhar and Meaghan English at the Patrick J. McGovern Foundation for throwing their support behind my work. Thank you to the Journalism Venture Capital Fund at NYU, which was started by Stephen Solomon—a truly generous colleague.

I also want to thank Marina Walker Guevara, Boyoung Lim, their whole team, and the other fellows at the Pulitzer Center AI Accountability Network, who all encouraged me to keep going and helped me every step of the way.

I could not have done this work without all of your support!

And thanks to everyone else along the way who cheered me on and helped me in many ways!

NOTES

Prologue

1. Drew Harwell, "A Face-Scanning Algorithm Increasingly Decides Whether You Deserve the Job," *Washington Post*, November 6, 2019, https://www.washingtonpost.com/technology/2019/10/22/ai-hiring-face-scanning-algorithm-increasingly-decides-whether-you-deserve-job/.

2. James Hu, "99 Percent of Fortune 500 Companies Use Applicant Tracking Systems," *Jobscan*, 2019, https://www.jobscan.co/blog/99-percent-fortune-500-ats/.

3. HireVue, "HireVue Milestone and Major Company Growth," press release, November 2, 2022, https://www.hirevue.com/press-release/hirevue-supercharged-for-growth-hitting-33-million-interviews-milestone-and-appointing-chief-growth-officer-patrick-morrissey-chief-marketing-officer-amanda-hahn.

4. Eric Rosenbaum, "IBM Artificial Intelligence Can Predict with 95 Percent Accuracy Which Workers Are About to Quit Their Jobs," *CNBC*, April 3, 2019, https://www.cnbc.com/2019/04/03/ibm-ai-can-predict-with-95-percent-accuracy-which-employees-will-quit.html;

Ina Fried, "Google Received 3.3 Million Job Applications in 2019," *Axios*, January 9, 2020, https://www.axios.com/2020/01/09/google-2019-applications-backlash;

Max Nisen, "Here's Why You Only Have a 0.2 Percent Chance of Getting Hired at Google," *Quartz*, October 22, 2014, https://qz.com/285001/heres-why-you-only-have-a-0-2-chance-of-getting-hired-at-google.

5. Bernard Marr, "The Amazing Ways How Unilever Uses Artificial Intelligence to Recruit and Train Thousands of Employees," *Forbes*, December 14, 2018, https://www.forbes.com/sites/bernardmarr/2018/12/14/the-amazing-ways-how-unilever-uses-artificial-intelligence-to-recruit-train-thousands-of-employees/.

6. Steven Greenberg, "What Delta Wants in Job Seekers: New Skills," CBS News, May 30, 2018, https://www.cbsnews.com/news/what-delta-wants-in-job-seekers-new-skills/.

7. Hugh Son, "There's No Shortage of Aspiring Goldman Bankers as Record 236,000 Students Apply for Internships," *CNBC*, April 5, 2022, https://www.cnbc.com/2022/04/05/goldman-says-record-236000-students-apply-for-internships.html.

8.	Josh Bersin, "Google for Jobs: Disrupting the $200 Billion Recruiting Market?" *Josh Bersin* (blog), May 26, 2017, https://joshbersin.com/2017/05/google-jobs-disrupting -the-recruiting-market/.

9.	IBISWorld, "Global HR & Recruitment Services Industry—Market Research Report," updated January 3, 2023, https://www.ibisworld.com/global/market-research -reports/global-hr-recruitment-services-industry/.

10.	Rosenbaum, "IBM Artificial Intelligence Can Predict," https://www.cnbc.com /2019/04/03/ibm-ai-can-predict-with-95-percent-accuracy-which-employees-will-quit.html.

11.	Bart Ziegler, "Should Companies Track Workers with Monitoring Technology?" *Wall Street Journal*, August 20, 2022, https://www.wsj.com/articles/compa nies-track-workers-technology-11660935634.

12.	Jodi Kantor and Arya Sundaram, "The Rise of the Worker Productivity Score," *New York Times*, August 14, 2022, https://www.nytimes.com/interac tive/2022/08/14/business/worker-productivity-tracking.html.

13	Nina Reece, "Workers say no to increased surveillance since COVID-19," TUC, March 1, 2022, https://www.tuc.org.uk/blogs/ workers-say-no-increased-surveillance-covid-19.

14.	US Government Accountability Office, *Women in the Workforce: The Gender Pay Gap Is Greater for Certain Racial and Ethnic Groups and Varies by Education Level*, report no. GAO-23-106041 (Washington, DC: US GAO, December 15, 2022), https://www.gao.gov/products/gao-23-106041;

Bureau of Labor Statistics, "19.1 Percent of People with a Disability Were Employed in 2021," March 1, 2022, https://www.bls.gov/opub/ted/2022/19-1-percent-of-people-with-a-disability-were-employed-in-2021.htm.

15.	Joseph Fuller, Manjari Raman, Eva Sage-Gavin, and Kristen Hines, *Hidden Workers: Untapped Talent* (Cambridge, MA: Harvard Business School, September 3, 2021), https://www.hbs.edu/managing-the-future-of-work/Documents/research /hiddenworkers09032021.pdf.

16.	Leadership IQ, "Leadership IQ Study: Why New Hires Fail," press release, September 5, 2005, https://web.archive.org/web/20230510013958/https://www.prweb .com/releases/2005/09/prweb287275.htm.

Chapter 1

1.	Roy Maurer, "Labor Shortages Forecast to Persist for Years," SHRM.org, January 23, 2023, https://www.shrm.org/resourcesandtools/hr-topics/talent-acquisition /pages/labor-shortages-forecast-to-persist-2023.aspx.

2.	Jeffrey Dastin, "Amazon Scraps Secret AI Recruiting Tool That Showed Bias Against Women," Reuters, October 10, 2018, https://www.reuters.com/article /us-amazon-com-jobs-automation-insight/amazon-scraps-secret-ai-recruiting-tool -that-showed-bias-against-women-idUSKCN1MK08G.

3.   Hilke Schellmann, "Finding It Hard to Get a New Job? Robot Recruiters Might Be to Blame," *The Guardian*, May 11, 2022, https://www.theguardian.com /us-news/2022/may/11/artitifical-intelligence-job-applications-screen-robot-re cruiters.

4.   The Ladders, *Eye-Tracking Study* (New York: The Ladders, 2018), https://www .theladders.com/static/images/basicSite/pdfs/TheLadders-EyeTracking-StudyC2.pdf.

5.   Equal Employment Opportunity Commission (EEOC), "Part 1607— Uniform Guidelines on Employee Selection Procedures (1978)," *CFR*, Title 29: Labor, July 1, 2017, https://www.govinfo.gov/content/pkg/CFR-2017-title29-vol4/xml/CFR -2017-title29-vol4-part1607.xml.

6.   EEOC, "Prohibited Employment Policies/Practices," https://www.eeoc.gov /prohibited-employment-policiespractices.

7.   EEOC, "Questions and Answers to Clarify and Provide a Common Interpretation of the Uniform Guidelines on Employee Selection Procedures," March 1, 1979, https://www.eeoc.gov/laws/guidance/questions-and-answers-clarify-and-provide -common-interpretation-uniform-guidelines.

8.   EEOC, "EEOC Sues iTutorGroup for Age Discrimination," May 5, 2022, https://www.eeoc.gov/newsroom/eeoc-sues-itutorgroup-age-discrimination.

9.   Daniel Wiessner, "Tutoring Firm Settles US Agency's First Bias Lawsuit Involving AI Software," Reuters, August 10, 2023, https://www.reuters.com/legal /tutoring-firm-settles-us-agencys-first-bias-lawsuit-involving-ai-software-2023 -08-10.

10.   EEOC, "DHI Group, Inc. Conciliates EEOC National Origin Discrimination Finding," March 20, 2023, https://www.eeoc.gov/newsroom/dhi-group-inc-conciliates -eeoc-national-origin-discrimination-finding.

11.   Tara Sophia Mohr, "Why Women Don't Apply for Jobs Unless They're 100 Percent Qualified," *Harvard Business Review*, August 2014, https://hbr.org/2014/08 /why-women-dont-apply-for-jobs-unless-theyre-100-qualified.

12.   Sheridan Wall and Hilke Schellmann, "LinkedIn's Job-Matching AI Was Biased. The Company's Solution? More AI," *MIT Technology Review*, June 23, 2021, https://www.technologyreview.com/2021/06/23/1026825/linkedin-ai-bias-zipre cruiter-monster-artificial-intelligence/.

13.   Basileal Imana, Aleksandra Korolova, and John Heidemann, "Auditing for Discrimination in Algorithms Delivering Job Ads," *WWW '21 Proceedings of the Web Conference 2021*, April 2021, 3767–3778, https://doi.org/10.1145/3442381.3450077.

14.   Joseph Fuller, Manjari Raman, Eva Sage-Gavin, and Kristen Hines, *Hidden Workers: Untapped Talent* (Cambridge, MA: Harvard Business School, September 3, 2021), 3, https://www.hbs.edu/managing-the-future-of-work/Documents/research /hiddenworkers09032021.pdf.

15.   Fuller et al., *Hidden Workers*, 3.

16.   Fuller et al., *Hidden Workers*, 22.

17.   Misty L. Heggeness, Jason Fields, Yazmin A. García Trejo, and Anthony Schulzetenberg, "Tracking Job Losses for Mothers of School-Age Children During a Health Crisis," US Census Bureau, March 3, 2021, https://www.census.gov/library /stories/2021/03/moms-work-and-the-pandemic.html.

18.   Fuller et al., *Hidden Workers*, 39.

19.   Fuller et al., *Hidden Workers*, 38.

Chapter 2

1.   Nicholas Confessore and Danny Hakim, "Data Firm Says 'Secret Sauce' Aided Trump; Many Scoff," *New York Times*, March 6, 2017, https://www.nytimes .com/2017/03/06/us/politics/cambridge-analytica.html.

2.   Ben Frasier, "Rethinking Reskilling: Investing in Critical Skills vs. Critical Roles," *The SHRM Blog*, SHRM, May 10, 2022, https://blog.shrm.org/blog /rethinking-reskilling-investing-in-critical-skills-vs-critical-roles.

3.   Laura LaBerge, Clayton O'Toole, Jeremy Schneider, and Kate Smaje, "How COVID-19 Has Pushed Companies over the Technology Tipping Point—and Transformed Business Forever," McKinsey & Company, October 5, 2020, https://www .mckinsey.com/capabilities/strategy-and-corporate-finance/our-insights/how -covid-19-has-pushed-companies-over-the-technology-tipping-point-and-trans formed-business-forever.

4.   Emma Goldberg, "The $2 Billion Question of Who You Are at Work," *New York Times*, March 5, 2023, https://www.nytimes.com/2023/03/05/business /remote-work-personality-tests.html;

Eben Harrell, "A Brief History of Personality Tests," *Harvard Business Review*, March 2017, https://hbr.org/2017/03/a-brief-history-of-personality-tests.html.

5.   Emma Goldberg, "Personality Tests Are the Astrology of the Office," *New York Times*, September 17, 2019, https://www.nytimes.com/2019/09/17/style /personality-tests-office.html.

6.   Goldberg, "Personality Tests Are the Astrology of the Office," https://www .nytimes.com/2019/09/17/style/personality-tests-office.html.

7.   Rebecca Heilweil, "Beware of These Futuristic Background Checks," *Vox*, May 11, 2020, https://www.vox.com/recode/2020/5/11/21166291/artificial-intelligence -ai-background-check-checkr-fama.

8.   Kathryn Vasel, "This Company Uses AI to Flag Racist and Sexist Comments from Potential Hires," *CNN Business*, April 12, 2019, https://www.cnn.com/2019 /04/12/success/fama-prescreen-employment/index.html.

9.   Vasel, "This Company Uses AI," https://www.cnn.com/2019/04/12/success /fama-prescreen-employment/index.html.

10.   Ben Mones, "Protecting Your Brand with Social Media Screening," webinar, HireRight, November 12, 2020, https://www.hireright.com/resources/protecting-your -brand-with-social-media-screening.

11. Drew Harwell, "Wanted: The 'Perfect Babysitter.' Must Pass AI Scan for Respect and Attitude," *Washington Post*, November 16, 2018, https://www.washingtonpost.com/technology/2018/11/16/wanted-perfect-babysitter-must-pass-ai-scan-respect-attitude/.

12. Kaveh Waddell, "'Extreme Vetting' for Hiring," *Axios*, November 2, 2018, https://www.axios.com/2018/11/02/artificial-intelligence-ai-hiring.

13. Heilweil, "Beware of These Futuristic Background Checks," https://www.vox.com/recode/2020/5/11/21166291artificial-intelligence-ai-background-check-checkr-fama.

14. Lyft, "Driver and Passenger Ratings," https://help.lyft.com/hc/e/all/articles/115013079948-Driver-and-passenger-ratings.

15. Lyft, "Driver and Passenger Ratings," https://help.lyft.com/hc/e/all/articles/115013079948-Driver-and-passenger-ratings.

16. Dylan Curran, "Are You Ready? Here Is All the Data Facebook and Google Have on You," *The Guardian*, March 30, 2018, https://www.theguardian.com/commentisfree/2018/mar/28/all-the-data-facebook-google-has-on-you-privacy.

17. Matt Burgess, "All the Data Google's Apps Collect About You and How to Stop It," *Wired*, May 4, 2021, https://www.wired.co.uk/article/google-app-gmail-chrome-data; Brian Resnick, "Cambridge Analytica's 'Psychographic Microtargeting': What's Bullshit and What's Legit," *Vox*, March 23, 2018, https://www.vox.com/science-and-health/2018/3/23/17152564/cambridge-analytica-psychographic-microtargeting-what.

18. Alex Hern, "Cambridge Analytica Did Work for Leave.EU, Emails Confirm," *The Guardian*, July 30, 2019, https://www.theguardian.com/uk-news/2019/jul/30/cambridge-analytica-did-work-for-leave-eu-emails-confirm.

19. Patrick Svitek and Haley Samsel, "Ted Cruz Says Cambridge Analytica Told His Presidential Campaign Its Data Use Was Legal," *Texas Tribune*, March 20, 2018, https://www.texastribune.org/2018/03/20/ted-cruz-campaign-cambridge-analytica; Billy House, "Cambridge Analytica's Promotion of Discontent Tied to Bannon," *Bloomberg*, April 25, 2018, https://www.bloomberg.com/news/articles/2018-04-25/cambridge-analytica-s-promotion-of-discontent-tied-to-bannon#xj4y7vzkg.

20. Harry Davies, "Ted Cruz Using Firm That Harvested Data on Millions of Unwitting Facebook Users," *The Guardian*, December 11, 2015, https://www.theguardian.com/us-news/2015/dec/11/senator-ted-cruz-president-campaign-facebook-user-data.

21. Carole Cadwalladr, "'I Made Steve Bannon's Psychological Warfare Tool': Meet the Data War Whistleblower," *The Guardian*, March 28, 2018, https://www.theguardian.com/news/2018/mar/17/data-war-whistleblower-christopher-wylie-faceook-nix-bannon-trump.

22. Erin Brodwin, "Here's the Personality Test Cambridge Analytica Had Facebook Users Take," *Insider*, March 19, 2018, https://www.businessinsider.com/facebook-personality-test-cambridge-analytica-data-trump-election-2018-3.

23. Michal Kosinski, David Stillwell, and Thore Graepel, "Private Traits and Attributes Are Predictable from Digital Records of Human Behavior," *Proceedings of the National Academy of Sciences of the United States of America* 110, no. 15 (April 2013): 5802–5805, https://doi.org/10.1073/pnas.1218772110.

24. Sandra Matz, Michal Kosinski, Gideon Nave, and David Stillwell, "Psychological Targeting as an Effective Approach to Digital Mass Persuasion," *Proceedings of the National Academy of Sciences of the United States of America* 114, no. 48 (November 2017): 12714–12719, https://doi.org/10.1073/pnas.1710966114.

25. Kosinski, Stillwell, and Graepel, "Private Traits and Attributes Are Predictable," 5802–5805.

26. Resnick, "Cambridge Analytica's 'Psychographic Microtargeting,'" https://www.vox.com/science-and-health/2018/3/23/17152564/cambridge-analytica-psychographic-microtargeting-what.

27. Paul Robinette, Wenchen Li, Robert Allen, Ayanna Howard, and Alan Wagner, "Overtrust of Robots in Emergency Evacuation Scenarios," *2016 11th ACM/IEEE International Conference on Human-Robot Interaction* (HRI), Christchurch, New Zealand, March 2016, 101–108, https://doi.org/10.1109/HRI.2016.7451740.

28. Kashmir Hill, "Wrongfully Accused by an Algorithm," *New York Times*, June 24, 2020, https://www.nytimes.com/2020/06/24/technology/facial-recognition-arrest.html.

29. Alene K. Rhea, Kelsey Markey, Lauren D'Arinzo, Hilke Schellmann, Mona Sloane, Paul Squires, Falaah Arif Khan, and Julia Stoyanovich, "An External Stability Audit Framework to Test the Validity of Personality Prediction in AI Hiring," April 2022, https://arxiv.org/pdf/2201.09151.pdf.

30. Olivia Atherton, Emily Grijalva, Brent Roberts, and Richard Robins, "Stability and Change in Personality Traits and Major Life Goals from College to Midlife," *Personality and Social Psychology Bulletin* 47, no. 5 (August 2020): 841–858, https://doi.org/10.1177/0146167220949362.

Chapter 3

1. Harver, "Harver Acquires Pymetrics, Further Enhancing Talent Decision Capabilities Across the Employee Lifecycle," press release, August 11, 2022, https://harver.com/press/harver-acquires-pymetrics/.

2. Emma Goldberg, "The $2 Billion Question of Who You Are at Work," *New York Times*, March 5, 2023, https://www.nytimes.com/2023/03/05/business/remote-work-personality-tests.html.

3. Sonia Malik, "Skills Transformation for the 2021 Workplace," *IBM Learning Blog*, IBM, December 7, 2020, https://www.ibm.com/blogs/ibm-training/skills-transformation-2021-workplace/.

4. Katharina Salmen and Marion Festing, "Employee Agility: What It Entails and How to Nurture It," ESCP Business School, November 22, 2022, https://escp.eu/news/employee-agility-what-it-entails-and-how-nurture-it.

5. Joan Williams, Denise Loyd, Mikayla Boginsky, and Frances Armas-Edwards, "How One Company Worked to Root Out Bias from Performance Reviews," *Harvard Business Review*, April 21, 2021, https://hbr.org/2021/04/how-one-company-worked-to-root-out-bias-from-performance-reviews.

6. EEOC, "Pre-Employment Inquiries and Medical Questions & Examinations," https://www.eeoc.gov/pre-employment-inquiries-and-medical-questions-examinations.

7. Recce Akthar, Franziska Leutner, and Tomas Chamorro-Premuzic, *The Future of Recruitment: Using the New Science of Talent Analytics to Get Your Hiring Right* (Bingley, UK: Emerald Publishing, 2022), 131.

8. Felix Wu, Evan Mulfinger, Leo Alexander III, Andrea Sinclair, Rodney McCloy, and Frederick Oswald, "Individual Differences at Play: An Investigation into Measuring Big Five Personality Facets with Game-Based Assessments," *International Journal of Selection and Assessment*, December 2021, https://doi.org/10.1111/ijsa.12360.

9. Information Commissioner's Office (ICO), "What Does the UK GDPR Say About Automated Decision-Making and Profiling?" https://ico.org.uk/for-organisations/uk-gdpr-guidance-and-resources/individual-rights/automated-decision-making-and-profiling/what-does-the-uk-gdpr-say-about-automated-decision-making-and-profiling/.

10. H. Beau Beaz III, "Personality Tests in Employment Selection: Use with Caution," *Cornell HR Review*, 2012, https://ecommons.cornell.edu/bitstream/handle/1813/72937/1_26_13_Personality_Tests_in_Employment_Selection.pdf.

Chapter 4

1. HireVue, "HireVue Milestone and Major Company Growth," press release, November 2, 2022, https://www.hirevue.com/press-release/hirevue-supercharged-for-growth-hitting-33-million-interviews-milestone-and-appointing-chief-growth-officer-patrick-morrissey-chief-marketing-officer-amanda-hahn;

Lindsey Zuloaga (chief data scientist, HireVue), in discussion with author, June 14, 2023.

2. Retorio, "The Science Behind Retorio's Behavioral Analytics AI," https://www.retorio.com/en/scienceai.

3. Jason Bellini and Hilke Schellmann, "Artificial Intelligence: The Robots Are Now Hiring," *Wall Street Journal*, September 20, 2018, https://www.wsj.com/articles/artificial-intelligence-the-robots-are-now-hiring-moving-upstream-1537435820.

4. Bellini and Schellmann, "Artificial Intelligence," https://www.wsj.com/articles/artificial-intelligence-the-robots-are-now-hiring-moving-upstream-1537435820.

5. Duke University, "Typical Questions from HireVue Interviews," https://econ.duke.edu/sites/econ.duke.edu/files/file-attachments/Typical%20Questions%20from%20HireVue%20Interviews.pdf.

6.   Lucia Mutikani, "US Labor Market Softens as Job Openings Drop, Layoffs at Highest Level in over Two Years," Reuters, May 2, 2023, https://www.reuters.com/markets/us/us-job-openings-post-third-straight-monthly-decline-march-2023-05-02/.

7.   HireVue, "HireVue Milestone and Major Company Growth," https://www.hirevue.com/press-release/hirevue-supercharged-for-growth-hitting-33-million-interviews-milestone-and-appointing-chief-growth-officer-patrick-morrissey-chief-marketing-officer-amanda-hahn.

8.   Bellini and Schellmann, "Artificial Intelligence : The Robots Are Now Hiring," https://www.wsj.com/articles/artificial-intelligence-the-robots-are-now-hiring-moving-upstream-1537435820.

9.   Elisa Harlan and Oliver Schnuck, "Objective or Biased: On the Questionable Use of Artificial Intelligence for Job Applications," *BR24*, February 16, 2021, https://interaktiv.br.de/ki-bewerbung/en.

10.   Federal Bureau of Investigation, "Deepfakes and Stolen PII Utilized to Apply for Remote Work Positions," public service announcement, June 28, 2022, https://www.ic3.gov/Media/Y2022/PSA220628.

Chapter 5

1.   Blaise Agüera y Arcas, Margaret Mitchell, and Alexander Todorov, "Physiognomy's New Clothes," *Medium*, May 6, 2017, https://medium.com/@blaisea/physiognomys-new-clothes-f2d4b59fdd6a.

2.   Agüera y Arcas et al., "Physiognomy's New Clothes," https://medium.com/@blaisea/physiognomys-new-clothes-f2d4b59fdd6a.

3.   Luke Stark and Jevan Hutson, "Physiognomic Artificial Intelligence," *Fordham Intellectual Property, Media & Entertainment Law Journal* 32, no. 4 (Summer 2022): 922–978.

4.   Stark and Hutson, "Physiognomic Artificial Intelligence," 922–978.

5.   Harrisburg University, "HU Facial Recognition Software Predicts Criminality," May 5, 2020, https://web.archive.org/web/20200506013352/harrisburgu.edu/hu-facial-recognition-software-identifies-potential-criminals/.

6.   Aaron Holmes, "Researchers Said Their 'Unbiased' Facial Recognition Could Identify Potential Future Criminals—Then Deleted the Announcement After Backlash," *Business Insider*, May 7, 2020, https://www.businessinsider.com/harrisburg-university-lab-facial-recognition-identify-future-criminals-2020-5.

7.   Yilun Wang and Michal Kosinski, "Deep Neural Networks Are More Accurate Than Humans at Detecting Sexual Orientation from Facial Images," *Journal of Personality and Social Psychology* 114, no. 2 (February 2018): 246–257, https://doi.org/10.1037/pspa0000098.

8.   Agüera y Arcas et al., "Physiognomy's New Clothes," https://medium.com/@blaisea/physiognomys-new-clothes-f2d4b59fdd6a.

9. Agüera y Arcas et al., "Physiognomy's New Clothes," https://medium.com /@blaisea/physiognomys-new-clothes-f2d4b59fdd6a.

10. Agüera y Arcas et al., "Physiognomy's New Clothes," https://medium.com /@blaisea/physiognomys-new-clothes-f2d4b59fdd6a.

11. Jackie Hyams, "Can Handwriting Get You the Job?" *Evening Standard*, June 8, 2004.

12. Catherine Quinn, "Handwritten Evidence," *The Guardian*, April, 15, 2009, https://www.theguardian.com/careers/handwriting-analysis.

13. "Be Careful Not to Write Yourself Off: GRAPHOLOGY: France Has Long Endorsed the Use of Handwriting Analysis in Recruitment. But the Practice Has Its Critics," *Financial Times*, August 15, 2001.

14. Abby Ellin, "What Your Handwriting Says About Your Career," *New York Times*, July 18, 2004, https://www.nytimes.com/2004/07/18/jobs/what-your-hand writing-says-about-your-career.html;

Barry Beyerstein and Dale F. Beyerstein, eds., *The Write Stuff: Evaluations of Graphology—the Study of Handwriting Analysis* (Buffalo, NY: Prometheus Books, 1992).

15. Jonathan Duffy and Giles Wilson, "Writing Wrongs," *BBC News*, February 1, 2005, http://news.bbc.co.uk/2/hi/uk_news/magazine/4223445.stm.

16. Hugh Schofield, "A French Love Affair . . . with Graphology," *BBC News*, April 29, 2013, https://www.bbc.com/news/magazine-22198554.

17. Mari Yamaguchi, "Hey Baby, What's Your Blood Type?" Associated Press, February 1, 2009.

Chapter 6

1. Centers for Disease Control and Prevention, "Disability Impacts All of Us," last reviewed May 15, 2023, https://www.cdc.gov/ncbddd/disabilityandhealth/info graphic-disability-impacts-all.html.

2 Esme Kirk-Wade, "UK disability statistics: Prevalence and life experiences," House of Commons Library, August 23, 2023, https://commonslibrary.parliament. uk/research-briefings/cbp-9602.

3. Maria Town, "Initiative on AI and Algorithmic Fairness: Disability-Focused Listening Session," TheEEOC, YouTube video, at 14:20 of 45:54, February 28, 2022, https://www.youtube.com/watch?v=LlqZCxKB05s.

4. Town, "Initiative on AI and Algorithmic Fairness," https://www.youtube .com/watch?v=LlqZCxKB05s.

5. EEOC, "Small Employers and Reasonable Accommodation," https://www .eeoc.gov/publications/small-employers-and-reasonable-accommodation.

6. Alexandra Reeve Givens, Hilke Schellmann, and Julia Stoyanovich, "We Need Laws to Take On Racism and Sexism in Hiring Technology," *New York Times*, March 17, 2021, https://www.nytimes.com/2021/03/17/opinion/ai-employment-bias -nyc.html.

7. Karen Hao, "Can You Make an AI That Isn't Ableist? IBM Researcher Shari Trewin on Why Bias Against Disability Is Much Harder to Squash Than Discrim-

ination Based on Gender or Race," *MIT Technology Review*, November 28, 2018, https://www.technologyreview.com/2018/11/28/1797/can-you-make-an-ai-that-isnt -ableist/.

8. Hao, "Can You Make an AI That Isn't Ableist?" https://www.technologyreview .com/2018/11/28/1797/can-you-make-an-ai-that-isnt-ableist/.

9. Roland Behm, "Initiative on AI and Algorithmic Fairness: Disability-Focused Listening Session," TheEEOC, YouTube video, at 22:49 of 45:54, February 28, 2022, https://www.youtube.com/watch?v=LlqZCxKB05s.

10. Strategic Organizing Center, *The Injury Machine: How Amazon's Production System Hurts Workers* (Washington, DC: Strategic Organizing Center, April 2022), 1, https://thesoc.org/wp-content/uploads/2022/04/The-Injury-Machine_How -Amazons-Production-System-Hurts-Workers.pdf.

11. Ifeoma Ajunwa, "Beware of Automated Hiring," *New York Times*, October 8, 2019, https://www.nytimes.com/2019/10/08/opinion/ai-hiring-discrimination.html.

12. Sheridan Wall and Hilke Schellmann, "Disability Rights Advocates Are Worried About Discrimination in AI Hiring Tools," *MIT Technology Review*, July 21, 2021, https://www.technologyreview.com/2021/07/21/1029860/disability-rights -employment-discrimination-ai-hiring/.

13. Senator Michael F. Bennet to Janet Dhillon, Chair of the Equal Employment Opportunity Commission, December 8, 2020, https://www.bennet.senate.gov/public /_cache/files/0/a/0a439d4b-e373-4451-84ed-ba333ce6d1dd/672D2E4304D63A04C C3465C3C8BF1D21.letter-to-chair-dhillon.pdf.

14. Wall and Schellmann, "Disability Rights Advocates Are Worried," https://www .technologyreview.com/2021/07/21/1029860/disability-rights-employment-discrimination -ai-hiring/.

15. Brett A. Brenner, Associate Director, Office of Communications and Legislative Affairs, to Michael F. Bennet, January 15, 2021, via *MIT Technology Review*, https://wp.technologyreview.com/wp-content/uploads/2021/07/EEOC-Response -Letter-January-2021.pdf.

16. Wall and Schellmann, "Disability Rights Advocates Are Worried," https://www .technologyreview.com/2021/07/21/1029860/disability-rights-employment-discrimina tion-ai-hiring/.

17. Aaron Rieke, Urmila Janardan, Mingwei Hsu, and Natasha Duarte, "Analyzing the Hiring Technologies of Large Hourly Employers," *Upturn*, July 6, 2021, 39, https://www.upturn.org/work/essential-work/.

18. EEOC, "The Americans with Disabilities Act and the Use of Software, Algorithms, and Artificial Intelligence to Assess Job Applicants and Employees," May 12, 2022, https://www.eeoc.gov/laws/guidance/americans-disabilities-act-and-use-software -algorithms-and-artificial-intelligence.

19. Khari Johnson, "Feds Warn Employers Against Discriminatory Hiring Algorithms," *Wired*, May 16, 2022, https://www.wired.com/story/ai-hiring-bias-doj -eecc-guidance/.

20. Hilke Schellmann, "Auditors Are Testing Hiring Algorithms for Bias, but There's No Easy Fix," *MIT Technology Review*, February 11, 2021, https://www.technologyreview.com/2021/02/11/1017955/auditors-testing-ai-hiring-algorithms-bias-big-questions-remain/.

21. HireVue, "HireVue Leads the Industry with Commitment to Transparent and Ethical Use of AI in Hiring," press release, January 12, 2021, https://www.hirevue.com/press-release/hirevue-leads-the-industry-with-commitment-to-transparent-and-ethical-use-of-ai-in-hiring.

22. Christo Wilson, A. Ghosh, Shan Jiang, A. Mislove, Lewis Baker, Janelle Szary, Kelly Trindel, and Frida Polli, "Building and Auditing Fair Algorithms: A Case Study in Candidate Screening," *Proceedings of the 2021 ACM Conference on Fairness, Accountability, and Transparency*, March 2021, https://doi.org/10.1145/3442188.3445928.

23. Meg Young, Michael Katell, and P. M. Krafft, "Confronting Power and Corporate Capture at the FAccT Conference," *Proceedings of the 2022 ACM Conference on Fairness, Accountability, and Transparency*, June 20, 2022, 1375–1386, https://doi.org/10.1145/3531146.3533194.

24. Joy Buolamwini and Timnit Gebru, "Gender Shades: Intersectional Accuracy Disparities in Commercial Gender Classification," *Proceedings of Machine Learning Research*, January 15, 2018, 81.

25. EEOC, "Select Issues: Assessing Adverse Impact in Software, Algorithms, and Artificial Intelligence Used in Employment Selection Procedures Under Title VII of the Civil Rights Act of 1964," https://www.eeoc.gov/select-issues-assessing-adverse-impact-software-algorithms-and-artificial-intelligence-used.

Chapter 7

1. Bureau of Labor Statistics, "More Job Openings Than Unemployed People Since May 2021," March 10, 2023, https://www.bls.gov/opub/ted/2023/more-job-openings-than-unemployed-people-since-may-2021.htm.

2. Manish Singh, "AI Startup Eightfold Valued at $2.1B in SoftBank-Led $220M Funding," *TechCrunch*, June 10, 2021, https://techcrunch.com/2021/06/10/ai-startup-eightfold-valued-at-2-1b-in-softbank-led-220m-funding/.

3. World Economic Forum, "The Future of Jobs Report 2020," October 20, 2020, https://www.weforum.org/reports/the-future-of-jobs-report-2020/in-full/infographics-e4e69e4de7.

4. Niket Nishant, "Canadian HR Tech Firm Visier Becomes Unicorn After Goldman-Led Investment," Reuters, June 29, 2021, https://www.reuters.com/technology/canadian-hr-tech-firm-visier-becomes-unicorn-after-goldman-led-investment-2021-06-29/.

5. Dave Zielinski, "The Dangers of Using Predictive Analytics to Gauge Employee Flight Risk," SHRM.org, March 12, 2020, https://www.shrm.org/resourcesandtools/hr-topics/technology/pages/dangers-using-predictive-analytics-employee-flight-risk.aspx.

6. Zielinski, "The Dangers of Using Predictive Analytics," https://www.shrm.org/resourcesandtools/hr-topics/technology/pages/dangers-using-predictive-analytics-employee-flight-risk.aspx.

Chapter 8
1. Jodi Kantor and Arya Sundaram, "The Rise of the Worker Productivity Score," *New York Times*, August 14, 2022, https://www.nytimes.com/interactive/2022/08/14/business/worker-productivity-tracking.html.
2. Adam Satariano "How My Boss Monitors Me While I Work from Home," *New York Times*, May 6, 2020, https://www.nytimes.com/2020/05/06/technology/employee-monitoring-work-from-home-virus.html.
3. "Hybrid Work Is Just Work. Are We Doing It Wrong?" special report, Microsoft Work Trend Index, September 22, 2022, https://www.microsoft.com/en-us/worklab/work-trend-index/hybrid-work-is-just-work.
4. Danielle Abril and Drew Harwell, "Keystroke Tracking, Screenshots, and Facial Recognition: The Boss May Be Watching Long After the Pandemic Ends," *Washington Post*, September 24, 2021, https://www.washingtonpost.com/technology/2021/09/24/remote-work-from-home-surveillance.
5. Jared Spataro, "Microsoft: 'Using Technology to Spy on People at Work Is Not the Answer,'" *Fortune*, September 22, 2022, https://fortune.com/2022/09/22/microsoft-technology-surveillance-employee-work-jared-spataro/.
6. Microsoft, "Overview of Microsoft Graph Data Connect," September 7, 2022, https://learn.microsoft.com/en-us/graph/data-connect-concept-overview.
7. Zoom, "Attendee Attention Tracking," last updated December 20, 2022, https://support.zoom.us/hc/en-us/articles/115000538083-Attendee-attention-tracking.
8. Alex Hern, "Microsoft Productivity Score Feature Criticised as Workplace Surveillance," *The Guardian*, November 26, 2020, https://www.theguardian.com/technology/2020/nov/26/microsoft-productivity-score-feature-criticised-workplace-surveillance.
9. Jared Spataro, "Our Commitment to Privacy in Microsoft Productivity Score," *Microsoft 365 Blog*, December 1, 2020, https://www.microsoft.com/en-us/microsoft-365/blog/2020/12/01/our-commitment-to-privacy-in-microsoft-productivity-score/.
10. Microsoft Mechanics, "Manage Data Risks from Employee Insiders with Microsoft Purview," YouTube video, 14:23, April 19, 2022, https://youtu.be/Ynkfu8OF0wQ?si=fTOV9hizRXGItl7C.
11. Privacy International, "WFH—Watched from Home: Office 365 and Workplace Surveillance Creep," June 15, 2022, https://privacyinternational.org/long-read/4909/wfh-watched-home-office-365-and-workplace-surveillance-creep.
12. Valerie Strauss, "Houston Teachers Sue over Controversial Teacher Evaluation Method," *Washington Post*, April 30, 2014, https://www.washingtonpost.com/news/answer-sheet/wp/2014/04/30/houston-teachers-sue-over-controversial-teacher-evaluation-method/.

13.   Jennifer Abruzzo, "Electronic Monitoring and Algorithmic Management of Employees Interfering with the Exercise of Section 7 Rights," National Labor Relations Board, Memorandum GC 23-02, October 31, 2022, https://apps.nlrb.gov/link /document.aspx/09031d45838de7e0.

Chapter 9

1.   Christopher Rowland, "With Fitness Trackers in the Workplace, Bosses Can Monitor Your Every Step—and Possibly More," *Washington Post*, February 16, 2019, https://www.washingtonpost.com/business/economy/with-fitness-trackers-in-the -workplace-bosses-can-monitor-your-every-step--and-possibly-more/2019/02 /15/75ee0848-2a45-11e9-b011-d8500644dc98_story.html.

2.   Rowland, "With Fitness Trackers in the Workplace," https://www.washington post.com/business/economy/with-fitness-trackers-in-the-workplace-bosses-can-mon itor-your-every-step—and-possibly-more/2019/02/15/75ee0848-2a45-11e9-b011 -d8500644dc98_story.html.

3.   Glassdoor, "Could Not Find a better Company If I Tried," Regal Plastic Supply reviews, accessed July 17, 2023, https://www.glassdoor.com/Reviews/Regal-Plastic -Supply-Reviews-E376248.htm.

4.   Thorin Klosowski, "The State of Consumer Data Privacy Laws in the US (and Why It Matters)," *New York Times*, September 6, 2021, https://www.nytimes .com/wirecutter/blog/state-of-privacy-laws-in-us/.

5.   Rachel Emma Silverman, "Bosses Tap Outside Firms to Predict Which Workers Might Get Sick," *Wall Street Journal*, February 17, 2016, https://www .wsj.com/articles/bosses-harness-big-data-to-predict-which-workers-might-get -sick-1455664940.

6.   Alisha Haridasani Gupta and Ruchika Tulshyan, "'You're the Problem': When They Spoke Up About Misconduct, They Were Offered Mental Health Services," *New York Times*, July 28, 2021, https://www.nytimes.com/2021/07/28/us/goo gle-workplace-complaints-counseling.html.

7.   Matthew Boyle, "Bank of America-Backed Scorecard Lets Companies Assess Workplace Mental Health," *Bloomberg*, October 3, 2022, https://www.bloomberg .com/news/articles/2022-10-03/bank-of-america-axa-back-new-workplace-mental -health-scorecard.

8.   Eleanor Hawkins, "New Tool for Assessing Mental Health in the Workplace," *Axios*, May 4, 2023, https://www.axios.com/2023/05/04/assessing-mental-health -in-the-workplace.

9.   Stephen Chen, "'Forget the Facebook Leak': China Is Mining Data Directly from Workers' Brains on an Industrial Scale," *South China Morning Post*, April 29, 2018, https://www.scmp.com/news/china/society/article/2143899 /forget-facebook-leak-china-mining-data-directly-workers-brains.

10. Yifan Wang, Shen Hong, and Crystal Tai, "China's Efforts to Lead the Way in AI Start in Its Classrooms," *Wall Street Journal*, updated October 24, 2019, https://www

.wsj.com/articles/chinas-efforts-to-lead-the-way-in-ai-start-in-its-classrooms
-11571958181.

11. Evan Ackerman and Eliza Strickland, "Are You Ready for Workplace Brain Scanning?" *IEEE Spectrum*, November 19, 2022, https://spectrum.ieee.org /neurotech-workplace-innereye-emotiv.

12. Andrew Wong, Erkin Otles, John P. Donnelly, Andrew Krumm, Jeffrey McCullough, Olivia DeTroyer-Cooley, Justin Pestrue, Marie Phillips, Judy Konye, Carleen Penoza, Muhammad Ghous, and Karandeep Singh, "External Validation of a Widely Implemented Proprietary Sepsis Prediction Model in Hospitalized Patients," *JAMA Internal Medicine* 181, no. 8 (August 2021): 1065–1070, https://doi.org/10.1001 /jamainternmed.2021.2626.

13. Lauren Kaori Gurley, "Amazon Delivery Drivers Forced to Sign 'Biometric Consent' Form or Lose Job," *Vice*, March 23, 2021, https://www.vice.com/en/article /dy8n3j/amazon-delivery-drivers-forced-to-sign-biometric-consent-form-or-lose -job.

14. Avi Asher-Schapiro, "For This Amazon Van Driver, AI Surveillance Was the Final Straw," Thomson Reuters Foundation, March 19, 2021, https://news.trust .org/item/20210319120214-n93hk.

15. Asher-Schapiro, "For This Amazon Van Driver," https://news.trust.org/item /20210319120214-n93hk.

Chapter 10

1. Gem Siocon, "Ways AI Is Changing HR Departments," *Business News Daily*, June 22, 2023, https://www.businessnewsdaily.com/how-ai-is-changing-hr.

2. Scott Miller, "Amazon Picker Job Description," Vocational Training HQ, last updated December 29, 2019, https://www.vocationaltraininghq.com/job-description /amazon-picker.

3. Colin Lecher, "How Amazon Automatically Tracks and Fires Warehouse Workers for 'Productivity,'" *The Verge*, April 25, 2019, https://www.theverge.com/2019 /4/25/18516004/amazon-warehouse-fulfillment-centers-productivity-firing-terminations.

4. Crystal S. Carey to Barbara Elizabeth Duvall, field attorney, National Labor Relations Board, September 4, 2018 (Amazon termination document obtained by *The Verge*, April 25, 2019), https://cdn.vox-cdn.com/uploads/chorus_asset/file/16190209 /amazon_terminations_documents.pdf.

5. Lecher, "How Amazon Automatically Tracks and Fires," https://www .theverge.com/2019/4/25/18516004/amazon-warehouse-fulfillment-centers-productivity -firing-terminations.

6. American Civil Liberties Union, "Briefing on Electronic Monitoring," December 31, 1997, https://www.aclu.org/documents/privacy-america-electronic -monitoring;

Max Freedman, "Spying on Your Employees? Better Understand the Law First," *Business News Daily*, March 29, 2023.

Epilogue

1.   Top Class Actions, "Dice Job Candidate Open Web Profiles Class Action Settlement," March 28, 2019, https://topclassactions.com/lawsuit-settlements /closed-settlements/dice-job-candidate-open-web-profiles-class-action-settlement/.

2.   Nicole Kobie, "The Complicated Truth About China's Social Credit System," *Wired*, July 6, 2019, https://www.wired.co.uk/article/china-social-credit -system-explained.

3.   Princeton University and Columbia University, "About the Future of Families and Child Wellbeing Study," https://ffcws.princeton.edu/about.

4.   Matthew J. Salganik, Ian Lundberg, Alexander T. Kindel, and Sara McLanahan, "Introduction to the Special Collection on the Fragile Families Challenge," *Socius* 5 (September 10, 2019), https://doi.org/10.1177/2378023119871580.

5.   Matthew J. Salganik, Ian Lundberg, Alexander T. Kindel, et al., "Measuring the Predictability of Life Outcomes with a Scientific Mass Collaboration," *Proceedings of the National Academy of Sciences* 117, no. 15 (March 30, 2020): 8398–8403, https://doi.org/10.1073/pnas.1915006117.

6.   Arvind Narayanan, "How to Recognize AI Snake Oil," Princeton University, 2019, https://www.cs.princeton.edu/~arvindn/talks/MIT-STS-AI-snakeoil.pdf.

7.   Narayanan, "How to Recognize AI Snake Oil," https://www.cs.princeton.edu /~arvindn/talks/MIT-STS-AI-snakeoil.pdf.

8.   Jonathan Kestenbaum, "NYC's New AI Bias Law Broadly Impacts Hiring and Requires Audits," *Bloomberg Law*, July 5, 2023, https://news.bloomberglaw.com/us -law-week/nycs-new-ai-bias-law-broadly-impacts-hiring-and-requires-audits.

9.   Pete Seeger, "Die Gedanken sind frei" lyrics, 1966, Lyrics on Demand, https://www.lyricsondemand.com/p/peteseegerlyrics/diegedankensindfreilyrics.html.

10.   Margaret Osborne, "Researchers Use A.I. to Decode Words from Brain Scans," *Smithsonian Magazine*, May 3, 2023, https://www.smithsonianmag.com/smart -news/researchers-use-ai-to-decode-words-from-brain-scans-180982097/.

INDEX

INDEX